Praise for
Deny Yourself and Follow Me

"This book exposes us to a forgotten tradition and contextualizes it in such a way that self-denial becomes desirable, not frightening. We are called to self-emptying, to be filled with Christ for the glory of the Father. Abnegation is a 'rubric' for the liturgy of our faith lives. All clerical formation should include this work in its reading list."—DCN JAMES KEATING, Professor of Spiritual Theology, Kenrick Glennon Seminary

"*Deny Yourself and Follow Me* is a deeply moving treatment of self-abnegation, Christ's invitation to empty ourselves and make room for Him. In an age that celebrates the self and seems obsessed with ever more transience, David Fagerberg challenges us to surrender our lives to find peace and meaning in the Lord. The book is also a treasure box full of the deep words of many unvalued and largely unread spiritual voices of the last few centuries—from Jean-Jacques Olier and Louis of Blois to Louis of Montfort and François Fenelon."—J. STEPHEN RUSSELL, professor emeritus of English, Hofstra University

"David W. Fagerberg's remarkable new work, *Deny Yourself and Follow Me*, is one of the most original and important developments in contemporary liturgical theology. When I first encountered Fagerberg's central idea of 'liturgical abnegation,' it immediately struck me as potentially as significant as his celebrated recovery of liturgy as *theologia prima*. Here, with extraordinary theological depth, spiritual insight, and historical range, he demonstrates how self-denial, asceticism, and deification belong intrinsically within the liturgical life of the Church."—REV. STEPHEN MORGAN, Rector and Professor of Theology, University of St Joseph, China

"This is a deeply moving reflection by David Fagerberg—personal, luminous, and threaded throughout with *pearls of wisdom*, both his own and those drawn from his long company of saints and spiritual masters. Across years of theological and liturgical inquiry, Fagerberg has forged an unwavering conviction—asceticism first, abnegation now. This is the treasure he unearthed in the field, and he offers it now with the open-handed generosity of a master who knows that wisdom is fulfilled only when shared."—REV. SŁAWOMIR NOWOSAD, Professor of Moral Theology, John Paul II Catholic University of Lublin

"Drawing on more than eighty Catholic spiritual masters between 1500 and 1900, David Fagerberg undertakes the formidable task of reframing the traditional language of annihilation, mortification, nothingness, crosses, and self-denial within the horizon of love and its perfection. He makes no apology for the hundreds of references gathered here; the book is intended less as a system than as an extended conversation with the great voices of the spiritual tradition. It is a veritable spiritual *vademecum.* The author invites the reader to enter the parlor from time to time for a conversation with his new friends, following the advice of Malaval, 'when you do read, to interrupt your reading, from time to time, in order to recollect yourself for a moment in God.'"—JAMES CHUKWUMA OKOYE, CSSp, Director of the Center for Spiritan Studies, Duquesne University

"Five years ago David Fagerberg first began to share with me excerpts from his inspiring engagement with the spiritual writers whom he would later call 'theologians of abnegation.' Beginning from Edward Leen (*Why the Cross?*) to Segneri (*Manna of the Soul*), for the next four years, reading these excerpts would feel like going on a retreat with these spiritual writers, the fruits of which have led me to a deeper appreciation of how destitute we are without humility, how empty until we allow God to be all in all for us! This book will be a theological and spiritual guide for the everyday practice of humility, self-denial, and love as a condition for the possibility of true worship of God. Here, Fagerberg offers us the quintessence of liturgical spirituality."—REV. KENNETH O. AMADI, Director, Church Life Africa, Concurrent Assistant Professor of Theology, Augustine Institute

Deny Yourself and Follow Me

Abnegation as a Liturgical Act of Love

David W. Fagerberg

Deny Yourself and Follow Me

Abnegation as a Liturgical Act of Love

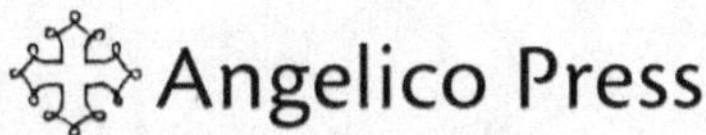

Angelico Press

First published
by Angelico Press 2026

For information, address:
Angelico Press
169 Monitor St.
Brooklyn, NY 11222
info@angelicopress.com

979-8-89280-189-8 (pbk)
979-8-89280-190-4 (cloth)
979-8-89280-191-1 (ebook)

Cover design: Michael Schrauzer

To my students of the past four decades

CONTENTS

Preface

Imagine a man walking in a large field. It is easy for me to imagine, for I am he. This man is in the field of theology, within which there are many landscapes. He has not seen them all, but he has visited a number of them during his career as an academic tramp in theology. On the highlands are the Church Fathers; contemporary discussions in the context of religious studies are a bog land; the lush pastures of Orthodox theology are in the same field, even if on the other side of a fence; and the plains of Catholic theology are vast. The gear the man carries in his backpack is liturgical theology, which is his specialty, and with this kit he examines artifacts he comes across. What he finds useful in the field are those things useful to liturgical theology.

And now, at the end of his career, he is visiting a pasture in the field he had not before, because whenever he looked at it from a distance, it seemed disorganized, unruly, untidy. The grass was more overgrown than the tidy lawns of systematic theology; the paths were not as well laid out as in dogmatic theology; the potential harvest here seemed sparse, and he gave it wide berth. This parcel is spiritual theology, and to him a precision had always appeared wanting. Furthermore, he found here a Western, Latin, Catholic crop of spirituality that had been planted between 1500 and 1900, which appeared especially harsh and unwelcoming. It is a land of annihilation, mortification, nothingness, abnegation, and crosses.

But this time it looks different to his eye. He supposes this is due to what the Orthodox tradition has taught him about asceticism. He had already devoted a book to exploring liturgical asceticism in Eastern Christianity, and if that *Orthodox asceticism* had given him a different way of looking at liturgy, that view of liturgy has given him a different way of looking at *Catholic abnegation*. Perhaps his rucksack of liturgical theology should be expanded to include mysticism and spirituality, he wonders. In liturgical theology he had asked "what happens in liturgy?" In liturgical asceticism he had asked "how can we be capacitated for liturgy?" In liturgical mysticism he had asked "what happens to us in liturgy?" Now he could ask of liturgical abnegation "what does liturgy do for the perfection of our souls?"

So into the corner of the field he treks, and what do you suppose he finds? A landscape of jewels waiting for collection. There are so many pearls of wisdom that it looks like so many hailstones after a storm. There is such an abundance of diamonds that his feet get sore from walking on them, as on a gravel driveway. Each jewel glitters while it describes the interior life and applies the mystery of abnegation to an individual life. Each reveals the therapy of the Cross for healing a damaged soul. Each encourages confidence in God's wisdom (faith), in God's goodness (hope), and in God's providence (love).

He did not walk into the field looking for any particular gem, and he does not possess a mineralogical field guide to teach him which ones to pick up. Many of his colleagues think this disqualifies him from being in the field at all. "You are not allowed in," they say, "without the permission granted by a program of study. The keepers of the academy have not stamped your passport." But his purpose is not to classify and codify what he finds. He is not organizing the treasures by century, or country of origin, or school of thought. He is just picking them up and looking at them. He did not enter with a list of what he wanted to find, rather, friends have introduced him to other friends. He knew the names of a few gems before entering: de Liguori, de Sales, and Faber. He had only heard of a few others: Fénelon, de Bérulle, and Libermann. But he knew nothing about most of them: Segneri, Nepveu, Tronson, Rigoleuc, de Chaugy, and so on. When someone made a favorable quotation, he went on to find their book.

He used to keep syllabi. That was part of the job. Whoever he read, it was with the intention of teaching that author to a classroom of students later. But now there is no more syllabus, no more classroom, no more students, so that purpose of reading has lost its motive. That is a frustrating dimension of retirement. He sighs, looking at all these abnegation authors he enjoys so much, having no one to share them with. Then one day an angel comes with this message: "The boss says He enjoys all these guys, too, and is happy to share them with you. Stop preparing to be a professor of your own course, and enroll as a student in his. He's writing your (mysterious) syllabus. Keep reading, and if the pressure grows too great, try writing a book." He did that once before,[1] but it was more academic and accumulative in nature. This one is more diminutive.

So that is how this book came to be: a pilgrim wanting to share the contents of his treasure chest. It is not a monologue, containing his ideas, his conclusions, his theories; it is a trialogue of the reader, the voices, and his observations. Therefore he does not apologize for the number of quotations in what follows. He is not teaching the reader, he is bringing his new friends into the parlor for a conversation with the reader, and all he wants to do is get out of the way. A jeweler does not claim credit for the diamond's brilliance when he sets the stone; neither does this visitor claim credit for collecting and mounting passages. Perhaps the reader will find a personal affinity with one of these friends. They might find such a rapport if they follow Malaval's advice:

> Remember also, when you do read, to interrupt your reading, from time to time, in order to recollect yourself for a moment in God; that will allow God, like a good and helpful Director, to use the matter you are reading, which you will thus offer Him by this interruption. He will give you the increase with interest, illuminating interiorly, either at that moment, or when you require it, whatever may be obscure in the book you are reading, and *perfecting your knowledge by His light in so admirable a way, that instead of remaining in your memory as it used to do, that which you read will pass unconsciously into your will*, and you will soon recognize what a wonderful benefit it is to read what one reads with God.[2]

1. *Take Up Your Cross* (Gastonia, NC: Sensus Fidelium Press, 2024).

2. François Malaval, *A Simple Method of Raising the Soul to Contemplation: In the Form of a Dialogue* (London: J. M. Dent and Sons Ltd., 1931), 28–29. Emphasis added.

1

What is Abnegation?

I have been thinking for a long time about a title for this book, and to my surprise, Jesus wrote one for me. Mark 8:34, Matthew 16:24, and Luke 9:23 are identical (except for Luke's addition of one word): "If any man would come after me, *let him deny himself* and take up his cross [daily] and *follow me*." I guess I shouldn't be surprised that Our Lord did the title, since he's also responsible for the contents.

Francis Libermann wants us never to forget that abnegation is Jesus's teaching, not our invention. "It is not I who preach abnegation, it is our Lord Himself who has set down the conditions under which He will receive us as His followers.... No doctrine has ever found more forceful expressions in the Gospels.... The words of our Savior allow of no quibbling."[1] Jean Grou makes the same point. "[Jesus] admitted no compromise. There is no middle course, He said; you must deny yourself, or I shall deny you; you can only belong to Me on that condition."[2] And Croiset also finds mortification to be "so necessary for the perfect love of Jesus Christ, that it is the first lesson that Jesus Christ Himself gives to those who wish to be His disciples. Without it, we can have no hope of ever being disciples of Jesus Christ."[3]

This book aims to do two things. First, to give an account of what certain Catholic spiritual writers have said about self-denial. The Vulgate translates "deny yourself" as *abneget se ipsum*, and you can recognize the term *abnegation* in the passage. My purpose in

1. Francis Libermann, *Instructions for Missionaries* (https://dsc.duq.edu/cgi/viewcontent.cgi?article=1021&context=spiritan-rc), 39.

2. Jean Grou, *The School of Jesus Christ* (London: Burns Oates & Washbourne Ltd., 1932), 81.

3. John Croiset, *Devotion to the Sacred Heart of Jesus* (London: Burns & Lambert, 1863), 77–78.

this chapter is to give it further definition, but for now it is enough to connect it with love's ultimate goal for every human being, namely, his or her deification. Saint-Jure says that in order "to render a man capable of being changed, and transformed into God, it is necessary that he strip himself of himself, that he die absolutely to his self-love, and to all that feeds self-love in him."[4] This is abnegation, and it is in the service of our transformation.

The second aim of this book is to give abnegation a home in liturgical theology. It has been a topic for Christian theologians and mystics throughout the history of the Church, in both the East and the West, but I am going to focus on Latin spiritual writers who lived between 1500–1900. I have only recently discovered these authors in a deeper way. For many years I was put off by their style of writing, but if the reader and I could together find another way into their language then we might better understand abnegation. That way in, I submit, is liturgy. Abnegation should be understood as an act of liturgy. Of course, I mean more than the cultic liturgy: I mean the liturgy that takes residence in the heart to be ritually enacted in the public cult. Liturgy invites abnegation, and abnegation enlarges liturgy. I think of it, therefore, as *liturgical abnegation*. It is mystical, not moralistic; it is pneumatological, not psychological; its home is in the whole Church, not only the cloister; it is glorification of God, not disparagement of man. Abnegation is liturgical because it is done in the name of Jesus, for Jesus, through Jesus, filled with Jesus, and in tune with Jesus's desire to glorify his Father in heaven. Abnegation flips a fallen state back to right side up, like a turtle on his back regaining his footing, to let us live our lives in constant celebration of God's honor and glory.

The reason for approaching abnegation from the altar is because otherwise the language used by these theologians seems distasteful to us. I mean language like *annihilation, austerity, indifference, resignation, mortification, abjection, abasement, abandonment, self-denial, self-renunciation, self-detachment, nothingness, contempt, hating the world, suffering,* and *bearing crosses*. Many people might

4. Jean Baptiste Saint-Jure, *The Religious: A Treatise on the Vows and Virtues of the Religious State*, vol. 1 (New York: P. O'Shea, 1882), 575.

close the book and move on when they come across such language. (I did, for many years.) It seems to come from a foreign land, or a different century, and because of the discomfort we feel, we hope to ignore it. But if it comes from Scripture, then we most certainly cannot ignore it. If it confronts our unnatural state of sin, then we cannot ignore it. If it is the price of growing perfect in love, then we cannot ignore it.

Biblical passages about the Cross have been worn so smooth by constant repetition that we hardly hear the words anymore, and are scarcely startled when Paul says that he has been crucified with Christ (Gal 2:20), that he dies daily (1 Cor 15:31), that those who belong to Christ have crucified the flesh (Gal 5:24), that our old self was crucified with Jesus (Rom 6:6), and that we must die with Christ (Rom 6:8). What does this mean? How deeply does the Cross penetrate? The overtones of asceticism and abnegation permeate the New Testament's entire description of the perfection of our salvation. It says to everyone, even those in our century, "join Christ where he is to be found, which is on the Cross."

Is the negative reputation of abnegation justified? When I finally dove into these spiritual writers, I found that they put the word in rather different company. I will make my point with examples from only one person, Francis Libermann. Consider the company to which he gives the word in the following passages. The spiritual person is advised to belong "totally to God in self-abnegation, peace, mildness and humility of heart";[5] to preserve "a spirit of humility, abnegation and confident abandonment to God";[6] to perform "an act that contains a movement of humility, abnegation, of oblation of yourself to God";[7] to pursue "a work of patience, abnegation, gentleness";[8] to attain virtues of "humility, obedience, charity, gentleness, simplicity, a life of prayer and abnegation";[9] to maintain a heart in perfect peace, which is "a quiet abnegation of

5. Francis Libermann, *Letters to Clergy and Religious*, Spiritan Series 7, vol. 3, (Pittsburgh: Duquesne University Press, 1963), 256.

6. Libermann, *Letters to Clergy and Religious*, Spiritan Series 7, vol. 3, 285.

7. Ibid., 158.

8. Ibid., 317.

9. Ibid., 319.

every sort of earthly affection and a total detachment from everything that is not God."[10]

One might not think to associate abnegation with peace, mildness, humility, confidence in God, patience, gentleness, simplicity, and perfect love—examples picked from the above list. But, in fact, abnegation is associated with love because love for another always involves denying oneself. Abbess Cécile Bruyère is convinced that "the higher the soul rises the less does God spare her. Divine love is in very truth a strong and generous wine, sustaining the soul in heights above herself, but that love ever enforces the law of total self-abnegation. . . . When she lives the true life, God adapts her to Himself, and then everything in her that is unfit for union must irremissibly disappear."[11] Spirituality is submission to God, and abnegation is the act of surrender. Abnegation is giving up our judgment, abandoning our way of thinking to adopt God's views and affections, to judge things as God judges them. Abnegation rises out of gratitude, says Faber. "We wish to annihilate our whole being to return Him thanks for it."[12]

If abnegation is difficult, it is because we do not realize the glory attached to it. Our Father in heaven keeps the doors of his kingdom open to everyone who desires to enter what Rogacci calls the happy country, the palace of the King of kings, the land of eternal and perfect joy. This thought should make the labors of God's service light. The saints knew it; do we? "If we, on the contrary, find it so difficult to avoid sin, to abstain from the pleasures of sense, to mortify our natural inclinations, and to bear even a slight trouble for the love of God, the real reason is, that either we do not consider, or do not vividly realize the vast and eternal glory which is to be attained by these means. For, if we kept it in sight, and had a right conception of it, it would be not only very easy to fulfill every one of God's

10. Francis Libermann, *Letters to Clergy and Religious*, Spiritan Series 8, vol. 4, (Pittsburgh: Duquesne University Press, 1964), 38.

11. Abbess Cécile Bruyère, *Spiritual Life and Prayer According to Holy Scripture and Monastic Tradition* (New York: Benziger Brothers, 1905), 280.

12. Frederick Faber, *All for Jesus: or, The Easy Ways of Divine Love* (Baltimore: John Murphy and Co., 1855), 364.

commandments, but all but impossible to transgress them."[13] Abnegation removes self-love to increase love for God. It empties in order to fill. It is a preparatory treatment, which removes anything that hinders giving God full glory. When Jesus sanctifies, Olier says he restores the heart to its original state of emptiness because "he cannot tolerate there anything but his Father and his Divine perfections. . . . That is why Jesus Christ came into the world. He wanted to purify the human heart, empty it of every creature and thus make reparation for the original misfortune and disorder into which we had fallen through the misery of sin and the goading of the devil."[14]

The Son of God is the Good Shepherd. He left his Father in heaven for the purpose of rescuing mankind, a flock of lost sheep, to lead them back to his Father by the Spirit. Mankind has strayed out of pasture, into dry desert, and become prey to three dangers: Satan, flesh, and the world. Man listened to the voice of a counterfeit shepherd (Satan), who promised a happiness based upon a false premise (the world), which led to rebellion (in the flesh). This so disoriented the soul that it was unable to focus upon spiritual things. As John of Ávila explains, the word *world* "does not refer here to the world created by God, which is good, created by the one who is the supreme Good. It is used for those who have no other feeling and no other love than for what is visible. Saint John calls this the 'pride of life, the concupiscence of the flesh, and the concupiscence of the eyes' (1 John 2:16–17)."[15] Put plainly, these branches of self-love are the love of pleasure, the love of riches, and the love of honor, and abnegation is multitherapeutic: it applies pressure against all of these.

The sheep could have grazed happily in the world. God made man for himself, and made the world for man, and under this good

13. Benedict Rogacci, *Christian Reformed in Mind and Manners* (London: Burns and Oates, 1877), 236–37.

14. Jean-Jacques Olier, *Introduction to the Christian Life and Virtues*, in *Bérulle and the French School: Selected Writings*, ed. William M. Thompson (New York: Paulist Press, 1989), 249.

15. John of Ávila, *Audi, Filia—Listen, O Daughter* (New York: Paulist Press, 2006), 275.

order, Bona observes that human beings were created with everything necessary for happiness. Man was created with "an understanding to know his maker, a will to love and obey him, a memory to think of his laws, faculties to serve him, and a tongue to praise him," and then "as he made man for himself, so he created the whole world for man, that he might use all things for his own happiness, and for the glory of God."[16] It could have continued so. Man might have used the whole world—all of it!—for his happiness and God's glory. But the Fall ruined man's relationship with creation. Instead of gratefully receiving it, we now seize it and surrender to it. The world now commands our attention, instead of directing our attention to God. The sinner demands rights to the gift, and the giver is forgotten. Nicholas Cross warns, "Beware of the world's smiles . . . we are never more in danger than when we appear to be its darlings."[17]

Abnegation is not required because there is something the matter with matter. What God desires is the death of sin, in order to liberate the whole person (body and soul). God's love never lets the heart rest after it has taken possession of it, which is why Alacoque advises us to surrender ourselves to the ardor of his pure love, "so that we may love Him with our whole being. Everything must be subservient to that, everything bend and yield before this holy love."[18] It is a great mystery (I think, perhaps, the mystery of iniquity) how nothing can be wrong with the world, yet we do the world wrongly. I will define "worldliness" as *taking the world without reference to God.* No thing in creation is bad, but every thing in creation can used badly by someone who has lost discipline of his appetites. No thing is sinful, but any thing can be used sinfully. Or, we may say, the problem is not money, sex, or beer; the problem is

16. Giovanni Bona, *Precepts and Practical Rules for a Truly Christian Life* (London: Printed by M. Clark, 1678), 32.

17. Nicolas of the Holy Cross [sic], *Pious Reflections, and Devout Prayers, on Several Points of Faith and Morality, from Man's Creation to His Consummation* (Doway: by M. Mairesse, 1695), 199. Most books are published with the name "Nicholas Cross," except this text of *Pious Reflections.*

18. Mary Margaret Alacoque, *The Letters of St. Margaret Mary Alacoque* (Charlotte, NC: TAN Books, 2012), Letter 24, Kindle edition.

avarice, lust, and gluttony. Then it is as if the world doesn't work right any more—which actually means that we do not work the world correctly because we do not use it for liturgy.

Adam and Eve were occupants of a paradise, a place of excellence, a garden of bliss—so long as they were in command of their appetites. Ullathorne reminds us that "every tree that God planted in Paradise was good. It was not, then, to any evil in the nature of the tree to which man gave his appetite, when he touched the forbidden tree, but he committed the evil act by deserting what was better."[19] Adam and Eve could not choose a sinful thing, for God had planted no sinful things in his garden to choose! But Adam and Eve could make a sinful choice, by hungering "for a good in the creature that could only be obtained by deserting his Creator."[20] The sin of Adam and Eve was touching the tree with the wrong motive, at the wrong time, in the wrong way. Their sin was worshiping the creature rather than the Creator, forsaking their status as liturgical agents in Paradise. The Fall consisted in disobedience, but it was caused by pride, and pride went on to poison everything. The Fall was the forfeiture of our liturgical career.

Ever after, men and women have stood in an ambiguous relationship to the world and to their own flesh, and all forms of love must be straightened out, refocused, and put back on target. All forms of love require purification, that is to say, perfection (from *perficere*: to accomplish, finish, complete). Libermann says perfected love will always prefer what "we believe to be most pleasing to God. We then still love the things of earth—we still have a taste for, and a delight in creatures and in the satisfactions and pleasures of this world—but we do it with moderation and without offense to God."[21] *When we love God above all things, then we can love all things in God.* Jacqueline Favre, the second Visitation Sister, made a vow "never to allow her mind to dwell voluntarily on any thought but of God, or the

19. William Ullathorne, *The Endowments of Man Considered in their Relations with His Final End* (London: Burns & Oates, 1880), 217.

20. Ibid.

21. Francis Libermann, *Letters to People in the World*, Spiritan Series 6, vol. 2 (Pittsburgh: Duquesne University Press, 1963), 218.

things of God, in her earnest desire to offer to Him, as a pure vase of gold or crystal, a heart thoroughly void of self, that He might fill it with His love."[22] John Peter Camus calls the objects that attract concupiscence "earthly trash" because it is a heavy burden that will "hinder those that strive to clime the mountaine of God. But if, by a holy contempt, we treade upon the same burden, it rayseth us thitherward."[23] Creation is a table full of gifts at the wedding reception, but love of the Bridegroom does not shut out all other loves. "Rather it admits them, and lifting them up to an alliance with itself, transforms them and elevates them, lending to them a share of its own excellence."[24] The difficulty of creatureliness for a worldling is put in the words of a confession by Duguet: "My desires ... have hitherto divided my heart, and, as it were, torn it into as many parts as there have been objects that have attracted it."[25] Abnegation restores simplicity, a progress which Swetchine describes as a series of steps from absence, to occasional glimpses, to God in the world, to, finally, God on the mountain alone.

> For a time, O my Lord,—a time which I cannot now conceive,—thou wert everywhere as now, and I saw thee nowhere. Yet at last I had glimpses of thee amid the crowd of objects which hid thee from my view, and soon thy adorable head lifted itself above others, and asserted its supremacy. . . . I began by often turning my eyes to thine; then oftener: at last, I removed them no more; but that dear sight became inseparably mingled with all others, and made me better and wiser. I had advanced so far, and thought to advance no farther, when it came to pass, I know not how, that

22. Françoise-Madeleine de Chaugy, *Life of Mother Marie Jacqueline Favre: To which is added Lives of Other Mothers of the First Religious of the Visitation of Holy Mary* (London: R. Washbourne, 1876), 88.

23. John Peter Camus, *A Draught of Eternitie* (Doway: by the Widow of Marke Wyon, 1632), 354.

24. Henry Collins, *Heaven Opened; or, Our Home in Heaven, and the Way Thither. A Manual of Guidance for Devout Souls* (London: Thomas Richardson and Son, 1880), 108.

25. Jacques Joseph Duguet, *The Principles of the Christian Faith*, vol. 1 (Edinburgh: Printed for G. Hamilton & J. Balfour, J. Traill, W. Miller, and J. Brown, 1755), 18.

> one day, one hour,—one swift and blissful hour, I ceased to see aught besides thee! . . . I saw my dear Jesus aright, and the poor sheep knew its true shepherd![26]

What God had planned by one design, had to be accomplished by another design. God never abandoned his plan to have mankind seated with him in heaven, and he always had a plan to repair the damage we did in Eden. Bona acknowledges that the first man could have come to bliss "by a free and lawful use of those good creatures which God had prepar'd for him, in the delights of Paradise: but after he had rebell'd against God and infected his unborn posterity with sin, the Divine Wisdom appointed another way to Bliss; that is, the way of the Cross and Self-denyal, through which *Christ* himself past."[27] That intended path is no longer open to us, and now the path to bliss is through abnegation. John of the Cross can give us a concise summary of the problem we face: "the more the heart is occupied with self, the less it is occupied with God."[28] This is the problem Jesus was addressing when he commanded us to deny the self.

Olier says the reason why "our Lord put abnegation in his gospel as the first step we must take in the Christian life … [is] because self-centeredness, being filled with the self, blocks Jesus Christ and the fullness of his divine life from entering us. It is the inexhaustible source of every evil and every sin."[29] Abnegation does not narrow a person, it enlarges a person so that Jesus can enter. It clears and expands; it purges and protracts. Abnegation's constriction of passions is for the liberation of the soul, and this is why it stands front and center in the gospel that Christ proclaims.

Abnegation and renunciation are synonyms, but what is

26. Frederic Alfred Pierre, Comte de Falloux, *Life and Letters of Madame Swetchine* (New York: The Catholic Publication House, 1869), 145.

27. Bona, *Precepts and Practical Rules for a Truly Christian Life* , 47.

28. John of the Cross, *Spiritual Canticle Between the Soul and Christ* in *The Complete Works of Saint John of the Cross*, vol. 2 (London: Longman, Green, Longman, Roberts & Green, 1864), 49.

29. Olier, *Introduction to the Christian Life and Virtues*, in *Bérulle and the French School*, 262–63.

renounced in self-denial? Not the good things of creation, only the misuse of creation. Not proper love of self, only faulty self-love. Not our neighbor, only selfish manipulation of our neighbor. We may picture redemption as a counterattack on the enemy. Disobedience is countered by obedience; pride is countered by humility; self-centeredness is countered by self-denial. Where Satan has planted the weeds of pride, abnegation grows a crop of humility, and humility must be marked by self-abnegation, says Leen, "which aims at purging from [the soul] everything that is not God, so that 'conformed to the image of His Son' it may live its life in full accord with the designs of Providence in its regard."[30] The spiritual warfare is fought to the death, so another synonym for abnegation is *mortification*. This means more than denying some peripheral possession, it involves killing all boasting, self-reliance, self-conceit. It replaces self-possession with piety.

If the sheep cease the senseless wandering that has been caused by the three inheritances of sin (pride of life, the lust of the flesh, and the lust of the eyes), it is because their Good Shepherd has shown them a better path, a better life. We follow Jesus because we want to be like him, and Eudes thinks that when Jesus commands "deny yourself," he is simply applying to us the conditions under which he, himself, lived. Jesus has "given you the perfect example of self-abnegation. While He was on earth, He never acted according to His own desires, but rather He did the will of His Father. He never sought His own satisfaction nor His own interests, but those of His Father. 'For Christ did not please himself' (Rom. 15, 3)."[31] This deserves our adoration, and he marvels at the design Jesus "had in your regard when He said these words. Ask His pardon for placing any obstacle in the way of its fulfilment. Give yourself to Him . . . and realize that He Himself first did what He asks of you, having given you the perfect example of self-abnegation."[32]

30. Edward Leen, *Progress Through Mental Prayer* (New York: Sheed and Ward, 1935), 15.

31. John Eudes, *The Priest: His Dignity and Obligations* (New York: P.J. Kenedy & Sons, 1947), 191.

32. Ibid.

To summarize, I have proposed two reasons for why we are obliged to practice self-abnegation. First, the Fall has left us disordered, and we need to be reconstructed from the inside out. Second, Jesus is our model: salvation means that what happened in Jesus should happen to us. Giffard reminds us that the Cross on Calvary waits to fit into our hearts. "What *Jesus* did to save us, we must do to be saved by *Jesus*."[33] Salvation does not mean letting Jesus do something *instead* of us, salvation means Jesus doing something *in* us. When the Word became incarnate, he healed the human nature he assumed, and that healing should continue in every individual. Therefore, Saint-Jure says the Word Incarnate "should empty us of ourselves, replenish us with His Divinity, imprint on us traces of His perfections; that He should unite us to Himself and cause us to live a life divinely human; that He should operate in us without resistance whatever He pleases, make us act in and by His spirit, [and] render us to His Father to be employed in His service now and forever."[34]

In other words, abnegation is a road of holiness. John of Ávila believes this should take our fear out of abnegation, because "holiness comes from love, and the greater the love, the greater the saint. The best proof we can give of our love for Christ is to obey His commands and bear the cross for Him. . . . Contempt for self and abnegation of our will are also signs of this love, for our Lord says: 'If any man will come after me, let him deny himself.'"[35] We need not grope in the dark to discover a pattern for our faith, because Christ has given us his own pattern of life to follow. Only start to follow the Good Shepherd, and Elizabeth of the Trinity says you will discover "the path is traced for us. We have but to deny ourselves, to die to self, to lose sight of self. Is not that the Master's meaning when

33. Bonaventure Giffard, "Of the Nativity of our Lord," in James Ayray et al., *A Select Collection of Catholick Sermons Preached before their Majesties King James II, Mary Queen-Consort, Catherine Queen-Dowager, etc.*, vol. 1 (London: s.n. 1741), 112.

34. Jean Baptiste Saint-Jure, *A Treatise on the Knowledge and Love of Our Lord Jesus Christ*, vol. 2 (New York: P. O'Shea, 1875), 407–8.

35. John of Ávila, *Letters of Blessed John of Ávila* (London: Burns & Oates Ltd., 1904), 98–99.

He says: 'If any man will come after Me, let him deny himself, and take up his cross, and follow Me'?"[36]

Christ's self-denial spanned an arc from the Incarnation to his crucifixion. He lived a life of self-detachment from Mary's womb to Calvary's hillside, and did so in order to give himself to his Father and to mankind. It is no small matter to renounce the world, Eudes admits, and yet

> our Lord cries out to us in a loud voice: "If any man will come after me, let him deny himself, and take up his cross, and follow me" (Matt. 16, 24). So, then, if you want to be among the followers of Christ and belong to Him, you have to renounce yourself, that is, your own mind, your own ideas, your own will, desires, inclinations and your self-love, because it is your self-love that leads you to hate and avoid anything that might cause pain or mortification to your spirit or your flesh and makes you love and seek out everything that may give them pleasure and contentment.[37]

How can we think ill of abnegation when it is a matter of uniting with Jesus to live life in his manner? How can we have an aversion to abnegation when its purpose is to create a similarity to Jesus? How can we avoid abnegation when it is the path Jesus, himself, took? How can we shun the Cross when it is the supreme exercise of faith, hope, and love? And yet we do, which puzzles Grou. "How is it that we dislike, and indeed have almost a horror of hearing about interior mortification, abnegation, poverty of spirit, or renunciation of every natural inclination, repugnance, desire, or fear? As though all this were not included in the saying of Jesus Christ: *If any man will come after Me let him deny himself!*"[38]

A sign of our fallen state is our secret dislike for the very idea of abnegation, which comes from the fact that self-denial is the opposite of self-seeking. When Leen wonders aloud, "What is self-

36. Elizabeth of the Trinity, *The Praise of Glory: Reminiscences of Sr. Elizabeth of the Trinity* (London: R. & T. Washbourne, Ltd., 1914), 244.

37. John Eudes, *The Life and the Kingdom of Jesus in Christian Souls* (New York: P. J. Kenedy & Sons, 1946), 19.

38. Grou, *The School of Jesus Christ*, 432.

denial?" he comes through with a brilliant summary. "To 'deny self' is the contrary of 'to assert self' or 'to put self forward.' Self-seeking in all its forms is an evil tendency surviving in men as an effect of original sin.... Instead of glorifying God, [fallen man] has an inveterate inclination to glorify himself."[39] Abnegation denies anything that denies God's right to everything.

If we have a natural aversion to abnegation (I mean an aversion that comes from a fallen nature!) then embracing it will require courage, and every spiritual theologian admits it. But there is no other way, or else Christ would have used it, says de Ravignan. "If there were any better means, our Saviour when consummating His sacrifice upon Calvary, for the expiation of our hardness of heart, in order that we might gain every grace and that the world might be saved, would assuredly have commanded and taught it to us."[40] If Jesus requires crosses of us, he also bestows the power to bear them, meaning that no abnegation happens by some energy we summon up from ourselves. It relies upon a strengthening by God; grace opens the door for it. And waiting for that strengthening is a form of patient surrender to Providence, de Sales thinks.

> You must see and speak to God amid the thunders and the whirlwinds; you must see him in the bush, and amid the thorns; and to do this, the truth is that we must take off our shoes, and make a great abnegation of our wills and affections. But the Divine goodness has not called you to the state in which you are, without strengthening you for all this. It is for him to perfect his work. True, it is a little long, because the matter requires it; but patience.[41]

Or, in the briefer words of de Sales's disciple, Jane de Chantal, the state of submission means "to *refuse nothing* that the Providence of

39. Edward Leen, *The True Vine and Its Branches* (New York: P.J. Kenedy & Sons, 1938), 178.

40. Gustave de Ravignan, *Conferences on the Spiritual Life* (London: R. Washbourne, 1873), 169–70.

41. Francis de Sales, *Library of St. Francis de Sales: vol. 1, Letters to Persons in the World* (London: Burns & Oates, Ltd., 1894), 259.

God shall present for our perfection, and *not to desire* that which it will not give us."[42]

The glory of his Father required the Cross, so Jesus welcomed it. The glory of the Father will require crosses for us, so we welcome whatever abnegation is required. Grou observes this liturgical trait in persons of abnegation: "provided God be glorified, no matter by what instrument, they are happy, and if permitted to select the means of promoting His glory in their own persons, they would choose such as are most humiliating and most calculated to lead to self-abnegation."[43] We do not often put "abnegation" and "happiness" in the same sentence, but Jesus did, and the saints do.

Have I succeeded in expanding the definition of abnegation by digging down deeper to its roots? These authors do not equate self-abnegation with self-denigration, or self-ridicule, or self-reviling. How could they, when it was Jesus himself who taught us to empty ourselves in order to glorify God, and be filled with the Holy Spirit? Grou can't understand how we could dislike abnegation when it is Christ's condition for following him. "As though this renunciation, carried to the highest pitch of perfection, were not the characteristic of Jesus Christ's holiness, and ought not to be the characteristic of our own!"[44]

Christianity is the life of Christ perpetuated in his followers, more fully in some, less fully in others, just barely in a few. The Apostle Paul uses the phrase *en Christo* (in Christ) 164 times in his epistles. The Church is not another one of Adam's cults that have been scattered across the historical landscape. The Church is the cult of the New Adam mystically perpetuated in us. Liturgy is the religion of Christ perpetuated in his followers. "Deny yourselves and *follow* me." Follow him where? Where is the Good Shepherd leading his flock? To the Father, to the throne of heaven, to eternal life, to the waters of regeneration, to the sacrament of love.

42. Jane de Chantal, *Saint Jane Frances Frémyot de Chantal: Her Exhortations, Conferences and Instructions* (Westminster, MD: The Newman Bookshop, 1947), 448.

43. Jean Grou, *The Interior of Jesus and Mary*, vol. 1 (New York: Benziger Brothers, 1893), 233–34.

44. Grou, *The School of Jesus Christ*, 432.

If I were looking for a term to encompass the purpose and rewards of abnegation, I would suggest the term *deification.* Our authors of liturgical abnegation use it freely. De Sales says when our minds are illuminated by the blessed light of glory "then will the soul be deified, filled with God, and made like to God."[45] Eudes speaks of our Savior's heart as "a burning furnace of most pure love for us; a furnace of purifying love, of illuminating love, of sanctifying love, of transforming love, and of deifying love."[46] Again from Eudes, Christ is formed in the hearts of the faithful, "transforming them into His children, deifying them as it were, according to the words of Sacred Scripture: 'He called them gods, to whom the word of God was spoken' (John 10, 35)."[47] And Saint-Jure says Our Lord promised to illuminate us interiorly, inflaming the will and enlightening the understanding, "that He may be truly our *Emanuel, God with us*, to dwell in us, to sanctify us, and to deify us."[48] Union is at stake, one which Jean de Bernières-Louvigny describes as deification. "This union is a perfect assimilation to his states and mysteries. And this assimilation is what they call a transformation into God, which renders a person wholly divine, and devoted to the interests of the Almighty. By this privileged grace we become divine—having no other inclinations than those of God—living by the life of God—and desiring nothing but the love and glory of God."[49]

Only God's Incarnation could cause man's deification. I could put it in clumsy English by saying God *man-ified* himself so we could be *dei-fied.* Bossuet expresses it without clumsiness by summarizing the Fathers and saying, "He took our flesh, that we might

45. Francis de Sales, *The Consoling Thoughts of Saint Francis de Sales: Gathered from His Writings, and Arranged in Order, by the Rev. Père Huguet* (Dublin: M. H. Gill & Son, 1877), 319.

46. John Eudes, *The Sacred Heart of Jesus* (New York: P. J. Kenedy & Sons, 1946), 133.

47. Eudes, *The Priest*, 75.

48. Jean Baptiste Saint-Jure, *The Spiritual Man; or, The Spiritual Life Reduced to its First Principles* (London: Burns and Oates, 1878), 39.

49. Jean de Bernières-Louvigny, *The Interior Christian in Eight Books* (New York: The Catholic Publication Society, 1843), 191.

take His spirit."[50] Jesus imitates our human nature by taking it on, so we may imitate him in his sanctity by taking him on. Saint-Jure sees the exchange in a similar manner: Christ became man "so that he may do for us what his divinity did for his humanity, which was to sanctify it, strengthen it, deify it."[51]

It might be tempting at this stage to let our thoughts wander directly to heaven, but we must rein them in. Glories then require trials now. This is where abnegation makes its appearance. Our only way to glory is through the Cross, and our trials are used to unite us to the Cross. Of this, Saint-Jure is certain. "Our Lord's cross and sufferings are able to sanctify ours and render them salutary.... [Therefore we should] take great pains to unite to our Lord afflicted, suffering and dying, and to beg him to bless, to purify, to sanctify and deify our afflictions and sufferings."[52] Deification does not spare us from trial, it uses trials to attain its end. This mortification is bitter at first, but sweetens as it achieves its purposes. The mystical union requires a mystical death.

Liturgy is an activity of love, love is the substance of liturgy, and for the love of Christ we accept all sorts of abnegations. Unified will is a sign of love, while preserving one's own will is a sign of estrangement. Attached to himself, man is detached from God; detached from self, man can be attached to God. And then we can approach the Lord with what Tronson says is "lively faith, a deep humility, a burning love, a total abnegation of self, and a fervent longing to be wholly united to Thee in time and in eternity."[53] All things serve love: abnegation's service to love is to purify it. Wanting us for himself, God strips other things away.

There is a worldly drag on our heavenward flight. John Evangelist of Boisleduc pictures the soul of man as "created to live in God as the bird in the air, but ... hindered in its heavenward flight by attach-

50. Jacques-Bénigne Bossuet, *Great French Sermons from Bossuet, Bourdaloue, and Massillon* (London: Sands and Co., 1917), 50–51.

51. Jean Baptiste Saint-Jure, *Union With Our Lord Jesus Christ in His Principal Mysteries for All Seasons of the Year* (New York: D. & J. Sadlier & Co., 1876), 72.

52. Ibid., 183–84.

53. Louis Tronson, *Examination of Conscience Upon Special Subjects* (Oxford: Rivingtons, 1870), 115.

ments to creatures, be that attachment [ever] so slight."[54] He goes on to picture the soul as a pilgrim who could run faster if she discarded the useless weights she is carrying, but that is not an end in itself. The abnegation of all creatures should "be done purely for the love of God. When this pure love of God is joined to the perfect detachment, the soul is lifted above herself unto God. . . . This pure love of God consists herein, that a man absolutely deny himself all created things, and render up himself wholly unto God without seeking therein any merit, comfort, profit or benefit, interior or exterior, temporal or spiritual, but purely for God."[55] The soul is lifted above herself into God.

Abnegation is a scouring, a straightening, a smoothing. It is the front line battle with idolatry and is intended to protect monogamy in the heart. Challoner starts with the Old Testament truth that God is a jealous God, and therefore "will not suffer a rival in his kingdom, a partner in his throne, or an idol in his temple. . . . If we follow any other lovers, we lose his love, and drive him away from us. . . . Ah! the bed is too narrow; it will not hold two."[56] When the Son of God came down from heaven to be born into this world, it was, Challoner says, *for you.* And "though he did not disdain the stable nor the crib, the ox nor the ass, he will not endure a heart divided, or occupied by unclean affections, which will not allow him the whole bed."[57] The passage being referred to is Isaiah 28:20, which most translations (King James, New Revised Standard Version, and a dozen more) depict as "the bed is too short on which to stretch out." But the Douay-Rheims translation says, "the bed is straitened," meaning squeezed or confined, "so that one must fall out," and our authors take the verse in this sense. Diego de Estella:

54. John Evangelist of Boisleduc (Balduke), *The Kingdom of God in the Soul* (London: Sheed & Ward, 1930), 65–66.

55. Ibid., *The Kingdom of God in the Soul*, 80.

56. Richard Challoner, *Considerations Upon Christian Truths and Christian Duties*, part I (Philadelphia: Eugene Cummiskey, 1874), 204.

57. Richard Challoner, *Considerations Upon Christian Truths and Christian Duties*, part II (Philadelphia: Eugene Cummiskey, 1874), 294.

> No one can serve two masters, says our Saviour. A heart has not room for two contrary loves and therefore it is proper that he who wants to serve God should despise and hate the works of the devil and the love of this world. Isaias says: "Too narrow a bed and one or the other must fall out; a short cloak is no covering for two." If the love of the world dwells in you, there is no place into which the love of God can fit. . . . If you realize that you cannot serve both, for they order contrary things, there is no doubt that you should serve Jesus Christ and throw off the heavy yoke of the world.

He says you cannot *serve* these two masters. To serve God and *use* the world is a thing that is very possible, but to serve the world, making yourself its servant and slave, giving way to your appetites, and together with all this to serve God, is a thing impossible.[58]

Jesus made denying oneself his principal requirement on the path to perfection. Indeed, this book could be retitled that—"The Path to Perfection"—if we remember that we are talking about a *perfection of love*. It is love that we are trying to perfect, and that depends upon the union of our will with Christ's, says Vincent de Paul:

> The perfection of love does not consist in ecstasies, but in fulfilling the will of God. Whoever would be the most perfect of all is the one who has best conformed his own will to God's in such a way that no distinction remains between his own will and God's. Whoever would excel on this point would be the most perfect. When our Lord wished to instruct the man spoken of in the Gospel about how best to arrive at perfection, he said: "if anyone wishes to come after me, let him renounce himself, take up his cross, and follow me." Now I ask you, who renounces himself more, or who carries the cross of mortification better, or follows Jesus Christ more perfectly than he who seeks to follow the will of God rather than his own will?[59]

58. Diego de Estella, from *Treatise on the Vanity of the World* in Kathleen Pond, *The Spirit of Spanish Mystics: An Anthology of Spanish Religious Prose from the Fifteenth to the Seventeenth Century* (London: Burns & Oates, 1958), 91–92.

59. Vincent de Paul, in Louis Abelly, *The Life of the Venerable Servant of God: Vincent de Paul*, vol. 3 (New York: New City Press, 1993), 41–42.

When the vocabulary of abnegation, self-denial, annihilation, and mortification is put against a limited horizon, it sounds like a very grim and gloomy moral program. But when the vocabulary is placed against a more transcendent horizon, it sounds completely different. That horizon, I propose, is the act of liturgy before a God who deserves and demands our total worship. I have hinted that abnegation and liturgy are connected, but we must turn to this more directly and explicitly.

2

The Liturgical Home for Abnegation

Deny yourself and follow me. Be dead to sin and alive to me. Empty yourself and be filled with me. Annihilate the old Adam and come alive in me. Negate your self-will and obey my Father's will. Renounce false gods and believe the truth. Recant your selfishness. Love your neighbor as I have loved you. Have faith in me, not in yourself. Have hope in me, not in the world. Love me, not yourself. The language of liturgy and the language of abnegation coincide: consecrating is renouncing, oblation is surrender, sacrifice is annihilation, attending God's will is denying self-will, liturgizing is abnegating. A turn toward is also a turn away. Liturgy is embracing, turning toward, and conversion, while abnegation is denial, turning away, and aversion. Having taken measure of the Uncreated horizon, vanities evaporate, self-will is subdued by obedience, possessions are held in contrast, honors are evaluated by a different measure, slavery yields to freedom, and success is no longer appraised by the opinion of the world. All these things will be weighed "on the scales of the sanctuary," the meaning of which is explained by Segneri.

> As, under the Old Law, no weights were reckoned just, or lawful to be used, but such as had been accurately examined in the famous balance of the sanctuary; so, in order that the value which we set upon things, or the weight, so to speak, which we give them in our judgments, must be just and true, it must be brought to the infallible test of the Divine Judgment, and there weighed by the esteem in which Almighty God Himself holds them.[1]

1. Paul Segneri, *The Devout Client of Mary Instructed in the Motives and Means of Serving Her Well* (London: Burns & Lambert, 1857), 3.

We can only take just measure of ourselves in the light of God's truth and under the scrutiny of his justice. "How many actions," asks Nepveu, "that appear good in the eyes of men will be found wanting when weighed on the scales of the temple!"[2] The spiritual soul that is formed by liturgy discovers the logic of abnegation, which will explain the grammar of a spirituality that otherwise disturbs us. Elizabeth of the Trinity finds abnegation perfecting love and improving liturgy (glorification of God) when she says "a praise of glory is a soul that lives in God, that loves Him with a pure and disinterested love, without seeking itself in the sweetness of this love; that loves Him beyond all His gifts and even though it would not have received anything from Him, it desires the good of the Object thus loved."[3] She makes the connections we seek: to love God beyond all his gifts is abnegation; that God's will orders everything for his greater glory is liturgy.

The abnegation we are talking about is not inspired by philosophy, or society, or nature, it is inspired by the Holy Spirit with which Jesus has infused his disciples. We belong to Jesus, and Jesus gives us permission—rights!—to use him when we fulfill our duty to worship the Father. Lebrun explains the teaching of Eudes by saying "the Saint reminds us that the life of Jesus belongs to us, and that we can use it as our own for fulfilling our obligations. In actual fact in giving Himself to us Our Lord conferred on us a real right over all His works. Besides, He is our head and we are His members."[4] The head works his will in his members, and the members can make use of what belongs to the head. Christ's liturgy is his sacrificial love that glorifies the Father, and our liturgy occurs by uniting our sacrificial love to his (if it does not, it is not Christian liturgy). So Eudes composes this prayer: "O Holy Father, O Divine Spirit, I offer you all the love and honour that my Jesus gave You throughout His life by all His divine thoughts, words and deeds, by

2. François Nepveu, *Meditations for Every Day in the Month* (New York: Benziger Brothers, 1911), 27.

3. Elizabeth of the Trinity, *I have Found God: Complete Works*, vol. 1 (Washington DC, ICS Publications, 1984), 112.

4. Charles Lebrun, *The Spiritual Teaching of St. John Eudes* (London: Sands & Co., 1934), 127.

the divine use He made of all the parts of His body and soul."[5] This requires joining ourselves to Christ's interior dispositions, and those dispositions involved a self-emptying that he did throughout his life, for the glory of his Father and the salvation of mankind. This is the liturgical pattern for his disciples' lives of self-emptying.

Asking "Whose liturgy are we doing?" is the same as asking "Who is doing our liturgy?" It is not us. Bona says, "sweet Heart of my Saviour Jesus Christ, watching over me with careful keeping all the night, I salute Thee with praise and glory for ever. Do Thou to the Father pay for me my debt of praises and thanksgiving."[6] Jesus is the only one who can liturgize adequately, satisfactorily, and properly; we beg him to pay our debt of liturgy. In the Incarnation, says Faber, "creation thus completed turned round as it were to the Face of the Creator, and worshipped Him with a worship equal to Himself."[7] Turned round. Turned away from autolatry to theolatry with adequacy for the first time. We can ask, and he will do so, because in the hypostatic union the Incarnation has united the divine liturgy of the Son of God with the human liturgy of a man. Men and women of all lands and ages are invited to join their brother in liturgy. By the power of the Holy Spirit, our liturgy is a cooperation in the liturgy the incarnate Son gives to the Father. He and we co-operate the liturgy: we work it together.

I propose that this exchange of love between God and man should be called the liturgical life. Therefore, liturgical abnegation is ultimately about true worship versus idolatry. Idolatry is the problem of a false love in the heart of man, and liturgical abnegation is its elimination. The King of Heaven brings love, and what does he want from us in return? Scupoli eavesdrops on the liturgical-abnegation conversation:

> "O King of heaven, Who art most high, what has led Thee within me, who am wretched, poor, blind, and naked?" And He will answer you: "Love."

5. Ibid., 127.
6. Giovanni Bona, *The Easy Way to God* (London: R. Washbourne, 1876), 207.
7. Frederick Faber, *Bethlehem* (London: Thomas Richardson and Son, 1860), 77.

> And you in reply will say: "O uncreated Love, O blessed Love, what dost Thou wish of me?"
>
> "Nothing else," He will say to you, "but Love; nor do I wish that other fire should burn on the altar of your heart and in your sacrifices and in all your works than the fire of my love, that consuming all other love and all your self-will, it may give me the sweetest fervor. . . .
>
> "And this can never be as long as you do not make that resignation of yourself which so much delights me, and remain attached to the love of yourself, to your own opinion, and to every wish and fancy of your own."[8]

Liturgy is a fire, a furnace, a brazier, but the wood only burns clean if it is dried by abnegation. "As a fire is not kindled in green wood still full of sap, but in dry wood," observes Bellarmine, "so the fire of charity demands hearts purified from earthly love and from empty confidence in one's own abilities."[9] And which comes first: the dry wood or the fire? Abnegation or liturgy? It would seem to be abnegation in order to have dry wood to burn, yet it is the liturgical fire

8. Lorenzo Scupoli, *The Spiritual Combat of Dom Lorenzo Scupoli* (London: Methuen & Co., 1909), 264–65. This book is a classic in ascetic theology with a confusing history. Several seventeenth-century editions were published under the name of the Spanish Benedictine John of Castañiza, but most critics consider Scupoli to be the author. One of de Sales's biographers says Scupoli himself gave him a copy when de Sales was in Padua 1587–1591. The admiration de Sales had for the book has been recorded multiple times. One day when the Bishop of Belley asked him who had been his director, he pulled this book from his pocket and said "There he is; it is the one who, with God, teaches me: From my youth, he has been my master in the things of the mind and of the inner life." Biographer Ravier says he insisted on its regular reading to Jane de Chantal, saying, "that is my dearest book and that I have carried in my pocket for at least eighteen years, and have never read it without benefit; in fact, the virtue of strength and the strength of virtue are never acquired in peace." Andre Ravier, *Saint Francis de Sales* (Rome: Salesians of Don Bosco, 2021), 177.

To complete the story, although outside of our scope here, the Orthodox ascetic, Nicodemus of the Holy Mountain published *Unseen Warfare, Being the Spiritual Combat and Path to Paradise of Lorenzo Scupoli*, revised by Theophan the Recluse (New York: St. Vladimir's Seminary Press, 1987).

9. Robert Bellarmine, *The Art of Dying Well* in *Robert Bellarmine Spiritual Writings* (New York: Paulist Press, 1989), 159.

that dries the wood. "When fire works upon green wood, it first expels the cold and moisture, which are obstacles to its operation," says Bona; "then it infuses dryness and heat, as necessary prerequisites to its own entrance; then, lastly, it is united intimately to the wood. So for the union of the soul with God, first all impediments must be removed out of the way, then the requisite predispositions must be procured; and, these things being done, union infallibly follows."[10] Abnegation is removal of all impediments out of the way, expelling cold and moisture, so that the soul can be united intimately to the flame of God (deification).

To be filled with God, we must be emptied of self. To let God sit upon the throne of our hearts, we must evacuate that throne we have stolen from him. To let God enter, we must not resent or resist him. To live under his rule, we must cease our self-rule. To obey his will, we must substitute it for our self-will. And to burn with the fire of his love on the altar of our heart, we must let it consume our self-love. Gregory de Lopez spent the first years of his hermitage praying "Thy will be done on earth as it is in heaven." For three years he said these words mentally, and when asked how soon the words presented themselves to his mind, he answered "I never breathe twice, after waking, before they are brought to my remembrance."[11] And his biographer (de Losa) said it was because these words "contain the most sublime and the most difficult doctrine in the whole spiritual life; for they contain a fixed resolution to do all that God requires, whether temporal or spiritual things, and an entire submission to his orders, by receiving at his hands, with tranquility of spirit, whatever he pleases, how rough soever it might be."[12]

So, on the one hand, abnegation cannot be understood apart from liturgy. On the other hand, liturgy expands abnegation. I am putting abnegation forward as an *act of liturgy* because liturgy is an act of love, and abnegation is a consequence of love. We should approach the Sunday liturgy already in a state of liturgy, one we have

10. Bona, *The Easy Way to God*, 60.

11. Francisco de Losa, *The Life of Gregory Lopez, A Hermit in America* (Boston: Henry V. Degen, 1856), 24–25.

12. Ibid., 89.

been conducting in our hearts throughout the week, at every moment. The liturgical heart-sacrifice (submission to the will of God) is constant. Liturgy has therefore been given expanded scope: it is no longer confined to the temple, but accompanies us through our lives, like a good friend. But as we have been saying, two things must happen for the perfection of this liturgy: we must dethrone ourselves, and let God be seated upon it because, observes Saint-Jure, "We must necessarily empty ourselves of *self*, if we wish to fill ourselves with God."[13]

If we place abnegation in the orbit of liturgy, then we can finally see its purpose. Liturgy stirs abnegation, and abnegation purifies liturgy. When the light of Mount Tabor shines from the altar, says de Granada, and "when our eyes are once cleared up by this heavenly brightness, we discover a new light, which represents things quite different from what they appear to us at first."[14] Abnegation is a matter of training love, correcting love, expanding love—all requiring a renunciation of self-love in order to revel in true love. Blosius says a soul that is humble and resigned to God is carried above itself. "All liquefied by love, and, as it were, reduced to nothing, it melts away into God."[15] Liturgical abnegation is being liquefied by the love of God.

We have all had experiences of this on a natural plane, and can use them to better understand the supernatural experience. A lover who is smitten by the beloved becomes less preoccupied with himself; the love a parent has for a newborn baby liquefies the mother and father so they pour themselves out in the care of the child; if a friendship is deep, it willingly makes sacrifice for the good of the other. Our eyes are taken off ourselves when fixed upon something greater. It is called conversion when our eyes are taken off ourselves (abnegation) and fixed on Jesus (liturgy). Abnegation is the result of being swept up in liturgy, leaving the soul to swoon with prayer.

13. Saint-Jure, *The Religious*, vol. 1, 574.

14. Luis de Granada, *The Sinner's Guide* (Philadelphia: Henry McGrath, 1845), 95.

15. Blosius (Louis of Blois), *Spiritual Works of Louis of Blois*, ed. John Bowden (London: R. & T. Washbourne, 1903), 185.

Sin has bent our love; abnegation will bend it back again. Then we can offer true worship to God. Liturgical abnegation is the cooperative movement of liturgy and abnegation for the perfection of the spiritual life. Every moment of life is a choice between fraudulent idolatry or true liturgy. Every moment is a choice as to whether we prefer self-will to God's will, self-love to his love, our own glory to his glory. It is a liturgical crisis (from *krinein* "to separate, decide, judge") and requires the solution of abnegation. Fixing our eyes on God requires taking them off idols, including ourselves. Practicing abnegation turns us toward what is pleasing to God, and away from what is displeasing to him. Or, in Tronson's words, "our eyes, wholly fixed upon our Dying Lord, refuse to be drawn aside by any outward object; so shall our hearts, filled with the love of God, urge us to cast away all self-love, to crucify in ourselves whatever is displeasing to Him."[16] Abnegation denies self-will its control, and withdraws our self-esteem so it may be directed to God. We can certainly love and respect creatures, but not to such a degree, or in such a manner, that any creature replaces the Creator. It is a matter of balance—a liturgical proportionality as we recover the balance upset by original sin.

Question: Why abnegation? Answer: Liturgy. Question: How does our liturgy become truer, simpler, and more spiritual? Answer: Abnegation.

Grou says every true Christian must have realized at some time that he had never found final happiness in the enjoyment of this world's goods.

> It was then that he really saw the nothingness of earthly things, and understood that they were capable indeed of exciting his passions, but never of satisfying his heart. Then a deep secret touch of grace taught him that man's true happiness lies in God. . . . The world has been crucified to him and he to the world; he has been attracted to God alone; he has sought Him, and found Him within his own soul, which is God's very temple.[17]

16. Tronson, *Examination of Conscience*, 122.

17. Jean Grou, *The Spiritual Maxims of Père Grou* (London: J.T. Hayes, 1874), 95–96.

This experience on the mountaintop of liturgy gives a new view of the world, one which undoes worldliness and demotes it from the position of idol to the position of servant.

Abnegation goes forth in full liturgical stride, indifferent to the distraction of creatures, and detached from self-love. God's grace is leading a two-step dance. First, God gives us a touch. It can be dramatic or quiet, stern or gentle, pulling from the front or pushing from the back. Second, God withdraws, which inflicts a wound of love that will draw the soul toward himself. Things of the world no longer magnetize a person, and Blosius says from that moment on, man is "unable to wander forth in search of spurious delight derived from created things, for all to him would be insipid and bitter which was not God."[18] God is love; love causes abnegation; abnegation flows willingly from love.

In his envy toward God and hatred of man, Satan does all he can to instigate idolatry. His activity is subtle, Grou acknowledges. "[Satan] does not immediately discover [reveal] himself and say, 'Fall down and adore me'; such an open invitation to rebel against God would produce only horror; but by concealing his ultimate object he is enabled the more securely to attain it, cautiously leading his unhappy votaries to transfer their adoration from God to their own illusions."[19] Hatred of sin and love of God are flip sides of the same coin. Sin arises from false worship—which is why battling sin is a liturgical warfare. Hatred of pride leads to meekness; hatred of self-will leads to obedience; hatred of self-esteem leads to humility; hatred of self-indulgence leads to renunciation; hatred of self-love leads to becoming true servants of God. Liturgical abnegation particularly combats sin in its twin forms of pride and idolatry.

This puts an eschatological question to us: What is our last end? Whom should we be worshiping? Man and woman got their answer wrong to these questions when they were first put to them in the Garden of Eden. There is a huge difference between *liturgizing* God and *utilizing* God. A person whose liturgy lacks purification by

18. Blosius (Louis of Blois), *A Book of Spiritual Instruction: Institutio Spiritualis* (St. Louis: B. Herder, 1900), 2.

19. Grou, *The Interior of Jesus and Mary*, vol. 1, 162–63.

abnegation has the following traits: he does not think of God alone, but always of God plus his own desires; his submission is not instantaneous; he accepts a cross only if he agrees to it, not because God imposes it; he expects God to persuade, not command; he hopes to persuade God, not obey him; his childlike spirit of sanctity is lost because he questions the ways of God; he expects God to flatter him; the refinement of obedience is gone. In summary, impure liturgy loses its liturgical purpose of adoration. Man's business is to adore God, not assail him, "otherwise the gracefulness of submission is gone," says Faber. "The right to more intimate union with God is forfeited. The waters of grace in their soul become shallow, and their spirit of prayer thin, peevish, vexed, and wailing. All this is because in their prayer they have had the habit of being something before God, instead of being nothing."[20]

Sin attempts to use God for one's own gain—and this is as true for the pious sinner as the worldly sinner. Sin is a disordered affection: being inclined and disposed to the wrong thing, in the wrong way, for the wrong reason, at the wrong time. Sin attaches self to the creature in place of the Creator, something true of both mortal and venial sins. The difference, says Saint-Jure, is that mortal sin "is directly opposed to the end of man," and excites man "to place in a creature his end and beatitude, which are to be found, not in the creature but in the Creator. The disorder of venial sin is not opposed to the end of man but to the means given him to attain that end."[21] All creatures were given as steps to beatitude, so the sinner not only commits an offense against God when he employs them in any other way, or for any other reason, the sinner also commits an offense against creation, which therefore groans in its bondage.

The world is a good creation, and we may use the things of this world, but only as a pathway to God. Creation is a ladder to its Creator, but, unfortunately, our disordered affections have rotted its rungs. Saint-Jure says, "Learn to love the Creator in His creature,

20. Frederick Faber, *The Foot of the Cross: or, The Sorrows of Mary* (London: Thomas Richardson and Son, 1858), 174.

21. Jean Baptiste Saint-Jure, *A Treatise on the Knowledge and Love of Our Lord Jesus Christ*, vol. 2 (New York: P. O'Shea, 1875), 357–58.

the workman in His work . . . [and] stop not at what he has done; go to Himself, lest you lose the Creator who has made these things, and you as well."[22] This life is a pathway, not a home; a trail, not a residence. So we are required to remain a pilgrim, and not become a squatter. A pilgrim does not set up permanent camp only a hundred feet from the beginning, and miles away from the ending. "Are you not children of God?" asks Bossuet. "Do you not carry the mark of his adoption, the sacred character of baptism? Is not the earth a place of exile? Is not heaven your home? Why do you so much admire the world? If you are from Jerusalem, why are you singing songs of Babylon? All that you say and think about the world is said in a foreign language learned during your exile. Forget that foreign language; learn to speak the language of your home."[23] Liturgy is a daily and weekly language camp.

We may use the world, but we must not be ruled by the world. De Liguori drives the point home.

> What folly would it not be for a traveler, if when traveling, he were only to think of making himself great in that country through which he only has to pass, without minding the being reduced to live miserably in that country where he will have to spend his whole life? And is he not foolish, who seeks his happiness in this world, where he has to remain but a few days, and who by so doing, runs the risk of being unhappy in the world to come, where he will have to remain for ever? He who possesses anything that is borrowed does not place his affections on it, knowing, as he does, that within a short time he will have to restore it. All the goods of this world are but given to us as a loan.[24]

Abnegation does not scorn temporal things, but the soul that has been made for eternal things cannot rest in temporal things. That is why our appetite for this world is affected when eternal things are

22. Saint-Jure, *A Treatise on the Knowledge and Love of Our Lord Jesus Christ*, vol. 1, 515.

23. Jacques-Bénigne Bossuet, *Meditations on Mary* (Manchester, NH: Sophia Institute Press, 2015), Kindle 25.

24. Alphonsus de Liguori, *Preparation for Death* (Philadelphia: J.B. Lippincott & Co, 1869), 27–28.

tasted in liturgy. When the saint overlooks the world, it is because he has looked it over and found it to be just the foreground of an eternal horizon.

Can we not all remember times when we became indifferent to an original desire because something more important arose? A certain scheme meant everything until we wed; then we happily change plans for one into plans for two. A certain expectation is well worked out until the child was born; then we happily change plans for two into plans for three. This is exactly what is happening on the supernatural plane. A certain temporal project is our entire hope until Jesus walks by; then we deny ourselves and follow him. Liturgy causes an indifference to the world because it presents the most important object of desire we can possibly have, namely, he who will give us beatitude. We do not know where our first steps are going when God draws us away from the world; we can only discover it on the journey, as Abraham did. Abraham was pulled, not pushed. Abnegation is not simple ignorance, it is holy ignorance. (Not a bad definition of faith).

In abnegation, the person of faith runs out of the world, and out of himself, in order to run after God, and into God. Pollien thus concludes that "one must go out of oneself to go to God."[25] But do not be sad! When someone runs out of creation and into God, then creation's own purpose is fulfilled. The cosmos becomes happy! The happiness of every creature consists of performing their part in God's design, and God's design for matter is to serve spirit. The design for truth, beauty, and goodness in nature is to bring the human person to the True One, the Beautiful One, the Good One. Natural creatures are happy to sacrifice themselves for our good, notices Fénelon. He asks God, "for what didst thou make all these Things?" and knows the answer already: "They were all made for Man, and Man was made for thee."[26] Your human growth should end in God, since you are made for God.

25. François Pollien, ed. Joseph Tissot, *The Interior Life Simplified and Reduced to Its Fundamental Principle* (London: Burns Oates & Washbourne Ltd., 1927), 170.

26. François Fénelon, *Pious Thoughts Concerning the Knowledge and Love of God* (London: W. and J. Innys, 1720), 8.

Many authors contrast the light of this world to the light of heaven, and search for illustrations. Blosius says love of God drowns out love of a temporal world, the way the sun drowns out the pale light of the stars when it rises in the morning. "When the uncreated light arises created light vanishes. Therefore the created light of the soul is changed into the light of eternity."[27] After this happens, the soul can find her way back to her first principle and last end. The world is privileged to show the way, but no creature pretends to be man's end. That is a lie Satan made up.

Liturgical abnegation is the extinguishment of any lamp that blinds us to God and impedes our union with him. Annihilation is death—but de Ravignan wants to know "what then is it that dies here?" He answers, "That which is not worthy to live . . . [namely] pride, frivolity, vanity, caprice, weakness, vice, and passion."[28] The liturgical soul takes a spiritual measure of the created horizon by placing it against the Uncreated horizon, and then everything changes. Life turns upside down, things turn around, souls turn their vision from downward to upward, inward to outward. The soul is converted (turns around) from creature to Creator, and John Evangelist of Boisleduc says God "infuses into her His divine light, irradiating the pure soul which, simply for His love, has put herself into such a state of poverty and detachment from all things."[29]

My thesis, to summarize, is that the liturgizing of God and the abnegation of self happen in one and the same motion. You look toward by looking away. Abnegating self liturgizes God; liturgizing God abnegates self. Here is my trail of thought: liturgy is oblation; oblation is giving your heart to God; giving your heart to God is uniting yourself with the will of Christ; uniting with Christ's will disunites you from your own will; this is liturgical abnegation. Surin describes the fruit of an abnegation of self as occurring "when, having put all our interests, temporal and spiritual, in the hands of the Lord, we desire only to obtain from Him what it is His will that we

27. Blosius, *A Book of Spiritual Instruction, Institutio Spiritualis*, 107.

28. Gustave de Ravignan, *On the Life and Institute of the Jesuits* (Philadelphia: W. J. Cunningham, 1845), 111.

29. John Evangelist of Boisleduc, *The Kingdom of God in the Soul*, 53.

should ask."[30] Liturgy is desiring to desire what God desires for us. Abnegation overcomes selfishness so liturgy can take place.

On the one hand, liturgy modifies an ordinary understanding of abnegation. Instead of viewing abnegation from a social, moral, or psychological viewpoint, liturgy assigns abnegation a completely new motive. On the other hand, abnegation modifies an ordinary understanding of liturgy. Liturgy's scope is expanded beyond the temple, to become constantly practiced in daily renunciations that raise the soul toward God. When a balloonist drops ballast, his basket rises. Jesus said we must deny something in order to follow him. Deny what? Ourselves. That is just shorthand for the many things Eudes says are included: "you have to renounce yourself, that is, your own mind, your own ideas, your own will, desires, inclinations and your self-love."[31] The reason to empty something is to receive something else. Saint-Jure explains that annihilation is required to be capacitated for union with God because it is impossible for a person to arrive at union with God otherwise. "In fact, how can you, says St. Augustine, fill a vase with honey, if you do not first empty it of that with which it is filled? We are all full of ourselves; we must necessarily empty ourselves of *self*, if we wish to fill ourselves with God: cast out what you have, in order to obtain what you have not."[32] There is no reason to annihilate the old thing unless some new thing is scheduled to arrive. To deny a present good without expectation of a greater good is perverse: one must not abnegate without hope, and faith, and love. Abnegation is a chapter in the book of the theological virtues. And the new thing scheduled to arrive is Christ himself. In that case, what ought we not empty out, so he can have room? What ought we not abandon, so he can take possession? What ought we not abnegate, so we can liturgize? We are linked to God the Father by the mystical liturgical chain of Son, Holy Spirit, Church, sacrament, and our own abnegation.

30. John-Joseph Surin, *The Foundations of the Spiritual Life: Drawn from the Book of the Imitation of Jesus Christ* (London: James Burns, 1844), 24.

31. Eudes, *The Life and the Kingdom of Jesus in Christian Souls*, 19.

32. Saint-Jure, *The Religious*, vol. 1, 574.

This is a matter of justice. Justice means giving someone what he is due, and God is due everything. De Caussade says failing to honor God is "injustice because we deprive Him of the glory that belongs to Him; falsehood because we flatter ourselves in appropriating what can never belong to us."[33] For this reason, the authors repeatedly say that withholding liturgy is an act of robbery. For example, Segneri says the greatest robbery of God we can commit is "to rob Him of that glory which can only be due to Him."[34] For example, Grou says "all our love . . . is due to God and to God alone, and He ought to be the end of all our affections, without any exception. . . . Every kind of self-love, whatever its immediate object may be, is a robbery from God."[35] For example, John of the Cross says "One thought of man is of more value than the whole world; God alone is, for that reason, the worthy object of it, and to Him alone is it due; every thought of man, therefore, which is not given to God, is a robbery."[36]

In daily abnegation, creation is put under the reign of God again ("thy kingdom come, thy will be done") by a cosmic priesthood that Christ restored to man and woman after they had forfeited it. Christ won it back for them by his merits on the Cross so we could fulfill our liturgical responsibility with justice. Liturgical abnegation is performed on the altar of our hearts, where love's sacrificial fire burns a holocaust. Diversions that take us away from Almighty God are annihilated there until the day we die. The fire God kindles in the soul of the liturgist will devour all foreign love within her. We cannot glorify God, or enjoy peace, without submission to the adorable will of our Maker.

This abnegation is unpleasant and irritating to our corrupted nature, so the sinner finds the idea of abnegation repulsive, and cre-

33. Jean Pierre de Caussade, *Abandonment to Divine Providence* (St. Louis: B. Herder Book Co., 1921), 116.

34. Paul Segneri, *The Manna of the Soul: Meditations for Every Day of the Year*, vol. 2 (New York: Benziger Brothers, 1892), 732.

35. Jean Grou, *Manual for Interior Souls* (London: S. Anselm's Society, 1890), 347–48.

36. John of the Cross, *Spiritual Canticle Between the Soul and Christ* in *The Complete Works*, 369.

ates ingenious ways to cling to the honor and esteem he has crafted for himself in this world. However, it is all for naught. The world will pass away, and the only ultimate satisfaction for the soul is liturgizing the ultimate God, since she was created and joined to a body for exactly that purpose. Surin thinks our happiness "is the fruit of an entire abnegation of self," and that "a good man is fully satisfied when God is pleased; His whole pleasure is to see God's will done."[37] And Leen gives us this thought to chew on: "*Self-abnegation* is but *the practical acknowledgement* of the fatherhood of God."[38] "Practical acknowledgement" means an acknowledgement put into practice. By acknowledging this fatherhood practically, we are uniting with Jesus to be made co-sons, co-heirs.

Liturgical abnegation cannot be grasped apart from the mystery of the Son of God who did not consider equality with the Father a thing to be grasped, but emptied himself. He forsook his place in heaven to occupy a manger. Challoner calls the manger "the royal bed of state, in which he was first laid, upon his coming down amongst us. O how has the Word incarnate here annihilated himself for us."[39] Man fell by the affectation of a superior excellence, so the Son of God begins his mortal life by profound humility to cure our pride. He annihilated his glory to bear our iniquity, and he mortified his will in order to be perfectly obedient to the Father, even to the Cross. He was a man of abnegation (Is 53:3). The Incarnation reaches through Bethlehem, through Calvary, through the Eucharist, all the way into the heart in order to deify the soul.

Everyone is beckoned to drink from the river that the Book of Revelation says floods the world. This is liturgy flowing from the throne of God, and Blosius thinks there will be consequences if we taste it. Beware! This fountain of water (Jn 4:14) "is of such efficacy and sweetness that it can easily cast out all the bitterness of vice. . . . If we can taste but one little drop of it, we shall no longer thirst for vain things and failing creatures, but for God only, only for the love

37. Surin, *The Foundations of the Spiritual Life*, 24.

38. Leen, *The True Vine and Its Branches*, 222.

39. Challoner, *Considerations*, part II, 293.

of God."[40] We lose our taste for the world by this new taste in two ways, paradoxically united.

First, as has already been said, a drop of this water makes the world taste insipid. De Bernières-Louvigny understands that "this soul, thus illuminated, begins to be dead to the world . . . because the same light that brings her to know and taste God present gives her a disrelish for creatures. Neither is it so much the insufficiency of creatures that causes this disgust as the all-sufficiency of God, and the lively feeling of his divine presence. All this may take place as well among [the] crowd of men as in deserts."[41] The abnegation of which we are speaking is not confined to the desert, for monks who have left the world, it is a daily command for even Christians in the city, who are still in the world.

Second, although the creature cannot satisfy as once it did, the denial of self permits a new appreciation of the world. Freed for obedience, set at liberty, free in the face of death, we fearlessly walk through life, protected from the attacks of Satan, flesh, and the world. Then, says Saint-Jure, the soul will tend directly to God, and we can enjoy "all the assistance and pleasure creatures afford us, [such as] food for the taste, colors for the sight, music for the ears, perfumes for the smell, and in all the other sinless pleasures of the body," remembering that God is present in these creatures. God uses them to draw us to himself. "He sends us through these channels little drops of pleasure which make us sigh after the fountain of all joy, which is Himself."[42] When we talk about denying the self and the world, we mean denying selfish pride in them both. And that will require humility, to which we must next turn.

40. Blosius, *A Book of Spiritual Instruction, Institutio Spiritualis*, 111.

41. De Bernières-Louvigny, *The Interior Christian in Eight Books*, 72.

42. Saint-Jure, *A Treatise on the Knowledge and Love of Our Lord Jesus Christ*, vol. 1, 514–15.

3

Humility

De Bergamo highlights the importance of humility by saying "there are saints in paradise who were neither martyrs, nor doctors, nor contemplatives, nor virgins;—but there is not a single one there who was not humble."[1] Deny yourself and follow me; humble yourself and be like me. Humility must be housed in the temple of theology. "Humility, properly understood," says Teresa Gertrude, "is the virtue resulting from a full and complete recognition on the part of the creature of its position with respect to the Creator."[2] Abnegation humility is not understood by considering the creature's position with respect to a king, an employer, a clique, or some other ring of society. Abnegation humility is a recognition of the creature's position with respect to the Creator. Such understanding comes when liturgy celebrates and adores the Almighty who has stooped to redeem us.

We can therefore immediately clear away three misconceptions. First, humility does not mean believing we are worthless, it means believing we are unworthy. Unworthiness does not mean worthlessness. Abnegation works in proportion to grace: the more powerful the presence of grace, the more powerful the sense of unworthiness. But it is not the false effort to think of ourselves as worthless. This humility is not full of self-loathing, it is full of something altogether different. "This kind of humility is full of reverence," says Gay, and then all will become clear, easy, and unutterably sweet because "it is

1. Gaetano Maria de Bergamo, *Thoughts and Affections on the Passion of Jesus Christ For Every Day of the Year, Taken from Holy Scripture and the Writings of the Fathers of the Church* (New York: Benziger Brothers, 1905), 43.

2. Teresa Gertrude of the Blessed Sacrament, *Jesus, the All-Beautiful* (London: Burns and Oates, 1910), 80.

the practical fruit and the normal expression of our religion towards God."[3] You are unworthy of grace, but how can you think yourself worthless when the Son of God shed blood for your redemption? Doyle observes that abnegation has both a positive and negative side. Thomas says charity means "God alone," and Cassian says purity of heart means "no creature." "Both these express the same thing in different words, just as we might express the fact of the English ambassador's having gone to Paris, by stating either positively, that he has reached that city, or negatively that he has not stayed at any other."[4] Positively put, man's last end is deification; negatively put, man's last end is not here, not now. Charity and purity of heart are the same thing, and both are connected with humility, the subject of this chapter.

Second, humility does not mean denying the talents with which God gifts his sons and daughters. De Sales distinguishes the truly humble from those "who amuse themselves with a false and foppish humility, which hinders them from considering in themselves, the good gifts which God has bestowed on them; such men are much in the wrong; the goods which God has put in us, require to be acknowledged, esteemed, and highly honoured."[5] Although the world tends to think of humility as weak, small, and timid, the theologians of liturgical abnegation think of humility as powerful, tremendous, and brave. Bona summarizes it well. "This virtue, though it may seem by its very name to denote something mean and small, is nevertheless the virtue of the great, since it is the virtue of the perfect, and it does not lower the mind to base things, but raises it to those that are more noble; for while it attributes nothing to itself, it is wholly turned to God, believing it can do all things in him, by whom it is strengthened. Therefore, it is brave and magnanimous."[6]

3. Charles Gay, *The Christian Life and Virtues Considered in the Religious State*, vol. 1 (London: Burns & Oates, 1878), 318.

4. Francis Cuthbert Doyle, *Principles of Religious Life* (London: R.&T. Washbourne, Ltd., 1906), 2–3.

5. Francis de Sales, *The Spiritual Director of Devout and Religious Souls* (Dublin: Printed by James Mehain, 1777), 97.

6. Giovanni Bona, *A Treatise of Spiritual Life* (New York: Fr. Pustet & Co., 1901), 428–29.

And third, sin has turned the world upside down, and in this topsy-turvy world we think pride exalts and empowers a person, while humility abases and dishonors a person. The worldling thinks humility oppresses, while in fact it exalts. Lacordaire notes that even an egotistical being can say "I forgot myself!" because "he forgets himself when he is happy; he forgets himself at the moment of the greatest dilation of his existence. It is because God, who is his true happiness, has, in fact, created him to forget himself one day in him."[7] Humility is a taste of that.

Liturgical abnegation therefore has a radically different assessment of humility than the world has. May I record some of the words of praise given it? They have always struck me as reminiscent of the O antiphons.

- O holy humility! thou art the key of perfection, the gate of paradise, and the seat of divine grace (Barbanson).[8]

- O amiable humility, how necessary art thou for me, how pleasing to God and man! With what comfort and quiet dost thou enrich thy possessor! O heaven upon earth! What do I not get by humility! What do I lose by pride and presumption! (de Castañiza).[9]

- O humility! who understands thy value? who prefers thee before all treasures? who endeavours to reap from every occurrence of life the precious fruit of self-abjection? Such a soul is great in the sight of God (Grou).[10]

- O incomparable humility! I know thee not, and unless the strong, clear light of heaven reveals thee to my view, I never shall know thee (Grou).[11]

7. Jean-Baptiste Henri-Dominique Lacordaire, *Life: Conferences Delivered at Toulouse* (New York: P. O'Shea, 1875), 54.

8. Constantine Barbanson, *The Secret Paths of Divine Love* (London: Burns Oates and Washbourne Ltd., 1928), 22.

9. Juan de Castañiza, *The Spiritual Conflict and Conquest* (London: Burns and Oates, 1874), 416. His version of this book includes *Maxims of Mystical Divinity* and this is maxim 24, page 416, not found in Scupoli.

10. Grou, *The Interior of Jesus and Mary*, vol. 2 (Dublin: James Duffy, 1847), 160.

11. Ibid., 168.

- O humility! first virtue and first duty of the Christian, who shall fear to exceed in thee, seeing the extremes to which Christ carried thee even before his birth? (Grou).[12]
- Oh, how precious humility must be when God recompenses it with eternal glory! (de Bergamo).[13]

The theologians of liturgical abnegation exclaim the mysteries of humility with wonder and affection.

So what is the purpose and value of humility? De Sales says it protects the virtues, and "he who would lay up virtues without humility is like one who carries a precious dust in his hand exposed to the wind."[14] No matter how many the virtues, or how detailed the virtues, without humility they will be blown out of our hands. Worse than that: without humility the virtues become self-defeating because self-pride ruins them.

Certain people are called to imitate Jesus in special and exceptional ways. There are monks who imitate his desert solitude, apostles who imitate his teaching, saints who perform miracles like him, and martyrs who imitate his agony. To make these kinds of imitations requires a special vocation that comes from divine law, and usually requires permission by Church law. If this is not your vocation, then do not deprecate them out of envy, but rather heed the words of de Sales: "If a robe of gold does not suit you, will you say that therefore it is worth nothing? Or will you throw a ring into the dirt because it fits not your finger?"[15] But if an extraordinary vocation is not given you, de Bergamo says ordinary humility is. "He has not called every one to be doctors, preachers or priests, nor has He bestowed on all the gift of restoring sight to the blind, healing the sick, raising the dead or casting out devils, but to all He has said: 'Learn of Me to be humble of heart,' and to all He has given the

12. Grou, *The Interior of Jesus and Mary*, vol. 1, 62.

13. Gaetano Maria de Bergamo, *Humility of Heart* (Mandeville, LA: Founding Father Films Publishing, 2015), 81.

14. Francis de Sales, *Maxims and Counsels of St. Francis de Sales for Every Day of the Year* (Dublin: M.H. Gill & Son, 1884), 160.

15. Francis de Sales, *Treatise on the Love of God* (Blacksburg, VA: Wilder Publications, 2011), 277–78.

power to learn humility of Him. Innumerable things are worthy of imitation in the Incarnate Son of God, but He only asks us to imitate His humility."[16] He commands certain of his followers to perform certain ministries, but he commands all of his followers to "Learn from me; for I am gentle and lowly in heart" (Mt 11:29).

Come close to me, says Jesus. This is necessary because humility is not taught through some special technique, it is caught by being close to Jesus. Grou admits that "when all is said, I know no method equal to that which Jesus Christ expressed in the words: *Learn of Me.* You have *My lessons* in the Gospel: study them, and put them in practice. You have *My example*, for My whole life was a mirror of humility: make Me your pattern. You have *My interior grace*, which will persuade and help you to profit by My lessons and My example."[17] Jesus's humility should be studied closely by Christian souls who aspire to humility, he adds. "Follow Him from His Crib to His Cross, and as you mark His actions one by one, say to yourselves: This is what He was; this is what my Master, my Pattern, my Saviour, my Judge was willing to be."[18] Humility requires sincerity. "Do not pretend to wish to be last and least, unless you really and sincerely mean it"[19] (de Sales).

We shall meet Christ on his way to us if we are on our way to him. Christ emptied himself, taking the form of a servant; we shall deny ourselves, emptying our hearts of pride, self-aggrandizement, and vainglory. De Sales says, "our Lord, desiring to give Himself wholly to us, wishes that we, on our part, should give ourselves entirely to Him. . . . [He] finds our hearts all full of desires, affections, and petty wishes. This is not what He seeks, for He hopes to find them empty, that He may make Himself their Master and Ruler."[20] Jesus does not resent maturity and independence on our part. Not at all. Indeed, he is trying to create a fully-developed heart

16. De Bergamo, *Humility of Heart*, 2–3.

17. Grou, *The School of Jesus Christ*, 216.

18. Ibid., 219.

19. Francis de Sales, *Introduction to the Devout Life* (New York: Vintage Spiritual Classics, 2002), 99.

20. Francis de Sales, *Library of St. Francis de Sales: vol. 5, The Spiritual Conferences* (London: Burns & Oates, Ltd., 1909), 350–51.

over which he may be master and ruler. The objective is not to lessen us, but to elevate us.

Sin is sneaky. Many theologians, and even philosophers, have pointed out that we can become proud of our humility, and that false humility takes many disguises. It may take on the appearance of pious fear before God, which is actually self-justification. It may take on the appearance of modesty, which may actually be a secret feeling of superiority. Libermann analyzes the situation correctly when he says certain acts of humility "are sometimes sincere and sometimes not; but, fundamentally, such persons always think well of themselves in their own conduct. They have a certain self-satisfaction and self-complacency because they feel they have privileges that others do not possess. . . . The soul is puffed up as it were by that feeling of superiority, in a vague and indefinite fashion."[21] Any self-satisfaction over humility is a warning sign.

Paul said he feels two laws at work within himself: the first delights at God's law, while a second law holds him captive to sin (Rom 7:22–23). A similar conflict occurs in the case of humility. One part of us praises humility as a virtue, and delights in it, and desires it. But another part of us knows that the only way to attain humility is through humiliation, and this we do not like so much. One prays for humility—but one does not like to be humiliated! Ravignan observes that it is not difficult to desire humility, "but to practise, to accept, to go in quest of humiliation is another thing. Humility itself is sweet, very sweet; but it is a fruit, a product, and we must labour and work for a long time, and pray above all things before gathering it."[22] De Bergamo asks, "What avail fine thoughts and discourses on humility if, after all, we are not humble?"[23] If one wants a test whether the humility is true or false, Fénelon has one to recommend: "A humility that is still talkative does not run very deep."[24]

21. Libermann, *Letters to Clergy and Religious*, Spiritan Series 7, vol. 3, 93.

22. Gustave de Ravignan, *Ravignan's Last Retreat* (London: Burns and Oates, 1859), 106.

23. De Bergamo, *Thoughts and Affections on the Passion of Jesus Christ*, 330.

24. François Fénelon, *The Seeking Heart* (Jacksonville, FL: SeedSowers Publishing, 1992), 16.

Since humiliations are the necessary way to attain humility, we are fortunate to be given so many opportunities for practice. De Bergamo thinks we ought to be grateful "to any one who helps to keep me in humility by subjecting me to humiliations of word and deed, because he is co-operating with the divine mercy to fulfil the work of my eternal salvation."[25] Like Augustine, who midway through his conversion famously prayed "O Lord, help me to be pure, but not yet," so we pray "O Lord, help me to be humble, but do not humiliate me." What is the key here? Humility must be caused by Christ, not by self-exertion. Saint-Jure says, "as the mariner's compass does not turn to the pole till it is touched with the loadstone, so our will does not of itself incline to humility, to contempt, to opprobrium; it must first be touched with the humility of Jesus Christ, who, communicating His virtue, makes us perform cheerfully what we had previously held in horror."[26]

Humility neither means scrambling to place oneself lower than everyone else, nor to refuse to recognize abilities and talents with which God has gifted a person. It rather means accepting exactly the place where God has placed you. This is a constant theme in de Sales. "There are persons who give way to a false humility, which hinders them from regarding the good that God has really placed in them.... That humility which does not produce generosity is undoubtedly false."[27] First humility says, "I can do nothing, I am nothing," and immediately after generosity says, "there is nothing I cannot do since I put all my confidence in God."

In this sense, the opposite of humility is not only pride, but also envy. Envy means being saddened at someone's good fortune, and gladdened at someone's misfortune, but there will be no envy in heaven because everyone will be happy at the sight of someone else's beatitude. This happiness does not have to wait for heaven; Jesus put it first in his list of beatitudes. The poor in spirit are devoid of spiritual arrogance. Saint-Jure says "there is no people in the world more poor in spirit, than the truly humble, because they

25. De Bergamo, *Humility of Heart*, 85.

26. Saint-Jure, *The Spiritual Man*, 241.

27. Francis de Sales, *Practical Piety* (London: Burns and Lambert, 1851), 162–63.

account themselves to be nothing, to have nothing, to be able to do nothing, and to be worth nothing . . . not assuming any praise to themselves for any thing whatsoever."[28] Such persons are blessed.

The world regards humility as a useless virtue, but that is only because it goes against the grain of worldliness more than any other Christian virtue. The world can even become angry at the appearance of the humble person (perhaps angry enough to crucify him). Grou understands that when Jesus "unfolded to their view the glory of a kingdom it was of a heavenly kingdom, totally different in its elements from the kingdoms of the earth; of a kingdom whose long-sealed portals could be opened only by the cross, and whose low and narrow entrance could give admittance only to humility and detachment."[29] The happiness of humility in the kingdom of heaven comes from discovering how dependent, how reliant, and how much we are in need of God. De Bergamo says he learned the entire theory of this virtue from the Apostle "who, in two words, explains to me both the theory and practice of true humility. The whole secret is, to realize in myself and to be profoundly penetrated with two things: *What art Thou, O my God, and what am I?*"[30] He who is truly humble is never ashamed at his nothingness because he honors God by admitting it. The more total a person's dependence on God, the more humility leads him to profess he is nothing without him.

On the one hand, humility would appear to be easy because we have so much to be humble about. On the other hand, de Sales says achieving humility is a life-long labor.

> To-day we love humility, and exclaim, therefore: "Ah! what a lovable virtue is humility! It is surely the most admirable and the most necessary of all!" And so that day we are bent upon trying with all our strength to acquire it. But on the morrow we shall be disgusted with it; or, at least, not prize or esteem it as we did yesterday. We shall say that it is certainly a very great virtue, but not

28. Jean Baptiste Saint-Jure, *The Holy Life of Monsieur de Renty* (London: printed for Benj. Tooke, 1684), 53.

29. Grou, *The Interior of Jesus and Mary*, vol. 1, 170.

30. De Bergamo, *Thoughts and Affections on the Passion of Jesus Christ*, 41.

> the most lovable of all; and then it is really quite piteous to think of all the trouble that must be taken to acquire it, with such small results, or even none at all. See how changeable and inconstant we are![31]

A life of humility requires stability, continuance, fixity, and an affection in the heart. It is not a virtue for the weak.

Liturgical abnegation relies upon humility, and humility arises from liturgical abnegation. John of Ávila knows that "nothing so offends its Creator as a self-satisfied heart, because it contains no empty vessel into which He can pour the riches of His mercy. It will remain in its natural poverty, for it can offer no place into which the waters of grace may flow, to make it live happily with God, and bring forth much fruit, like a well-watered garden."[32] Deny yourself and follow me; empty yourself and be filled with me; humble yourself and live with me; unlock your pride and open your door to me, and I will come in. Grou says our obligation to obey God comes from God's dominion over us, and this simply proves "that humility is the natural appendage of humanity."[33] Adam and Eve had natural reasons to be humble before God. It was natural to their humanity. But when they lost sight of those reasons, they forsook their reliance upon, and submission to, God. Alas, sinners don't do nature naturally anymore.

So what good is humility? How does it profit a person? The answer is two-sided: it enables someone to flee Satan and to adhere to Christ. About the former, de Bergamo says "humility causes the evil one to flee because he cannot face the humble on account of his great pride, and it causes every temptation to vanish suddenly because there can be no temptation without a touch of pride."[34] About the latter, Blosius asks for the grace "to take hold of the cross of self-denial with ardent devotion, and to imitate, with the most fervent charity, the example of Thy virtues, and to follow Thee in

31. De Sales, *Library of St. Francis de Sales: vol. 5, The Spiritual Conferences*, footnote 1, 321.

32. John of Ávila, *Letters of Blessed John of Ávila*, 152.

33. Grou, *The Interior of Jesus and Mary*, vol. 1, 266.

34. De Bergamo, *Humility of Heart*, 46.

all humility even unto death."[35] They happen simultaneously, the former being a condition for the latter, and let us consider both goods.

First, Satan hates it. De Sales imagines it hurting the devil's ears. "The swallow with its sharp cry and keen glance has the power of frightening away birds of prey, and for that reason the dove prefers it to all other birds, and lives surely beside it; even so humility drives Satan away, and cherishes the gifts and graces of the Holy Spirit within us."[36] Satan finds humility offensive because he finds submission oppressive. The great divide between angels and demons is humility, Blosius thinks. "Remember that our Lord Jesus Christ, and the blessed angelic spirits, and all the citizens of heaven are humble and detest pride; that, on the contrary, the wicked demons are proud and pursue humility with hatred."[37] The revelations to de Agreda made known to her what urged Lucifer and his confederates to sin, and it amounts to loss of humility which torpedoed worship. He would not liturgize God.

> [Lucifer] fell into a most disorderly self-love, which arose from the consciousness of being endowed with greater gifts and greater beauty of nature and grace, than the other inferior angels. He tarried with inordinate pleasure in this consciousness; and thus self-satisfied he became lax and remiss in the gratitude, which was due to God as the sole cause of all that he had received. Turning again and again in admiration toward himself, he took pleasure in his own beauty and grace, attributing them to himself and loving them as his own. This disorderly self-love not only caused him to exalt himself on account of the superior virtues, which he had received, but also induced him to harbor envy and covetousness for other gifts and for excellences not his own. Then, because he could not attain them, he conceived a mortal hatred and indignation against God, who created him out of nothing, and against all his creatures.[38]

35. Blosius, *Oratory of the Faithful Soul* (London: Richardson and Son, 1848), 51.

36. De Sales, *Introduction to the Devout Life*, 96.

37. Blosius, *Spiritual Works of Louis of Blois*, 120.

38. Mary de Agreda, *The Mystical City of God: Complete Edition* (London: Catholic Way Publishing, 2013), paragraph 85, Kindle page 96.

What strategy is left to Satan? He can neither create nor destroy, but he can corrupt. He is a deceiver, a liar, and has only too much latitude in corrupting how a sinner approaches the true, the good, and the beautiful. He opposes his devilish humility to divine humility, causing Teresa of Ávila to recognize that "the humility the devil leaves behind is false, unquiet, and without sweetness."[39] The devil's faux humility causes despondence; true humility causes trust. The humiliations the devil causes will lower the soul to despair, but Scaramelli finds the humility that God causes will raise the soul to hope, and leave it in great calm.

> The humility, however, which is counterfeit and from the devil, brings with it, in like manner, a knowledge of our own sins and weakness; but it has this most injurious quality, that while it bends low the soul, it takes away hope, or at least diminishes it, and leaves us full of cowardice, diffidence and discouragement. The humility which is God's gift, is holy. That which comes from the devil, is wicked. The former disposes us for pardon; the latter prevents forgiveness.[40]

Satan's counterfeit humility is ultimately an exercise of vainglory, proven by the fact that the counterfeit virtue leaves one further estranged from God.

Satan's hatred is not stronger than God's love, and Satan's seeds of doubt are not stronger than the theological virtue of faith God infuses. So what can the devil do? Teresa of Ávila thinks his strategy is to present a false picture of God. (Idolatry always was the devil's strong suit.) He makes it seem to the soul

> as if God were ready to put every one to fire and the sword. He represents the divine justice to her, and though she has faith in God's mercy, because the devil has no power to destroy that, yet, she believes in such a manner, that her faith gives her no comfort; but rather when she considers God's great mercy, the tempter

39. Teresa of Ávila, *Life of Saint Teresa, Written by Herself* (New York: P.J. Kenedy & Sons, 1870), 227.

40. John Baptist Scaramelli, *Directorium Asceticum; or, Guide to the Spiritual Life*, vol. 1 (New York: Benziger Bros., 1902), 497.

> makes this serve for her greater torment, because she thinks she ought to have served God so much the more.
>
> This is a stratagem of the devil, and one of the most painful, the most subtle, and disguised that I have ever known.[41]

The devil suggests to the soul that she is unworthy to converse with God in prayer, to beg mercy, or to ask for the merits of Christ's Cross.

If the first good of humility is that Satan hates it, the second good of humility is that Christ loves it. Humility adheres to Christ in virtue and worship. Fénelon gives the basis for giving homage to God when he says "there are only two truths in the world, that God is all, and the creature nothing. In order that humility be true, we need to give continual homage to God in our lowliness, and to stay in our place, which is to love being nothing."[42] So how do our theologians begin? They turn to Christ in prayer. I will let Eudes speak for them.

> I give myself to Thee, my Lord Jesus, that I may enter into Thy spirit of humility. I wish to spend all the days of my life with Thee, in this holy virtue. I call down upon myself the power of Thy spirit of humility in order to annihilate my pride and bind me close to Thee in humility. I offer up to Thee all the opportunities for humility that shall present themselves in my life. Deign, I beseech Thee, to bless them. I renounce myself and all things which may prevent me from sharing in the grace of Thy humility.[43]

Instead of fuming and fussing over your humiliations, turn the humility they produce into an occasion of liturgy.

Humility calms the mind and quiets the spirit so it can see truth, and accept it. De Lombez says "as in a quiet stream, we may distinguish the very smallest grains of sand, so when the soul is at peace, we can perceive our smallest imperfections; we see ourselves as we are."[44] And what are we? *Sinners befriended by a righteous God.* That

41. Teresa of Ávila, *Life of Saint Teresa, Written by Herself*, 269–70.

42. François Fénelon, *Christian Perfection* (New York: Harper & Brothers, 1947), 205.

43. Eudes, *The Life and the Kingdom of Jesus in Christian Souls*, 50.

44. Ambrose de Lombez, *A Treatise on Interior Peace* (NY: Alba House, 1996), 9.

is the truest assessment of man. Humility and charity are connected, described by de Sales with his typical use of natural imagery. "These are the mother virtues, which the others follow as little chickens do the mother hen."[45] "Charity is an ascending humility, and humility is a descending charity."[46] Humility and charity intertwine like the strands making up a rope capable of holding the anchor of a ship. Or, to use de Sales's example, they are like the ladder of Jacob by which angels ascended and descended. "This was not done simultaneously, but alternately; the Angels descending first, and then ascending afterwards. Similarly, as soon as humility has abased us, charity quickly raises us up towards heaven."[47] We see it in Mary: the Lady with the most ardent charity had the most profound humility. But wait, we protest: Doesn't one soar on high while the other abases itself? The Virgin corrects us by her living example. "Charity raised her soul above all creatures, and humility based it below them all, and yet the union of these two virtues was continuous."[48] She attained both of these at the moment of the Incarnation, so de Sales would teach us from her that "humility does not merely consist in diffidence in ourselves, but it must be accompanied by confidence in God."[49]

The mind dwells in truth; the heart dwells in goodness; the soul dwells in God. And out of this household clan comes liturgical prayer. Crasset describes prayer the way the Fathers do, as "an elevation of our soul to God by the union of our mind with supreme truth and of our heart with supreme goodness. It is a respectful homage which we render to the divine grandeur and majesty by the submission of all our powers."[50] Truth, plus charity, plus humility, plus obedience are the pillars holding up the house of liturgy. Paul connected

45. De Sales, *Maxims and Counsels*, 156.

46. De Sales, *Library of St. Francis de Sales: vol. 5, The Spiritual Conferences*, 136.

47. Francis de Sales in Don Gaspar Gilli, *The Month of Mary According to the Spirit of St. Francis of Sales* (London: Robert Washbourne, 1890), 81.

48. Ibid., 139.

49. Ibid., 140.

50. Jean Crasset, in Francis de Sales and Jean Crasset, *The Secret of Sanctity According to St. Francis de Sales and Father Crasset* (New York: Benziger Brothers, 1892), 153.

humility and obedience in Philippians 2:8: "And being found in human form he *humbled himself and became obedient*," and Camus remembers de Sales saying about this passage, "do you see . . . by what scale humility must be measured? By obedience. If you obey promptly, frankly, cheerfully, without murmuring, expostulating, or replying, you are truly humble."[51] One obeys promptly and cheerfully if one loves the person who commands. One obeys tardily and grudgingly if one does not love the person who commands. Why did Jesus obey willingly and eagerly? Because he loved his Father.

This invites us to ask why Jesus loved humility and we hate it? De Bergamo thinks the question deserves a liturgical answer. "He chose the way of humility as the most suitable one for rendering unto God, by His own humility, that honour of which the pride of man has deprived Him."[52] "Humility is in reality a confession of the greatness of God, who after His voluntary self annihilation was exalted and glorified."[53] Humility glorifies God; Jesus wants to glorify his Father; we imitate Jesus out of thankfulness for salvation; we practice humility as a life-liturgy.

At the Fall, Adam and Eve forsook their liturgical vocation. They were created to be cosmic priests of the world, to be the tongue of mute creation so as to join the cosmic liturgy to the angelic harmonies of praise in heaven. But the devil too easily seduced them into his rebellion, and envy entered their hearts. If the glory of God the Father is to be restored, Jesus must heal our soul and deliver us from our present condition, says de Sales. "Our first parents, and almost all others who have sinned, were led to do so by pride. For this reason our Lord, as the wise and loving Physician of our souls, goes to the root of the evil, and instead of pride He comes to plant, first of all, the very beautiful and useful plant of holy humility, a virtue that is all the more necessary because the contrary vice is so general amongst men."[54]

51. Jean Pierre Camus, *The Spirit of St. Francis de Sales* (London: Burns, Oates & Washbourne Ltd., 1925), 154.

52. De Bergamo, *Humility of Heart*, 132.

53. Ibid., 4.

54. Francis de Sales, *The Mystical Flora: The Christian Life Under the Emblem of Plants* (Dublin: M.H. Gill & Son, 1877), 38–39.

Jesus's temptation in the wilderness after his baptism was a kind of do-over of Eden. The first Adam surrendered to temptation in a garden; the second Adam was victorious over temptation in a desert. "What we have lost through the sin of the first Adam, we can regain through the grace of the second Adam," says de Granada, and "as the first Adam, by his pride and disobedience, has wounded our nature, the second Adam, by His humility and obedience, has given a remedy for these wounds."[55] In what way is Jesus our example? In what he chose. What way was that? "Poverty and humiliation," de Ravignan replies. Why did he do so? "It was to expiate your pride, your self-love, and to teach you a great lesson. What did He constantly preach? what has He taught? Always humility, that is to say the love of God, even unto sacrifice and contempt of oneself."[56] Christ's humility exceeds ours, in order to equip ours. Saint-Jure describes Jesus as possessing a life of liturgical humility from the moment of his conception. "The soul of Our Lord was, in the first moments of its creation, and will be for all eternity, the most humble of all creatures, rendering to God the most perfect submission, the most profound respect, the most excellent adorations, the greatest homages, the most ardent thanksgiving."[57] Faber summarizes the existence which began the night of the Annunciation as being a life of oblation, victim, incense, priest, imprisonment, silence, weakness, and poverty.[58] If we are worshippers, we are priests; in the Christian case, priests are also victims. The liturgist must mortify himself with a divine bravery.

Humility is lesson number one in the science of the saints, and the foundation of the whole curriculum of the Christian life. When Grou enrolls us in this school, he begins by reminding us "what man can dare to reject a doctrine that is taught by a God, that is

55. Luis de Granada, *Summa of the Christian Life: Selected Texts from the Writings of Venerable Louis of Granada, O.P.*, adapted by Jordan Aumann, 3 volumes combined (Rockford, IL: TAN eBook 1979), 191.

56. De Ravignan, *Conferences on the Spiritual Life*, 130–31.

57. Saint-Jure, *A Treatise on the Knowledge and Love of Our Lord Jesus Christ*, vol. 2, 626.

58. Faber, *Bethlehem*, 79–82.

practiced by a God, even to the highest degree of perfection?"[59] And Barbanson describes the first day of class. "The first lesson in the school of our Lord Jesus Christ is the virtue of humility, the contempt of ourselves, pronounced by his sacred lips in these words, so clear, so serious, so important: ... Unless ye become like unto little ones, ye shall not enter into the kingdom of heaven. Whence we may gather that without humility it is impossible to please God, and that there is no other way of gaining heaven."[60]

The divine science of the gospel cannot be learned by speculative knowledge. What Jesus meant by "deny yourself and follow me" cannot be learned in this book, that I wrote and that you are reading now. Grou thinks many Catholics believe classroom catechesis is enough, but they are mistaken. If they have not viewed their knowledge of religion "under the aspect of humility, directing their principal attention to this grand point; if they have not commenced the sacred study by the humiliation of mind and heart, although they may argue profoundly on theological questions, they are ignorant of the first elements of that Divine science which forms humble saints, not subtle disputants."[61] Christ assumed human nature in order to teach with his actions, not by words alone. "His whole life was nothing else than a long example and living model of humility,"[62] says Rodríguez. He is the master instructor.

Scaramelli speaks of the humble person as having two eyes. One eye should be "fixed on himself and on his own miseries, that the sight may humble him and fill him with confusion, by bringing home to him his unworthiness to receive any favour." And the other eye "must rest upon God's mercy, His liberality and His promises, so as to make the heart expand with a lively hope of receiving every good and perfect gift. Humility and confidence are the two wings on which prayer soars aloft to God; the two arms which force His hands to shed every blessing."[63] True humility makes alliance with

59. Jean Grou, *Morality, Extracted from the Confessions of Saint Austin*, vol. 2 (London: J. P. Coghlan, 1791), 117.

60. Barbanson, *The Secret Paths of Divine Love*, 19.

61. Grou, *The Interior of Jesus and Mary*, vol. 1, 338.

62. Alphonsus Rodríguez, *The Practice of Christian and Religious Perfection*, vol. 2 (Dublin: James Duffy, 1861), 133.

confident faith and hope, because they are welded together by love. When one sees with both eyes, then humility quietly perfects prayer—as quietly as yeast acts in the dough—which is why de Sales calls humility the first condition for praying well. "We must, in our humility, be little in our own eyes.... And as this humility raises the soul nearer to God, it makes the angels say: 'Who is she that goeth up out of the desert?'"[64] Prayer, like all liturgy, must be free of vainglory and self-esteem and self-justification. Vainglory is not a benign state; it opposes meekness, which is the very thing the Son of God embraced by his Incarnation.

Mary's humility is admired by all her children, but perhaps no one sees the power of her humility more than John of the Angels when he describes it in a startling way (the mystics have nerve to say things I couldn't). Humility conquers God. Ancient zoology described the unicorn as an agile, fierce, untamed animal, and the ploy that hunters would use to trap him was to place a beautiful maiden before him. Seeing her, the unicorn would

> lose his ferocity, and wounded in love, appeased and subdued, would abandon himself in her bosom only to be tied up and made the hunters' prey. O Divine Unicorn, the Son of the Eternal Father! For though fierce, untamed and restrained by no one, when this maiden Mary was put before him, wounded by her look and chained by her humility he was made tame, and forgetting his majesty and magnificence took flesh in her womb and was made man.[65]

63. Scaramelli, *Directorium Asceticum; or, Guide to the Spiritual Life*, vol. 1, 390–91.

64. De Sales, *The Mystical Flora*, 52–53.

65. Juan de los Angeles, *The Loving Struggle between God and the Soul in which the triumphs and greatness of love are treated and by which is taught the most excellent way for the affections* (London: The Saint Austin Press, 2001), 43. He adds a second image, which I hope to use in my Christmas cards one day. "He abandoned himself in her bosom, as Samson had done in Delilah's, and his head was shaven and was left ready to be mocked and derided by men. This is why St. Augustine said: *Had he not allowed himself to become man, no one could have captured him, no one could have scorned him, flogged him, or put him on a Cross.* The divine Delilah cut his hair and, dressing him with flesh, concealed the eternity, immensity, wisdom, fortitude and power which, like hair, adorned his head. O sacred and divine Delilah, you who so tied up the strong and weakened the mighty! And with what? With your faith and your humility."

How does the master instructor in this school teach us humility? He infuses his own into us, answers Olier. "This is what constitutes the humility of God and that of Jesus Christ, in which we should commune and which he pours forth in the heart of Christians, to whom he gives the same tendency and the same inclination toward lowly things. This is true Christian humility."[66] Why is humility so necessary that the Son of God would come from heaven to earth to teach it to us? Because John of Ávila recognizes it as the passageway from earth to heaven. "The Son of God came down from heaven and taught us by His life and words the way to heaven, and that way is humility."[67] It is a reversal of worldliness: now the gentle downward slope of humility leads up to heaven, and the upward slope of pride leads down to hell.

But this humility does not arrive companionless. It is accompanied first by nothingness, then by crosses, which are the subjects of our next chapters.

66. Olier, *Introduction to the Christian Life and Virtues*, in *Bérulle and the French School*, 235.

67. John of Ávila, *Letters of Blessed John of Ávila*, 121.

4
Nothingness

We have spent time in the house of humility; it is time to go into the basement and see its foundation. "Humility is based on a true sense of our own nothingness." That is Mother Drane's succinct definition, and she goes on to unpack its consequence. "For this reason it is safer to accustom ourselves to be familiar with the thought of our nothingness than of our faults. For self-love has something in it so inherently perverse that it will contrive to get satisfaction out of producing faults before the eyes of others, if it cannot produce virtues. The real cure and the real mortification to self is the putting self in oblivion."[1] Nothingness is not a moral category (faults), it is a liturgical category that arises from two coordinated truths: the greatness of God and a sense of our nothingness. The latter without the former sounds like self-contempt, or shame, or disgrace. The former without the latter rings hollow, incomplete, self-protected. But when ears are attuned by liturgical theology to hear both truths, then one can hear the admission of nothingness soberly and honestly. We dishonor God if we say we are not worth his trouble; we also dishonor God if we say his greatness does not recalibrate everything. Our confession of nothingness meets with a reply from God, thinks Marie of the Incarnation. "All I could say was, 'O my great God! O most adorable Abyss! I am mere nothingness!' And then I heard this reply, 'Even though you are mere nothingness, nevertheless you belong entirely to Me.'"[2]

1. Augusta Theodosia Drane, *A Memoir of Mother Francis Raphael* (London: Longmans, Green and Co., 1904), 184. Her name in Religion was Mother Francis Raphael; most books are listed under Drane, but one is listed under Francis Raphael.

2. Marie of the Incarnation, *The Autobiography of Venerable Marie of the Incarnation, O.S.U. Mystic and Missionary* (Chicago: Loyola University Press, 1964), 80.

We will wrestle with the concept of nothingness in this chapter, and do so in two parts. Nothingness is first an ontological fact, and second a liturgical fact.

Nothingness as an Ontological Fact: the Power of God

Where were you, and where was I, a hundred years ago? Nowhere. What were you, and what was I, a hundred years ago? Nothing. We were not. Nothingness recognizes God as a necessary being, and acknowledges every other bit of creation as contingent on him. De Agreda records that the greater the gift, the greater the debt. "My daughter [says the Virgin Mary to her], he that received more ought to consider himself more needy, since his debt becomes so much the greater. . . . Let man acknowledge his condition: for no one can say: I have made myself, I preserve myself in existence, I can prolong my life or postpone death."[3] Nothingness means that God alone has necessary being, and of our own accord we revert to nihility. Confessing nothingness is not a melancholic expression, it is recognition of an ontological fact, which means it concerns the nature of being. How did you come to have existence? asks Segneri.

> If thou hast an existence, it is only because God gave it thee, and preserves thee in it. And if this is so, thou hast no existence of thyself. Wouldst thou say that the reflection in a mirror has any existence of itself, vividly as it represents thy person? Certainly not: and why? Because it is entirely dependent on thee. Just so art thou with regard to God, Whose image thou bearest. . . . If He does but turn His face away from thee for a moment, thou returnest at once to thy original nothingness.[4]

The shortest ontological dialogue in philosophical history would go like this. Yahweh says "I am." Man replies, "I am not, and if I am, it is because my being is from you." (We do not find the word "being" odd because it means "able to be;" we could just as well find man replying with other neologisms, like my "is-ing" is from He who is, and my "am-ing" is from Yahweh.) De Ponte starts with the fact that

3. De Agreda, *The Mystical City of God*, paragraph 385, Kindle 266.
4. Segneri, *The Manna of the Soul*, vol. 2, 168–69.

the essence of God is to be *He that is*, and "this cannot be said of any other whatever besides Himself." All other things receive their existence from God, and "are capable of not being . . . and shall come to perish, if God do not always give them being, and preserve them in it."[5] Being and nothingness is the fundamental difference between Creator and creature, and this is the fact being recognized when we admit our nothingness. Ullathorne adds, "the word *being* in its absolute sense belongs to God alone: the word existence properly belongs to the creation. God *is*, the creation *exists* from Him."[6]

Philosophy, the handmaiden to the Queen of Sciences (which is Theology), lends us the useful word "contingency." God is necessary, creation is not. God is essential Being, creatures are contingent beings. This is why Pollien says we may define a creature as not-Creator. "By creatures, I mean universally all that is not God, all created things. . . . The word 'creatures' has, then, an absolutely universal sense, and denotes all that is not God, all that is between God and me, all that is, and all that takes place and happens around me, in me, for me or against me."[7] The more one feels one's dependence on God, the more complete can be the profession of nothingness (an ontological position). The more complete the profession of nothingness, the more one feels one's dependence on God (a liturgical disposition).

Olier says if God stopped creating—even for an instant—the creation would return to *nihilo*. "We are so totally and truly nothingness that if God does not communicate existence to us at all times, then there is nothing in us. Only nothingness remains. This is our core and our true reality."[8] We can speak of the Creator sustaining us, with Eudes ("if God were to withdraw His Almighty Hand which sustains me, and were to cease for a single moment to preserve me, I would at that very instant return to the nothingness from which

5. Louis de Ponte, *Meditations on the Mysteries of Our Holy Faith*, vol. 6 (London: Richardson and Son, 1854), 24.

6. Ullathorne, *The Endowments of Man*, 81.

7. Pollien, *The Interior Life*, 23.

8. Olier, *Introduction to the Christian Life and Virtues*, in *Bérulle and the French School*, 237.

He drew me"[9]); or preserving us, with Blosius ("if He by His power preserved not the things which He hath made, all would presently go back into nothingness; for of themselves they are nothing, and are altogether dependent upon God, by whom they were made"[10]); or preventing a relapse, with Eudes again ("At every successive moment, He has prevented it from falling back into the nothingness from which He drew it and He continually preserves it, which preservation is a perpetual creation"[11]); or being more involved in his work than an artisan is in his, with Froget: ("God, then, is not present to the world like the artisan or the artist" who is external to his work and can withdraw from it. Rather, "God is so intimately united to the works of His hands that if, after calling a created thing into being, He should withdraw from it and cease to sustain it, it would immediately fall into the nothingness out of which it was made"[12]).

Canfield gives a brilliant illustration of what nothing's dependence on something's reality (creation's dependence on God) means:

> 'Tis such as cannot well bee exprest in words: yet by a similitude we may come to some Notion thereof. So then is the Creature to God, as the Beame to the Sun, or heat to the Fire. For, as the Beame and heat doe so absolutely owe themselves to their productive Causes, as that without their perpetual sustentation and communicating, they cannot subsist: Even, in like manner, so omnimodous is the creatures depending on God, that without his continuall preservation they cannot endure.... The Sun is no sooner hid, but the Beames cease to be; So, if God hide himselfe, and withdraw his hand from the Creatures, they suddenly returne to their Nothing.[13]

9. John Eudes, *Meditation on Various Subjects* (New York: P.J. Kennedy & Sons, 1947), 47.

10. Blosius, *The Manual of the Spiritual Life* (London: John Hodges, 1871), 65.

11. Eudes, *Meditation on Various Subjects*, 52.

12. Barthelemy Froget, *The Indwelling of the Holy Spirit in the Souls of the Just* (New York: Paulist Press, 1921), 4.

13. Benedict Canfield, *A Bright Starre, Leading to, & Centering in, Christ our perfection. The third part of the Rule of Perfection* (London: Henry Overton, 1646), 76–77.

Nothingness is not only a past fact (where were we a hundred years ago?), it is a present possibility. Existence depends upon God the way a ray of light depends upon the sun. We cannot preserve our existence independently of God, any more than, as Saint-Jure says, a ray of light can be "produced or preserved independently of the sun: if separated for a moment from its source, it immediately flickers and dies out."[14] Grou pictures us living as though suspended over nothingness, "and unless we were drawn out of it by an almighty Hand should sink into it with all our weight."[15] We are sustained in being at every moment, thinks Fénelon. "He would only have to withdraw that which has continued his being, every moment from his birth, to replunge him into the nothingness from whence he originally drew him, as a man would merely open his hand to let a stone fall that he had held in the air."[16] And Eudes says, provocatively, that "by counting every moment that has elapsed since you came into the world, you may know how many times you would have been annihilated if God had not performed as great a miracle to preserve you as He did to create you."[17]

Grou thinks every person must admit that "throughout eternity I was not, and there was no reason why I should exist, nor why I should be what I am. My existence is the simple effect of God's Will."[18] But this conclusion becomes even more clear when that philosophical proposition is put into prayerful praise by Saint-Jure.

> I believe most firmly, O my God, that Thou art essentially a necessary Being, sovereign and independent; and I believe with equal firmness that I am essentially a mere nothing, a miserable being, entirely dependent on Thee; that Thou hast drawn me out of nothing, in the obscurity of which I had dwelt for eternity, to call me to life by giving me the being I have, and which Thou dost preserve to me; that I am in such absolute and continual dependence

14. Saint-Jure, *The Spiritual Man*, 33.

15. Grou, *The School of Jesus Christ*, 197.

16. François Fénelon, *Letters and Reflections of François de Fénelon*, ed. Thomas Kepler (New York: The World Publishing Co., 1955), 108.

17. Eudes, *Meditation on Various Subjects*, 104.

18. Grou, *The Spiritual Maxims*, 6.

> on Thee, that if Thou shouldst cease for a moment to sustain me, I should immediately fall back into my original nothingness, and so remain for all eternity. I believe that of my self I am nothing as to soul or body, as to the goods of nature, grace and glory; and that whatever I have or am is Thy gift, the result of Thy bounty.[19]

The sparks spraying out from this collision of divine being and creaturely contingency spread in every direction across the field of abnegation. Admitting nothingness is stitched into nearly every element of liturgical abnegation: humility, adoration, mortification, and the correction of self-will and self-love. We will find the concept in all our chapters, therefore, but let me name a few here.

First, admission of nothingness is an expression of humility. Alacoque recalls God addressing her vanity with a look of severity when they were alone together: "What hast thou to boast of, O dust and ashes, since of thyself thou art but nothingness and misery!"[20] Confessing nothingness is confessing that God is God, so she concludes "He is pleased only with souls that are reduced to nothingness, souls that are all in Him and find everything in Him, since they are nothing in themselves."[21] Blosius says, therefore, "the servant of God, considering the abyss of his own nothingness, and plunging himself into it, must dwell in the deepest valley of humility."[22] Saint-Jure agrees, saying, "another means proper to make us practise humility is, to approach God in thought, to consider ourselves in His presence, to measure our being with His, to compare ourselves with Him, for thus shall we clearly see our nothingness in His being, and our littleness in His grandeur."[23]

Nothingness is distasteful to the proud man. It is a simple (ontological) fact, but the proud find it revolting to count themselves as

19. Saint-Jure, *A Treatise on the Knowledge and Love of Our Lord Jesus Christ*, vol. 2, 491–92.

20. Mary Margaret Alacoque, *The Autobiography of Saint Margaret Mary* (Charlotte, NC: TAN Books, 2012), chapter 62, Kindle.

21. Mary Margaret Alacoque, *The Letters of St. Margaret Mary Alacoque*, Letter 106, Kindle.

22. Blosius, *A Book of Spiritual Instruction*, 18.

23. Saint-Jure, *A Treatise on the Knowledge and Love of Our Lord Jesus Christ*, vol. 2, 589.

nothing. Fénelon had to guide his spiritual students to this, asking them to "recall the interior difficulty which you felt, and which you very naturally testified when I directed you always to count as *nothing* this self which is so dear to us. *To abandon one's self* is to count one's self as nought; and he who has perceived the difficulty of doing it, has already learned what that renunciation is, which so revolts our nature."[24] Rodríguez says the saints are so humble because "as they increase in sanctity, they increase in humility, and in a contempt of themselves. The more God enlightens them, and communicates himself to them, the more they perceive that they have of their own only nothingness and sin."[25] Saint-Jure thinks it is "a brave humility to see nothing in ones self but Nothingness."[26]

Second, nothingness is the key to understanding the Incarnation. Related to nothingness is the Latin term *annihilare*, which means "reducing to nothing, bringing low, humbling." This connection leads Saint-Jure to summarize the Incarnation this way: "as the essence of the Name of God is *to be*, the name of creature is *not to be*, because the creature is nothing of itself. Hence, St. Paul had great reason to say that Jesus Christ, in becoming a creature, *annihilated Himself*."[27] His annihilation (kenosis) is the model for our nothingness (abnegation). The disciple must follow his path to nothingness in imitation of Christ's path from glory to Bethlehem. Startling as the thought is, admits Lallemant, "it may be said that the Divinity in some wise annihilated itself in this mystery of the incarnation, by uniting itself personally to a nature drawn from nothingness."[28] Christ's kenosis was a self-emptying, a sort of annihilation, and in this Christians should imitate him, leading Alacoque to say we honor Christ's abjection through our own abjection. "Love, then, of our own abjection in the love of Our Lord Jesus Christ is sufficient for us, in order to honor the mysteries of His holy Passion and

24. François Fénelon, *Spiritual Progress* (New York: M.W. Dodd, 1853), 30.

25. Rodríguez, *The Practice of Christian and Religious Perfection*, vol. 2, 163.

26. Saint-Jure, *The Holy Life of Monsieur de Renty*, 55.

27. Saint-Jure, *A Treatise on the Knowledge and Love of Our Lord Jesus Christ*, vol. 1, 282.

28. Louis Lallemant, *The Spiritual Doctrine of Father Louis Lallemant*, ed. Frederick Faber (London: Burns & Lambert, 1855), 236.

death. These He wishes us to honor. And we must observe a holy silence, as He did, in all humiliations and sufferings."[29]

The choice of Incarnation is an enigma to us. Why would he humble himself to such depths? What could possibly be his motive? What should possibly be our response? Alacoque hazards a guess.

> Ah, my beloved Sister, if only you realized the honor and partiality the King of Heaven is showing you in so lowering Himself as to come down into your heart! . . . He wishes to mean everything to you, wishes you to take these humiliations as a sign that He is waiting for you in the depths of your heart. . . . These are like so many stairs by which you can go down into the depths of your own nothingness, there to find your pleasure with Him. For this Sovereign of our souls takes pleasure only in souls empty of self. . . . To belong entirely to Him one must no longer retain anything of self.[30]

Third, nothingness is the foundation of the spiritual life, as de Ponte explains. The entire spiritual life is grounded upon "that *profound humility* which we ought to feel in the presence of God, and which is felt by the angels, the blessed spirits, the Virgin our Lady, and even by the soul of Christ our Lord. I have, therefore great reason to study to attain the same humility, by considering that as God alone is *He that is*, even so I am *he that is not*."[31] In order to elevate us, God must humble us; in order to show us the sublime, he must show us our nothingness; in order to give us true knowledge of himself and ourselves, he must break through the false revelations with which we incarcerate ourselves. Saint-Jure thinks "pride is inseparable from false revelations, because, in proportion as God elevates a soul to sublime favors, He humbles her by communicating His light more abundantly, to enable her clearly to see her sins, defects and nothingness."[32]

Fourth, nothingness challenges our perception of the world. We

29. Alacoque, *The Letters of St. Margaret Mary Alacoque*, Letter 101, Kindle.
30. Ibid., Letter 80, Kindle.
31. De Ponte, *Meditations*, vol. 6, 24.
32. Saint-Jure, *The Spiritual Man*, 100.

think it is something; we hope to become something in the eyes of others; we set ourselves the goal of being honored by the world. False revelations (from the evil one) tell us lies about the world, and lies about ourselves, from which we must be disabused, which will involve embracing nothingness, according to Libermann. "All here is vanity and nothingness. *God alone* must be our entire happiness. Blessed are we if, in the end, we are totally His. Let us not put our confidence in men. *God alone*!"[33] The name for choosing between a true and false assessment of the world is *conversion*. According to Fénelon, a new vision of the world either gets through to us, or it doesn't. If it doesn't, then it only grazes the heart.

> Show as much as you please of the vanity and nothingness of the creature by the faults of creatures. Call to notice the brevity and uncertainty of life, the fickleness of fortune, the faithlessness of friends, the illusion of great places, the bitterness which is inevitable there, the disappointment of the most beautiful hopes, the emptiness of all the good things we possess, the reality of all the evils we suffer: all this moralizing, true and reasonable as it is, only skims the heart. It does not sink in. The inner man is not changed at all. He sighs to see himself a slave to vanity, and does not get out of his slavery.[34]

But if it does, then it penetrates the heart.

> If the ray of the divine light shines within, he sees the abyss of good which is God, the abyss of nothingness and evil which is the corrupted creature. He despises himself. He hates himself. He leaves himself. He flees himself. He fears himself. He renounces himself. He gives himself up to God. He loses himself in him. Happy loss![35]

Nothingness as a Liturgical Fact: the Holiness of God

Nothingness is not a threat, it is a cause for gratitude. This means the nothingness revealed by liturgical abnegation is not a lesson

33. Libermann, *Letters to People in the World*, Spiritan Series 6, vol. 2, 146.
34. Fénelon, *Christian Perfection*, 146.
35. Ibid.

from the world, it is a lesson to learn from the holiness of God. Nothingness nerves and strengthens our worship, for the liturgist actually rejoices in the fact that God is Almighty, and he is not; that God deserves glorification, and he does not; that God rules, and he does not. We see God's All-might in creation, especially if we do not confine it to the past tense. Scaramelli suggests we should see the first chapter of Genesis outside our window every morning: "He repeats the gift at every instant, and preserves us by the working of a power which yields in nothing to that by which He created us."[36] Why would one not give all glory to God? The answer, alas, is because one wishes to reserve some of this glory for the creature or for oneself. Challoner states adamantly that the love of God will not admit of a divided heart. He will not suffer a rival in his kingdom. What? exclaims Crasset. Will you give God only part of yourself? "There can be only one soul to a body, one sun to a universe, one king to a dominion, one governor to a state, one shepherd to a flock, one pilot to a boat, one love to a heart, and one God to love. You purpose to give Him a portion of your heart? This is unjust, injurious, and impossible. What, did He create it only in part? Will He save it only in part?"[37] Nothingness is a spear designed to puncture idolatry. That *we* are nothing means *God* is All.

Can't we divide our heart? No! exclaims Vianney. "As if we could divide our heart into two parts! No, my friend: you either belong wholly to God or wholly to the world."[38] Must our love for God push all other loves off the page? Yes! exclaims Guillore. "His jealous Love knows no limit, He is not content to let us have the smallest reserve from Him, nor will He endure that we divide our hearts which are His only."[39] Can we only return the sort of love we receive? Yes! exclaims de Liguori. "In order to increase our confidence, God emptied himself, became nothing (Phil 2:7)" and went

36. John Baptist Scaramelli, *Directorium Asceticum; or, Guide to the Spiritual Life*, vol. 3 (New York: Benziger Bros, 1902), 598.

37. John Crasset, *Christian Considerations; or, Devout Meditations for Every Day in the Year* (New York: P. O'Shea, 1864), 458–49.

38. John Vianney, *Sermons for the Sundays and Feasts of the Year* (Long Prairie, MN: The Neumann Press, 1995), 13–14.

39. François Guillore, *Self-Renunciation* (London: Rivingtons, 1871), 105.

further still to hide himself under bread and wine "in order to be our companion forever and to be united with us with the greatest intimacy. . . . In short, God loves you as much as if he had no other object of love except you alone. And so you should love none other than God."[40] This knowledge is of the heart, and not of the mind alone, requiring nothingness to be known by liturgical embrace, not by theory.

Why is this necessary? All our theologians follow the signpost of Scripture when it points to the problem of pride, the mother of disobedience. Libermann characterizes pride as misplacing the location of glory.

> Pride has an invincible tendency to seek glory, glory inherent in the creature as such. There follows from this another invincible tendency, to seek glory in the good opinions of others, a glory which is basically a lie, since the creature to which it relates has only its own nothingness and consequently is devoid of true glory. It is formally a lie, for it only exists in the form of an idea held by others of the one whom they esteem. The latter draws nothing authentic from this good repute to really enhance itself.[41]

Overcoming the swelling of pride is done by puncturing it with a confession of nothingness, and Scripture has its lance ready: "For if any one thinks he is something, when he is nothing, he deceives himself" (Gal 6:3). Do you want to know where this deception comes from? De Bergamo answers, "in reality a lie dwells essentially in that pride which makes us esteem ourselves above what we are. Whoever regards himself as more than mere nothingness is filled with pride, and is a liar."[42]

So the point of connection between liturgy and nothingness is truth. Liturgical adoration, homage, glorification, and so forth, depends upon overcoming a lie, which Tronson says easily fools us.

40. Alphonsus de Liguori, *A Way of Conversing Continually With God as With a Friend* in *Alphonsus de Liguori: Selected Writings* (New York: Paulist Press, 1999), 274.

41. Francis Libermann, *Jesus Through Jewish Eyes*, vol. 3, transl. Myles L. Fay, CSSp (Dublin: Paraclete Press, 2005), 219–20.

42. De Bergamo, *Humility of Heart*, 10.

"Do we not quickly lose this consciousness of our nothingness when we are flattered and applauded by the world; and do we not suffer ourselves to be dazzled and intoxicated by praise, instead of humbling ourselves?"[43] The point here is not to make us feel bad about ourselves. The point is obedience, submission, service, and oblation—all liturgical verities. To reference de Bergamo again:

> But when this person says of himself: "I have riches, I have health, and I have knowledge," etc., what is meant by this "I"? Nothingness; and yet this "I," this nothingness, that derives all it possesses from God, dares to disregard this same God by disobeying His sovereign commandments, saying to Him, if not in words most certainly in deeds, which is far worse, "I will not serve"; no, I will not obey. Oh, pride, pride! But, O my soul, "Why doth thy spirit swell against God?"[44]

Nothingness is concerned with giving latria to the right object, in the right way, for the right reason, in the right measure. In other words, Libermann says it is concerned with justice in worship. "When people glorify themselves before others on whatever good quality it may be, it is not God they glorify nor is God glorifying them; it is nothingness glorifying nothingness through another nothingness, and consequently the glory is nothing: 'it is nothing.'"[45] What receives glory before God? Nothing. What serves to glorify God? Everything. Therefore, Libermann finds it laughable to misdirect our worship to other contingent beings (including ourselves). "Moreover, this tiny being is so insignificant that it could be called nothingness, even during its brief existence. And how can one boast of nothingness in the presence of other nothingnesses? Humans esteem us: that's something to be content with! . . . Nothingnesses hold another nothingness in high esteem! Will we be any less feeble and wretched for it?"[46] That is why grace gives us "this

43. Tronson, *Examination of Conscience*, 53–54.

44. De Bergamo, *Humility of Heart*, 118.

45. Francis Libermann, *Jesus Through Jewish Eyes*, vol. 2 (Dublin: Paraclete Press, 1999), 214.

46. Francis Libermann, "Nature et excellence de l'humilité," *Écrits spirituelles*, 323–63.

true idea of our nothingness and the inclination to remain within it, touches us only with regard to our own abyss and nothingness."[47] Liturgical obeisance produces an abnegation that climaxes in claiming nothingness. Because we recognize God's omnipotence, we confess our nothingness; because we recognize our weakness, we confess God's sovereignty; because we recognize our helplessness, we confess God's supremacy.

Embracing our nothingness does not, therefore, distance us from God—it is, in fact, a tremendously strong link to God. Our poverty connects us to his grandeur, our powerlessness hangs upon his goodness, our nothingness permits a full liturgizing of the Creator-Savior. De Bergamo describes the truly humble soul as one "entirely dependent on the power, providence and mercy of God," and when it annihilates itself before God, it does so "to glorify Him continually, conforming with exact obedience to His laws and with perfect submission to His will."[48] To be on the Cross with Jesus is perfect love, which requires abnegation. "If I wish to come after Thee I must not only renounce all things, but my own self as well," notes Eudes. "To this end, I give myself to the power of divine love by which Thou didst reduce Thyself to nothingness, and in union with that same love I profess to renounce entirely and forever everything belonging to myself and to the old Adam; to annihilate at Thy feet, as far as possible, my mind, my self-love, my own will, my life and my being."[49]

We are perhaps surprised at associating nothingness with Jesus, but why would that be? We are not surprised at associating humility, meekness, and lowliness with him. The Son liturgizes the Father by his subordination and submission *and annihilation*—and this is the very liturgy to which the Holy Spirit wants to unite us. Baker says, "He submitted Himself to all creatures, yea, forasmuch as concerned suffering, even to the devil himself. As a creature, He saw nothing in Himself but the nothing of a creature, and in all other

47. Ibid.

48. De Bergamo, *Humility of Heart*, 40–41.

49. Eudes, *The Life and the Kingdom of Jesus in Christian Souls*, 145.

creatures He saw nothing but God."[50] Regrettably, we do not embrace our nothingness, even when we have seen Christ model humility for us. "Even after His infinite example of humility," Eudes regrets, "nothingness still wants to be exalted, and then, indeed, He finds this more than unendurable."[51] The Lord therefore imposes crosses upon us—pieces of his own Cross, really—and Surin warns us "not [to] be surprised to find that God loves to see His servants in a condition in which their own nothingness is forced upon them."[52] More on that in the next chapter on crosses.

For now, I am stressing the conformity of our worship of God with Christ's worship of the Father. If Christ is master, then rejoice in the very things he loved, and the world despised. Rejoice in weakness, says Libermann. ("Rejoice at the sight of your weakness, abjection, uselessness and nothingness. Remain thus absorbed in our Lord who is in you and become, as it were, annihilated in order that He alone may exist in you."[53]) Rejoice in our annihilation, admits de Lombez. ("Say to Him… *You delight, dear Lord, to work upon nothing; behold me, and if I am yet something in my own eyes, hasten my annihilation that You may begin your work.*"[54]) Rejoice in nothingness, concludes Saint-Jure, because it allows giving all to God. ("I esteem myself happy in being nothingness, that Thou mayest be all, in being darkness that Thou mayest be light, weakness that Thou mayest be strength, poverty that Thou mayest be riches, misery that Thou mayest be beatitude, an abyss of imperfections that Thou mayest be the sovereign perfection… I beg of Thee… that Thou wouldst unite Thy being to my nothingness, and work great things in me, for Thy own sake."[55])

50. Augustine Baker, *Holy Wisdom, Or Directions for the Prayer of Contemplation Extracted out of more than Forty Treatises*, ed. R.F. Serenus Cressy (New York: Burns & Oates, 1911), 313.

51. Eudes, *The Life and the Kingdom of Jesus in Christian Souls*, 43.

52. Surin, *The Foundations of the Spiritual Life*, 13.

53. Francis Libermann, *Letters to Clergy and Religious*, Spiritan Series 9, vol. 5 (Pittsburgh: Duquesne University Press, 1966), 71.

54. De Lombez, *A Treatise on Interior Peace*, 110–11.

55. Saint-Jure, *A Treatise on the Knowledge and Love of Our Lord Jesus Christ*, vol. 1, 263.

The world's assessment of nothingness is wrong. Nothingness does not belittle self, it forgets self. And it forgets self in the flood of brilliance from the throne of God. Forgetting self (denying self) is a release to serve God, as Alacoque discovered. "Once He said to me with a voice full of authority: 'I am going to make you so poor, so despicable, so abject in your own eyes, I am going to destroy your self-esteem so completely that upon your nothingness I shall be able to establish Myself.'"[56] Strange though it sounds to the ears of the world, our powerlessness renders liturgical homage to God's omnipotence. God desires a liturgy from us that rises from poverty, dependence, submission, and nothingness. This is the place the Son sought out by his Incarnation, and it led to the Cross, where we must follow if we want the Christ to live in us. "He knows how He lives in us, and His Father knows also," says Libermann; "why, then should we want to interfere?"[57]

The liturgical origin and liturgical purpose of nothingness is startling, I admit, but startling or not, Tronson says this is the very reason why Jesus displayed cruciform nothingness. "Let us adore our Lord Jesus Christ, Who, although, as God, He is co-equal with His Father, yet, as Man, shows us by His own Example how we should prostrate ourselves before the Divine Majesty, acknowledging our nothingness in His Presence."[58] The Cross is a school of liturgy, says Crasset, where prayer "gives us a knowledge of ourselves, which teaches us wise lessons of humility, makes us realize and appreciate our nothingness, and reveals to us the greatness and sanctity of God, before Whom our imaginary virtues have no existence, beauty, form, or measure."[59] Do you want to be taught how to glorify the Divine Majesty? Look to his Son in human being. If you stand on some other ground, you should distrust the liturgy you are presenting, says Grou. Do it like they do it in heaven. "If you do not approach God with a profound consciousness of your own nothingness; if—while the pure and holy beings in Heaven cover their

56. Alacoque, *The Letters of St. Margaret Mary Alacoque*, Letter 70, Kindle.
57. Libermann, *Letters to Clergy and Religious*, Spiritan Series 8, vol. 4, 220.
58. Tronson, *Examination of Conscience*, 51.
59. De Sales and Crasset, *The Secret of Sanctity*, 156.

faces with their wings in His presence—you, a sinner, be not possessed by religious awe, you should mistrust your prayer."[60]

Conclusion

Where have we wound up? What is the result of this contemplation upon nothingness? Several of our theologians point the way. Eudes says nothingness perfects the honor and homage we give to God. "O Most Lovable Jesus, I fall at Thy feet in the utmost depths of my nothingness. . . . I offer Thee all the honor that has been given Thee during this night in heaven and on earth."[61] It has an intercessory note. "I willingly consent to be reduced to nothingness now and forever, by means of Thy grace, so that the Sacred Heart of Jesus may be incessantly adored by the whole universe."[62] Libermann says we will put the world into confusion because instead of cherishing what raises us in the eyes of men, we will "esteem, love and seek only their knowledge of their nothingness, of their weakness, of their uselessness, of their profound wretchedness. Instead of being complacent about that which exalts them, they will try to establish themselves in true humility of heart, loving lowly things and being pleased to suffer the contempt of others. Love for God that is most pure, detachment from themselves, and perfect obedience will be the foundation of that so holy and humble life."[63]

Liturgy is a love-activity, a fact that should never be forgotten. And if we wish to perfect our love (*perficere*) we find ourselves going down a path of abnegation that leads to embracing nothingness. Though it sounds like a demanding liturgy, it is the only one the Father accepts. Grou describes the Christian soul as being deeply impressed "with the conviction of her Maker's sovereign perfection,

60. Grou, *The School of Jesus Christ*, 246.

61. Eudes, *The Life and the Kingdom of Jesus in Christian Souls*, 112.

62. Eudes, *The Sacred Heart of Jesus*, 91.

63. Francis Libermann, *The Birth of Missionary Spirituality: Provisional Rule of the Missionaries of Libermann* (https://dsc.duq.edu/cgi/viewcontent.cgi?article=1061&context=libermann-collection), 181–82. See now: *Provisional Rule of Father Libermann: Text and Commentary*, transl. Walter van de Putte, CSSp (Pittsburgh: Center for Spiritan Studies, 2015).

and her own absolute nothingness; which mortifies her pride, wounds her self-love, and annihilates her natural feelings and inclinations; in a word, which experimentally proves to her the folly of relying on her own efforts, and deprives her of all resources in self."[64] The love-activity of liturgy can only reach heaven if it bears the perfume of "not my will, but thine be done." Liturgical abnegation is a matter of retraining our homage so we can direct it to the right object, and Surin says that to saints who have learned to do so, "esteem appears as nothing in their eyes.... Then they lift up their eyes to Heaven, they admire the greatness of God, they contemplate Him in His glory; and, dazzled with the splendour of Its rays, they hide themselves in their own nothingness, and would descend, if it were possible, to the very centre of the world, to humble themselves more profoundly before His Supreme Majesty."[65] Retraining esteem means forsaking self-esteem, and this means annihilation of self.

Accepting nothingness is concession to God. Nothingness means "nothing else"—nothing else but God, God alone. De la Colombière drives the point home with repetition (emphases added): "perfection consists in seeking to please God, *and only God*, in all things"; "it is *He alone* whom I wish to please"; "it is a great happiness to *belong altogether* to God"; "he wished his *friendship entire*";[66] "*you alone* are worthy of being loved, served, and praised";[67] "I do not know where to go *to serve anyone but Thee* who art my God";[68] "Dear God, *alone* good, *alone* lovable, must I sacrifice [my friends] to You, since You wish me to be *Yours entirely?*";[69] "when we find something *very perfect in any order*, we cannot bear with all the rest";[70] and if you feel a disturbance in your soul, cast yourself at the feet of Jesus and say, "What, my Jesus, I still desire something apart

64. Grou, *The Interior of Jesus and Mary*, vol. 1, 63.

65. Surin, *The Foundations of the Spiritual Life*, 232.

66. Claude de la Colombière, *Faithful Servant: Spiritual Retreats and Letters of Blessed Claude La Colombière* (St. Louis, MO: B. Herder Book Co., 1960), 56.

67. Ibid., 65.

68. Ibid., 66.

69. Ibid., 74–75.

70. Ibid., 76.

from You! *You alone* do not suffice for me, and I do not love *You alone*, and it isn't *enough* for me to be loved by You?"[71]

And the path to nothingness is marked by signposts. You will recognize them: they are shaped as crosses, to which we must turn to next.

71. Ibid., 112.

5

Crosses

The religious leaders saw Jesus on the Cross and challenged him to give a sign: "He saved others; he cannot save himself. Let the Christ, the King of Israel, come down now from the cross, that we may see and believe" (Mk 15:31–32). Teresa Gertrude suggests we ask for a similar, but different sign. The Pharisees would believe *if he* came down from the Cross, we would believe if he would *take us* down from the Cross.

> Such are souls who, not content with their Father's will, would fain demand a sign. . . . The Cross is to them a stumbling-block, and so they "would see a miracle." They can no longer demand of our Lord that He should come down from the Cross, wherefore they profess to believe in His power, or in His goodness, or in His love for them, but only on condition that He will let *them* descend from it. Souls such as these—and we ourselves are, or have been, perhaps of their number—were beheld afar off by our Lord "in the days of His flesh" and were among the motives of His sighs.[1]

It is time to notice that I omitted a phrase in my title. It is the phrase right in the middle. Jesus said, "If any man would come after me, let him deny himself *and take up his cross daily* and follow me." Denying oneself sounds less difficult if it does not involve a cross. It sounds less difficult if denying oneself is a self-improvement program, or prudential planning, or benefit cost analysis, or politics. But taking up a cross sounds more serious. And it sounds still more serious when our theologians speak of *crosses*, in the plural. Crosses happen repeatedly over the lifetime of liturgical abnegation, because virtues require repetition to become habit. God will use

1. Teresa Gertrude, *Jesus, the All Beautiful*, 451.

crosses as his instrument repeatedly, persistently, even stubbornly. Fénelon compares it to growing up. "God does not perform continual miracles in the order of grace any more than in the order of nature. It would be as great a miracle in the first sense were we to see one full of himself die suddenly to self-consciousness and self-interest, as to see a child go to bed a mere child, and rise up the next morning a man of thirty!"[2] At Golgotha they asked for the miracle of a Messiah without a cross; we ask for the miracle of being allowed to follow this Messiah without the cost of a cross. And John of Ávila says the crosses we need are the ones we do not seek. "If the troubles that come to us were those we sought, they would not be troubles, and we should be deprived of the company of our Redeemer's cross, which is the greatest ill that could happen to us. That which is most irksome to us has to come to us, for thus our self-will has to be cured until nothing that comes to us is irksome."[3]

The healing is slow and steady, de Caussade thinks, therefore it is "necessary to bear the little crosses we encounter every day, for by them God will enable us to destroy our self-love."[4] Grou describes crosses as "the great scourges by which self-love is destroyed," so our duty is to value, cherish, and actually desire them, "and to make it my happiness here below to glorify God by this great feature of resemblance to Jesus Christ."[5] Jesus taught us the use of crosses in the most powerful way possible: by fastening himself to one and making it a beacon of love. De Bergamo marvels at Christ's love that

> binds omnipotence and keeps Thee united and fastened to the cross more effectually than do the nails, more than could all the cords in the world! But how weak, on the other hand, is my love for Thee; scarcely does a cross befall me, than I am most impatient to shake it off. . . . We can not love the Crucified, if we do not love

2. François Fénelon, *Spiritual Letters of Archbishop Fénelon. Letters to Men* (London: Rivingtons, 1877), 298.

3. John of Ávila, "Letter 32 of the Cartas Espirituales" in Kathleen Pond, *The Spirit of the Spanish Mystics*, 62.

4. De Caussade, *Abandonment to Divine Providence*, 168.

5. Jean Grou, *Meditations Upon the Love of God* (London: J. T. Hayes, 1905), 174.

> the cross; and as I do not love the cross, this is an evident sign that neither do I love Thee, my most amiable Saviour![6]

If one wants to understand crosses, it will not be enough to just theorize about them. De Sales says: "it is better to bear the cross of our Lord, than only to think on it."[7]

Jesus is the High Priest and sacrificial victim, and from where did he exercise this priesthood of sacrifice with the most power and force in his lifetime? From the Cross, upon the Cross, by means of the Cross. So it is with his disciples: *liturgical abnegation is liturgy done from the cross.* Alacoque says, "The cross is the throne of the true lovers of Jesus Christ."[8] Daily abnegation becomes liturgy by undergoing mortifications in order to honor God, and the biggest question in life should be whether we are pleasing God or displeasing him. The glory of the Father required the Cross of Jesus, so he welcomed it. In imitation of Jesus, the glory of the Father will require crosses for us. Are we afraid of them? A bit. But Grou asks, "can you look at your Crucifix and complain that your religion costs too great a sacrifice? That God exacts too much of you? One glance there should surely silence all murmurs at the trifles which perplex and harass our daily life."[9]

How shall we define crosses? What are they? Grou can define them briefly—and comprehensively. "Crosses are the tests to which God puts our love, the sacrifices He expects it to make."[10] He can also explain them in more detail:

> As a rule when we speak of a cross we mean certain dispensations of Providence, either natural or supernatural, which thwart us, humiliate us, give us pain or sorrow, and try us in a variety of ways.... They attack our health, our possessions, our peace of mind, our reputation, our person or the persons of those we love; they mortify our feelings, our pride, our self-love; they exact a

6. De Bergamo, *Thoughts and Affections on the Passion of Jesus Christ*, 477.

7. De Sales, *The Spiritual Director*, 67.

8. Alacoque, *The Letters of St. Margaret Mary Alacoque*, Letter 16, Kindle.

9. Jean Grou, *The Hidden Life of the Soul*, selections by Henrietta Lear (London: Rivingtons, 1871), 115–16.

10. Grou, *The School of Jesus Christ*, 184.

> variety of sacrifices from us, some outward and some inward.... Everyone has his own; for some they are larger and more numerous; for others they are smaller and fewer. But no man is altogether exempt from them.[11]

In one of his sermons, Humberstone confirms that no one "obtains any Favour from God, by making the Sign of the Cross upon his Forehead with his Hand, unless at the same time he makes it inwardly in his Heart, by Faith."[12] He provides four examples. The Sign of the Cross is a sign of humility, but it will not benefit us if we have a proud heart within; it is a sign of patience, but will do no good while our minds are full of revenge; it is a sign of charity, but will be useless if the heart is angry with a neighbor, and void of pity toward the poor; it is a sign of suffering, but matters not so long as we live in pleasures. To sum up, "all outward Signs of Christianity, are but Lyes and do but make us Hypocrites, unless we have inwardly the Virtues we profess outwardly by these Signs."[13]

We have already applied Paul's confession that he has two laws at work within him to the difficulty of humility. Fénelon suggests it also applies to our attitude toward crosses. "The same hidden root of obstinate self-love which makes us need crosses makes us repulse them and hinder their work."[14] Instead of humbling ourselves to obediently accept the cross God assigns, he worries that "we are generally desirous of bargaining with God."[15]

That would explain the element of *suffering* in crosses. This word does not always refer to pain (physical or emotional), although it can. "To suffer" means "allowing to occur." It means "to permit" (as in the old translation of "suffer the little children to come to me"). Grou explains why it is necessary to *suffer crosses*: because "self can-

11. Ibid., 180.

12. Henry Humberstone, "Sermon 15, On the Sign of the Cross" in *A Select Collection of Catholic Sermons Preached Before their Majesties King James I, Mary Queen-Consort, Catherine Queen-Dowager, etc.*, vol. 2 (London: s.n., 1741), 83–84.

13. Humberstone, "Sermon 15, On the Sign of the Cross." The examples are across pages 84–85, this quote on 85.

14. Fénelon, *Letters to Men*, 99.

15. Fénelon, *Spiritual Progress*, 87.

not kill itself; the blow must be struck from elsewhere, and self must rest passive in receiving it."[16] Suffering means "permitting God," and Libermann picks up an image from Jeremiah 18 to explain what is going on. "You should remain in the Lord's presence like clay before the potter. . . . The clay offers no resistance; it leaves the potter perfect liberty to do with it what he wishes. The potter fashions a vase and it often happens that when it is half finished he breaks it up and reduces it to a shapeless mass. He then starts anew to make of it the particular vase he wants."[17]

It is necessary to stop bargaining with God, and accept what his providence designs. If this means accepting crosses in faith, then, de Sales says, crosses are entirely changed. De Chantal recalls him once writing to her: "The cross is from God, but it is a cross, because we do not unite ourselves thereto: for, when we are truly resolved to accept the cross God gives us, it is a cross no longer: it is only a cross because we do not accept it; and if it is from God, why do we not accept?"[18] We dare accept crosses only when we are thoroughly convinced that God always intends our good, never our harm. That is the faith required. God's end is our happiness, even if the means to it is a trial—just as a mother's end is the child's health, even if the means to it is a bitter medicine. As Jesus's Cross was the way to his Resurrection, so our crosses are the only way to our salvation. Crosses may be little and constant for some people; for other people, they may be large and singular. But whatever their size and frequency, crosses work to destroy self-love and make someone over in a resurrected state so he can love the Father, in the Spirit, as Jesus did.

Grou allows the question that is on our mind, and then answers it. "You may ask me: Why must we bear so many internal and external trials? Can we acquire holiness at no less price? No; the Gospel affirms that holiness is only to be attained by suffering, or at least by the will to suffer. Holiness consists in readiness to embrace all the crosses that it may please God to send us."[19] Faber says the saints no

16. Grou, *Meditations upon the Love of God*, 170.
17. Libermann, *Letters to Clergy and Religious*, Series 9, vol. 5, 116.
18. De Chantal, *Exhortations, Conferences and Instructions*, 343.
19. Grou, *The Spiritual Maxims*, 151.

longer doubt "that suffering is the one grand similitude of Christ," which actually leads them to love "that suffering which seems to be the golden coin in which Love repays our love."[20] Crosses take us out of ourselves and place us in the hands of God. The Cross can be imagined as a prybar God uses to leverage open a space for himself and to prepare us for beatitude. Libermann sees the Cross as "the shortest and straightest way to that goal. It is Jacob's ladder on which the angels of the earth—the children of God—must ascend to their Heavenly Father, and where angels of Heaven descend to lend their help to their earthly brothers, in the painful labor of ascent."[21] Vianney understands our fear, but tells us to take the leap of faith. "Whatever we do, the cross holds us tight—we cannot escape from it. What, then, have we to lose? Why not love our crosses and make use of them to take us to Heaven?"[22] "Do you dread trials?" Grou asks. But they "are indispensably necessary for your admission to heaven."[23]

It is remarkable, and perhaps the most difficult thing to grasp: that even our sufferings and sorrows can become liturgies. Blosius says the patience and submission with which we carry our cross can be ennobled and made worthy when the ascetical soul unites "her deeds as well as her sufferings, by her prayers or her desires, to the sorrows and actions of Our Lord. In this manner, these sufferings, and these actions . . . will become infinitely great, illustrious, and pleasing in the sight of God, for they will receive ineffable dignity from the merits of Jesus Christ, to which they will be united."[24] In the beginning crosses are hard and painful because they plow deep, but this is necessary if the Gardener is to plant the seed of life in us. It is like Christ's Cross has been turned upside down and turned into a plow so it can harrow the heart. Harrowing a field means to

20. Faber, *The Foot of the Cross*, 32.

21. Libermann, *Letters to Clergy and Religious*, Series 9, vol. 5, 290.

22. John Vianney, *The Little Catechism of the Curé of Ars* (Rockford, IL: TAN Books, 1951), 68.

23. Grou, *The Spiritual Maxims*, 151.

24. Blosius, quoted in Georges de Blois, *A Benedictine of the Sixteenth Century* (London: Burns and Oates, 1878), 151.

break up the hard soil for the planting, which is why Libermann says crosses "do away with our self-love and wicked affection for earthly things, that are like briars and thorns growing in, and covering the soil of our wretched soul. Those crosses have still another result: they soften the hardness of our heart and make it receptive for the seed which the Divine Master desires to cast in our soul."[25] As Christ harrowed hell, our hearts must be harrowed by abnegation. Though vexing, "nothing is more sanctifying than crosses."[26]

As you might have expected, the key to interpreting our many crosses is the one Cross of Calvary. Our many crosses are only splinters off his one Cross. The Son of God became incarnate, assumed human nature, delivered from sin by satisfying the justice of the Father, and just as he was raised upon the Cross, he will raise us by a cross to eternal life. Scaramelli describes the scene, and discovers the command contained in it.

> [Our blessed Savior] saw that the miserable earth on which we dwell is, so to speak, covered, sown broadcast with crosses. He knew that it was not possible to live in this vale of tears and in this painful exile, without trials and afflictions, grief and bitterness. What, then, did our good Captain do to encourage us to endurance? He took upon His own divine shoulders, the heaviest, the most weighty Cross, the Cross most full of pain; and, turning to us His soldiers, [he said]: "Do what you see Me do. Behold Me, laden with the Cross, groaning under its crushing weight, languishing and dying upon it. He who would boast of being My follower, let him take up his Cross, follow Me, tread in My footsteps, and become like unto Me."[27]

Our love must not only *respond* to Christ's love, it must *correspond* to his love. Or, as de Chantal says, "grace will never be wanting to us if we are faithful in seconding its attractions."[28] This is the reason why obedience is the strongest flavor on the plate of abnegation. We

25. Libermann, *Letters to Clergy and Religious*, Spiritan Series 8, vol. 4, 340.

26. Libermann, *Letters to People in the World*, Spiritan Series 6, vol. 2, 245.

27. Scaramelli, *Directorium Asceticum; or, Guide to the Spiritual Life*, vol. 3, 413–14.

28. De Chantal, *Exhortations, Conferences and Instructions*, 83.

do not watch Jesus die, we join Jesus actually dying by liturgically dying to ourselves. Dead to sin, we are alive to God in Christ Jesus (Rom 6:11). Libermann admits how difficult this would be if it were not for his aid with our crosses. "Oh! how difficult it is to go out of ourselves, to divest ourselves of self, to be unreservedly detached and abandoned! This we should never be able to attain, if God did not aid us with His almighty power. But, desiring to take pity on us, He overwhelms us with crosses and, whether we wish it or not, we must leave self, forget and lose ourselves, and thus belong to Him alone."[29]

Strange language to the ears of the world! But, then again, Bourdaloue says the world is deceived because it forms its "judgment of things according to the time in which we now are, and which passes away; but . . . the judgment of God is formed relatively to eternity, in which we shall hereafter be, and which will never pass away."[30] The world cannot understand suffering as precious, humiliation as desirable, afflictions as advantageous, because the world is short-sighted. Its vision is confined to the temporal and temporary, and it neglects the mystical and eternal, which is why Vianney asks us not to consider the labor, but the recompense. "A merchant does not consider the trouble he undergoes in his commerce, but the profit he gains by it. . . . What are twenty years, thirty years, compared to eternity? What, then, have we to suffer? A few humiliations, a few annoyances, a few sharp words; *that will not kill us*. It is glorious to be able to please God, so little as we are!"[31] This is an encouraging vision the Christian receives from the One Cross.

Love is friendly to crosses; they are not mutually exclusive. All our authors agree on this point. For example, de Sales: if you "plant in your heart Jesus Christ crucified, [then] all the crosses of this world will seem roses to you. Those who are pricked with the thorns of the crown of our Lord who is our head, scarcely feel of the

29. Libermann, *Letters to Clergy and Religious*, Spiritan Series 8, vol. 4, 327.

30. Louis Bourdaloue, *Sermons, and Moral Discourses, on the Important Duties of Christianity*, vol. 1 (Dublin: Published by James Duffy, 1843), 234.

31. Vianney, *The Little Catechism of the Curé of Ars*, "Catechetical Instruction of the Curé," xxi. Ellipses in original.

thorns."[32] For example, Libermann: the more crosses sent by our divine Spouse, "the more progress you will make in His holy love."[33] For example, Vianney: "crosses, transformed by the flames of love, are like a bundle of thorns thrown into the fire, and reduced by the fire to ashes. The thorns are hard, but the ashes are soft."[34] And, for example, Alacoque: Jesus "will make you see that He is not less lovable in the bitterness of Calvary than in the sweetness of Thabor."[35]

There are two mountains in Jesus's life, and on one he was transfigured, on the other he was crucified. On the former, a voice from heaven said, "this is My beloved Son, in whom I am well pleased," and when God looks upon Jesus on the latter mountain, de Bergamo believes the Father is no less pleased. Earth, angels, and men may be horrified at so strange a disfigurement, but when the God of glory looks down on Calvary he sees "the face of Thy beloved Son, resplendent as the sun! that face in which a short while before Thou didst take delight on Mount Tabor? . . . it is not a whit less fair and pleasing now than it was when it appeared in the Transfiguration, all dazzling with bright rays of glory. . . . It is not the beauty of the features, but of virtues, that gives delight to God."[36] All of us are drawn more to Tabor than to Calvary, but this is a mistake we must overcome, warns Huby. "Oh! how much is it to be lamented, that the science of the cross is so rare among the disciples of a crucified God. Many follow him to Mount Thabor: few to Mount Calvary."[37] If this is true, then Eymard can tell his spiritual daughter that he blesses her crosses and sufferings because "in this life they constitute the glory of God and his divine mercy, which overcomes the devil. Take heart, my dear daughter, inner desolation is more pleasing to

32. De Sales, *Library of St. Francis de Sales: vol. 1, Letters to Persons in the World*, 368–69.

33. Francis Libermann, *Letters to Religious Sisters and Aspirants*, Spiritan Series 5, vol. 1 (Pittsburgh: Duquesne University Press, 1962), 8.

34. Vianney, *The Little Catechism of the Curé of Ars*, 72.

35. Alacoque, *The Letters of St. Margaret Mary Alacoque*, Letter 3, Kindle.

36. De Bergamo, *Thoughts and Affections on the Passion of Jesus Christ*, 226.

37. Vincent Huby, *The Spiritual Retreat of the Reverend Father Vincent Huby* (Philadelphia: Printed for Mathew Carey, 1795), 184.

the heart of your divine Spouse than all the joy and brightness of Tabor."[38]

In order to follow Christ, his disciples must fix their attention where he fixed his. Chardon admits it is "marvelous to consider Christ in the midst of glory on Mt. Tabor, plunged into the divine essence, absorbed in a fullness of eternal happiness," but what did Jesus, himself, do? "Instead of fixing His mind on that which transfigured even His garments, He drew back, as it were, and turned to look from afar at scourges, thorns, nails, and a cruel death upon a cross.... Draughts of eternal glory cannot quench His thirst for suffering."[39] He presents it as a lesson for us to learn. "As the soul no longer considers anything but God, it follows that it no longer aspires to the sweetnesses of consolations, but abides peacefully in the God of all consolations. It no longer receives crosses as sources of affliction, but as the presence of the living God."[40]

Our crosses are not transformed by boasting (a strategy we frequently use), they are transformed by being united to Christ's Cross. What is bitter to nature is sweet to spirit—something experienced by saying "not my will, but Thine." In order to explain this sweetness, Vianney invokes the imagery of the Cross as a wine press. "If you put fine grapes into the wine press, there will come out a delicious juice: our soul, in the wine press of the Cross, gives out a juice that nourishes and strengthens it.... Thorns give out a perfume, and the Cross breathes forth sweetness. But we must squeeze the thorns in our hands, and press the Cross to our heart, that they may give out the juice they contain."[41] Crosses are totally changed when they become matters of love.

Could it be done in any easier way? No. Self-love is too deep not to require a deep cut. Could it be done in a way less painful? No. Self-love puts up too deep a resistance. Could we be made alive

38. Peter Eymard, *Life and Letters of Saint Peter Julian Eymard*, vol. 2 (Rome: Congregation of the Blessed Sacrament, 2010), 59.

39. Louis Chardon, *The Cross of Jesus*, vol. 1 (St. Louis, MO: B. Herder Book Co., 1957), 33.

40. Louis Chardon, *The Cross of Jesus*, vol. 2 (St. Louis, MO: B. Herder Book Co., 1959), 111.

41. Vianney, *The Little Catechism of the Curé of Ars*, 72.

without dying first? No. Self-love must be totally replaced. The only way forward is through crosses, submission, obedience, permitting God to act—in Fénelon's words, letting "love do whatsoever He will to root out self-love."[42] Crosses are remedies for pride. They mortify self-love. "Accept them, and you are cured,"[43] concludes Grou.

What we are talking about here is a contest for love. God wants our love; the sinner wants to keep his own love. God wants our willing obedience; the sinner wants to obey his own will. God wants to perfect our love, and direct it to the eternally true, beautiful, and good; the sinner wants to fix his love upon temporal goods that will wither like the grass (1 Pet 1:24, Is 40:6–8). Crosses are required to decrease our attachment to this world in order to permit an increase of attachment to God, which is why Libermann counsels us to "be humbly submissive to the divine will which crucifies you; love the hand of God that leads you with such severity. Have courage, this present life is nothing. The sorrows we suffer here pass quickly; this life is only a painful dream which will be followed by a joyful awakening. The more you suffer, the more detached you will become from yourselves and the world. This, at least, should be your aim."[44] Possessing one's soul with unwearied patience is only possible, says de Lombez, "because crosses are sown all over by the merciful hand of a God who knows their value and use."[45]

One can only imagine how this sounds to the world, which will flash from puzzlement, to sadness, to fear, to repulsion. Cruciform abnegation will forever confuse the worldling. There is a secret to crosses, hidden from Babylon, and Boudon composes a list of the kind of persons who cannot understand it: "lovers of themselves;" "delicate people, who love their ease;" "people interested in honor and eager for glory, who place their joy in the applause of men;" people who are "timid in the contradictions which can happen to them;" and, finally, people who are "even afraid of crucified per-

42. François Fénelon, *Spiritual Letters of Archbishop Fénelon. Letters to Women* (London: Longmans, Green, and Co., 1921), 178.

43. Grou, *The School of Jesus Christ*, 183.

44. Libermann, *Letters to Religious Sisters and Aspirants*, Spiritan Series 5, vol. 1, 28.

45. De Lombez, *A Treatise on Interior Peace*, 61.

sons: they would not dare to frequent them, from fear of sharing in their crosses."[46] Such persons will never find joy in crosses, but Languet says we should take no notice.

> Let the people of the world be saddened, O my good God, with Your chastisements; let them desire to turn them aside; let them seek in creatures, and in worldly amusement, their frivolous consolations; let them address to You their prayers to obtain deliverance from these salutary trials. For myself, I have but one prayer to offer You, and but one only desire—I wish to carry the amiable Cross of my Savior, to carry it with Him, to be attached to it with Him, to die on it with Him.[47]

Alacoque said a person should "kiss the hand that afflicts him,"[48] but it will take many years of immersion in the gospel—by reading, meditation, and prayer—to understand this liturgical reaction.

There is a warning given by these authors that I must mention before finishing: do not choose your own cross! You will choose one too heavy, or too light. If the whole purpose of your cross is to crucify vainglory, then de Sales warns against fashioning ones that will attract flattery from the world and feed our own self-esteem. "We do not love crosses, unless they are in gold, with pearls and enamel."[49] "Do not desire crosses, unless you have borne those already laid upon you well—it is an abuse to long after martyrdom while unable to bear an insult patiently."[50] His daughter in Religion, Jane de Chantal, learned the lesson well. "No, my dear Sisters, it is not permitted to choose our crosses. Let us bear the one that Divine Providence offers us, that is ours. But those we chose would be tainted with self-love, self-seeking, vain complacency; in a word,

46. Henri-Marie Boudon, *The Holy Slavery of the Admirable Mother of God* (CreateSpace Independent Publishing Platform, 2013), 194.

47. Jean-Joseph Languet de Gergy, *Confidence in the Mercy of God* (London: R. Washbourne, 1876), 232–33.

48. Alacoque, *The Letters of St. Margaret Mary Alacoque*, Letter 99, Kindle.

49. De Sales, *Library of St. Francis de Sales: vol. 1, Letters to Persons in the World*, 25.

50. De Sales, *Introduction to the Devout Life*, 171.

our choice spoils all."[51] This was a lesson learned by all the Visitation sisters with constant practice, and it permitted them to walk their path through life with steadiness. De Sales wrote to them:

> Those who walk on a rope hold a pole in their hands in order to keep their balance in the various movements they make on so dangerous a foothold, in like manner should you firmly hold the cross of our Lord in order to walk safely amidst the variety of perils that surround you, and the conversations that disturb you, so that all your movements may be balanced by the incomparable and sweet will of God to which you have consecrated both your body and your heart.[52]

Camus wonders what we could possibly be thinking when we want to trade in one of God's crosses for one we select ourselves.

> Where are your thoughtes, when you doe not onely wish for another Crosse, but even dare to demande it of God, as though you were wiser then that eternall wisdome, to discerne what is most convenient for you? O what a presumption, how blind an inconsideration, what an immortification is this! what irresignation, what selfe-love! No… not as thou wilt, but as God will: his will not yours be done.[53]

Sometimes we are too easy on ourselves, stopping before we should. Sometimes we are too hard on ourselves, trying to go further than God thinks wise at the moment. That accounts for why we are restless with our crosses. Libermann finds us saying, "'I do indeed desire to suffer, but I wish God would be pleased to give me some other cross than the one I have.' And [we] always find plausible reasons for this. This attitude is wrong. We should take the cross Jesus gives us and carry it wholeheartedly the way He hands it to us, never wearying."[54] It is a delusion to fantasize that we would carry

51. De Chantal, *Exhortations, Conferences and Instructions*, 458.

52. De Sales, quoted in *The Life of Jeanne Charlotte de Brechard* by the Sisters of the Visitation (New York: Longmans, Green and Co., 1924), 53.

53. Jean Pierre Camus, *A Spirituall Combat*, 1632 in *English Recusant Literature 1558–1640* vol. 189 (London: The Scolar Press, 1974), 153–54.

54. Libermann, *Letters to Clergy and Religious*, Spiritan Series 8, vol. 4, 116.

another cross more willingly than the ones we have been given, which is exactly how Grou analyzes the situation.

> [You say] the cross you are carrying is always the one you find heavy and particularly unpleasant. You would say the same of any other if it were laid on your shoulders, and perhaps you would find it heavier. . . . If crosses were left to your choice you would choose none, or else you would choose badly and repent of it afterwards. God knows better than you what is suitable for you; He loves you more than you love yourself. . . . If He strikes you on a sensitive spot it is because the malady is there and He is applying the remedy.[55]

The Cross has a sharp point because it must strike the sensitive spot. A blunt Cross would be of no use to anyone. Abnegation is resigning from self-will in order to glorify God by doing his will, which is why it is liturgical *abnegation*. Glorifying God is done by faith in his goodness and trust in his providence, which is why it is *liturgical* abnegation. The whole purpose of crosses is to change a will, which is why Libermann advises not to "set limits to the crosses you are willing to bear. Accept all that come as so many precious stones and be afraid to let any escape from your grasp. What are you afraid of? Haven't you the Heart of Jesus on which to rest where you will find the strength and love necessary to bear them?"[56] God knows what he is doing; let him choose your crosses for you.

A few saints have been given the privilege of bearing very hard, very heavy, very serious crosses. Most often it is for the purpose of encouraging the Church as an admirable example. But de Sales wisely knows human natures, and says extraordinary inspirations are often "more admirable than imitable."[57] Grou even warns against mimicking such saints out of personal vainglory.

> Such feelings as these are experienced only by the very few, and are the result, either of a very high degree of acquired perfection, or of a special inspiration. What is required of you is to expect crosses

55. Grou, *The School of Jesus Christ*, 182.
56. Libermann, *Letters to Religious Sisters and Aspirants*, Spiritan Series 5, vol. 1, 144.
57. De Sales, *Treatise on the Love of God*, 285.

> without going out to meet them, and not to be surprised when they come to you, as though you were especially privileged to be free from them; to submit humbly to them when they cannot be avoided; to bear them patiently, with the help of the great motives that religion supplies; to appeal confidently to God for His support, and hope steadfastly that He will not forsake you.[58]

The goal is not suffering; the goal is love. And to love as God wants us to love means preferring the crosses he chooses over the one we would choose for ourselves. Fénelon fears that "the crosses which originate with ourselves, are not near as efficient in eradicating self-love, as those which come in the daily allotments of God."[59]

The sinner and the believer have different reactions to crosses. Vianney thinks it is because they move in different directions, the former away from crosses, the latter toward them. "Most men turn their backs upon crosses, and fly before them. The more they run, the more the cross pursues them, the more it strikes and crushes them with burdens." But the believer

> who goes to meet the cross, goes in the opposite direction to crosses; he meets them, perhaps, but he is pleased to meet them; he loves them; he carries them courageously. They unite him to Our Lord; they purify him; they detach him from this world; they remove all obstacles from his heart; they help him to pass through life, as a bridge helps us to pass over water.[60]

In liturgical abnegation, our crosses fasten us to Christ, not only as we find him in the manger, and on the hills of Galilee, and on Mount Tabor, but especially when he is on his Cross. Somehow, there is room for two. The soul suffers—permits—God to remake her without complaint, ill humor, or regret. It is the very climax of the life of the soul. Christ shed his blood to restore perfect liturgy to the world, and Nicholas Cross traces the connection.

> He hath saved the World by the *effusion* of his precious *blood*, and nothing is more *glorious* to God than the *Salvation* of Mankind;

58. Grou, *The School of Jesus Christ*, 181–82.
59. Fénelon, *Spiritual Progress*, 53.
60. Vianney, *The Little Catechism of the Curé of Ars*, 68.

> for good and holy persons will praise, love, admire, contemplate, enjoy, and adore his perfections in the vast spaces of *Eternity*: Now had he not dyed for Man, no *Paradise*, no *felicity* could have been for them; so that God had remained under the *privation* of that *glory*, he doth and is to receive from *blessed Spirits* for all Eternity.[61]

By Christ's Cross heaven's liturgy is gladdened by glory. Tronson says the individual soul "is willing to suffer whatever crosses may be appointed for her, and to endure them joyfully, if she may thereby contribute to the glory of God."[62] Only liturgy explains crosses: they contribute to the glory of God. Suffering is liturgized.

Crosses appear as trials in the eyes of the world, but Christians are not of this world. They seek to please God, not the world. They hope to be rewarded by God, not by the world. We have already observed them abnegating this world in favor of their Father's house. Experience teaches that crosses are inevitable; Christianity goes further, and teaches they are covetable. They become precious insofar as they give a resemblance to Jesus Christ. The Cross has been taken down from Calvary and its wood refashioned into a yoke, and de Montfort rejoices that we can be joined to Christ by it.

> But if you suffer as you should, your cross will be a sweet yoke (Matt. 11:30), for Christ will share it with you. Your soul will be borne on it as on a pair of wings to the portals of Heaven. It will be the mast on your ship guiding you happily and easily to the harbor of salvation.
>
> Carry your cross with patience: a cross patiently borne will be your light in spiritual darkness, for he knows naught who knows not how to suffer (Eccli. 34:9).
>
> Carry your cross with joy and you will be inflamed with divine love, for only in suffering can we dwell in the pure love of Christ.[63]

61. Nicholas Cross, *The Cynosura, or A Saving Star That Leads to Eternity* (London: I. Redmayne for Thomas Books, 1679), 342–43.

62. Tronson, *Examination of Conscience*, 20.

63. Louis-Marie de Montfort, "Letters to Friends of the Cross," in *The Saint Louis de Montfort Collection* (London: Catholic Way Publishing, 2013), Kindle 459.

Thus Camus encourages us to "hearken to him who promiseth us to lighten our burden, by putting himselfe into the yoake with us."[64] Jesus did not say, "here is your cross; I have my own." Any more than he said, "here is your yoke; I have my own." A yoke is made for two, Francisco de Osuna reminds us, and "the one with the highest collar does most work and draws the heavier weight. Christ first undertook his part and is figured by Saul who had higher shoulders than the rest of the people and consequently, in his extreme humility and meekness, did more work."[65] The yoke is sweet because the Lord carries the chief part. He says, "take *my* yoke, *my* Cross—the one I bore first, the one I am still bearing, and we will share it together."

I come away from this chapter with various images of crosses. They are the timber columns on which the Church stands. They are a ratchet by which God elevates us. They are plows to overturn briars and plant divine seeds. They are balance beams to steady our pilgrimage. They are the bridges over which we cross from this temporal life to eternal life. They are crowbars that God uses to pry us loose from sin. They are kindling wood Jesus will use to cast fire upon the earth (Lk 12:49). They are the wood of the tree by which mankind fell, retooled to be the wood of the Cross. Jesus was a carpenter—he knew how to work with wood—and has recarved the tree of death into the tree of life. They are crutches of wood which aid our crippled pilgrim's gait. They are the wooden swords with which Christ beats upon the gates of hell, which shall not prevail against them. They are ladders (better than Jacob's) that scale heaven. They are the wooden door on which we can knock to request entrance into heaven.

64. Camus, *A Spirituall Combat*, 99.

65. Francisco de Osuna, *The Third Spiritual Alphabet* (New York: Benziger Brothers, 1931), 360.

6

Patience

De Granada makes the connection to this chapter by giving us one last image of the Cross. "Patience (as the holie fathers affirme) was the weddinge garmente wherewith the sonne of almightie God clothed himselfe when he came to be affyaunced [engaged] with the Catholike Churche, and to be married with her. . . . Our Savior Christe shyned most brightly with the garmente of all vertues, when he came to celebrate matrimonie with the Catholike Churche upon the bedde of the crosse, yet did he most principally shyne there with the robe of patience."[1] On the bed of the Cross, the splendor of Jesus's patience shines. *Splendere* means "to be bright, to shine" and his patience splendors from the Cross. We have found humility weaving its woof through every chapter's warp, and it is no different here: "Ah! patience is nothing else than humility in practice" exclaims Eymard. "Patience consists in confidence in God and the humbling of self."[2]

The modern definition of patience seems to understand it as tolerating a delay. A train is not on time, but the passenger is patient; the repairman won't arrive until this afternoon, but the housewife is patient. However, the root of the word actually emphasizes something else. *Pacience* meant the quality of "being willing to bear adversities; calm tranquility in the face of misfortune; submissiveness, humility."[3] The emphasis is on immovability, constancy, endurance. Gallwey underscores this. "*Patient*, as we see from the

1. Luis de Granada, *Of Prayer and Meditation* in *English Recusant Literature 1558–1640*, vol. 64 (Menston: The Scolar Press, 1971), 321.

2. Peter Eymard, *The Divine Eucharist: Fourth Series, the Eucharist and Christian Perfection* (New York: Fathers of the Blessed Sacrament, 1912), 651.

3. https://www.etymonline.com/search?q=patience.

Latin, is only another word for suffering. The Heart of our Lord is a suffering Heart. His love is a suffering love. We sometimes are kind and charitable as far as we can be *conveniently*, that is, till charity begins to cost, and brings suffering."[4] To lose patience is the beginning of disorder, says Ullathorne, but to remain patient "rests the soul on God, and establishes order, strength, and peace within the soul,"[5] and whenever we rest on God, we are resting on love. "True patience for the love of God is therefore the highest test and most evident proof of the presence of a noble degree of charity; because patience is its perfecting quality."[6] That is why Jesus could be so patient: he rested with his love upon the loving arms of the Father.

Patience-Endurance-Perseverance—it would be nice if I could create a word that stitched these three together, because we could use it to do the three tasks proposed in this chapter: (1) offer some definitions of patience in order to learn how to practice it, (2) marvel again at the patience of Christ on the Cross, (3) consider the patience of God toward us.

First, here are some brief definitions that get directly to the point.

- "Patience . . . is the virtue that endures all adversity without giving way"[7] (Segneri).

- "Patience means loving God with humility. . . . You must learn to leave time for your roots to go deep in the earth in order that you may be able to grow"[8] (Eymard).

- "Patience is a virtue that causes us to bear difficulties and sufferings in peace and gives us joy in the tribulations that God chooses to send us"[9] (Olier).

4. Peter Gallwey, *The Watches of the Sacred Passion with Before and After*, vol. 1 (London: Art and Book Company and Leamington, 1896), 372.

5. William Ullathorne, *Christian Patience: The Strength and Discipline of the Soul* (London: Burns & Oates, 1886), 93.

6. Ibid., 7.

7. Paul Segneri, *The Manna of the Soul: Meditations for Every Day of the Year*, vol. 1 (New York: Benziger Brothers, 1892), 378–79.

8. Peter Eymard, *Holy Communion* (New York: The Sentinel Press, 1940), 301.

9. Olier, *Introduction to the Christian Life and Virtues*, in *Bérulle and the French School*, 242.

- "Patience is a virtue by which we endure the evils of this world with even temper"[10] (Bona).
- "Where would patience be without the cross? Patience is synonymous with the cross"[11] (de Ravignan).
- And "patience is derived from adhering to the unchangeable strength of God"[12] (Ullathorne).

Patience is perseverance to the end. Without patience, the artist will not complete his drawing, the mechanic will not complete his repair, the craftsman will not complete his house, and the Christian will not complete his life. I don't just mean "reach the finish line," I mean finish building his life, with grace and virtues, in order to present it as an offering to God. We are born unfinished so we can cooperate with God in the attainment of virtues that will complete our character. It requires patience to become a Christian, because, Eymard says, "to sanctify self is to form Jesus Christ in self. That shapeless block of rough, hard stone, which is yourself, must be wrought upon. To chisel it, polish it, bring it in some degree to resemble the model, is not the affair of a day. Observation, study, labor are necessary. It has to be demolished, cut, repaired, and reconstructed. It is the work of a whole lifetime, and so patience is needed. And what is this patience? It is confidence in God and diffidence in self."[13] Christian life requires patience—not in the sense of waiting idly, but in the sense of steady, consistent, constant growth in grace.

If one believes—truly believes—that deification is man's end and purpose, then that changes everything. We speak of sin and pride as imperfections precisely because they prevent man's perfection. We are created in the image of God, and Ullathorne says "that . . . which is the living image of another can only be perfect in so far as it has the life of that other."[14] It "is a very imperfect creature until it has

10. Bona, *A Treatise of Spiritual Life*, 411.

11. De Ravignan, *Ravignan's Last Retreat*, 192.

12. Ullathorne, *Christian Patience*, 12.

13. Eymard, *The Divine Eucharist, Fourth Series: The Eucharist and Christian Perfection*, 648.

14. William Ullathorne, *The Groundwork of the Christian Virtues* (London: Burns & Oates, 1890), 265–66.

received the nobler existence for which it is made."[15] Pride is an inordinate appetite for one's own greatness, in *substitution* for the greatness man will receive from God. A garden is imperfect if it grows weeds instead of flowers and fruits; a house is imperfect if it is empty instead of having someone living in it; a dead body is imperfect if has not the soul for which it was made a habitation. And a soul? What would be an imperfect soul? A soul is imperfect when it is on its own, absent its inhabitant: God. "A soul, then, without the Spirit of God, is an existence without its object, a mere failure from the reason of its existence"[16] (Ullathorne).

This involves time because, as de Bernières-Louvigny says, "Christian perfection is not the work of a day. We must bear with our frailties and imperfections for many years. It is a gross mistake, arising from self-love, to think to march more speedily in ways of grace than God would have us. We must chiefly look to God, and, such as we are, cast ourselves into the arms of Jesus Christ."[17] Lallemant adds, "We wish to become saints in a day; we have not patience to await the ordinary course of grace. This proceeds from our pride and cowardice."[18] And "if there be any virtue which is acquired by degrees, it is patience,"[19] says Segneri, because overcoming our hesitancy to embrace the Cross must be done under God's providential guidance.

Fénelon says "the world cannot understand that patience can be a road to our true aim" because the world "persists in imagining patience to be mere inaction." [20] But the world is wrong. Patience is not waiting for God to do something, it is collaborating with the work God does to liberate us from sin, envy, malice, deceitfulness, lust, pride, and all the vices that estrange us from him. That takes time, so yes, be patient—which means "suffer; do not give up."

Let us take one example of the challenging patience Jesus asks of his disciples: turning the other cheek. De Bergamo says this is not

15. Ibid., 265.

16. Ibid.

17. De Bernières-Louvigny, *The Interior Christian*, 224.

18. Lallemant, *The Spiritual Doctrine of Father Louis Lallemant*, 171.

19. Segneri, *The Manna of the Soul*, vol. 1, 113.

20. Fénelon, *Letters to Men*, 198.

to be understood literally, because "Christian patience dwells not on the face, but in the heart." It would not fulfill Christ's intention if "a man would offer the other cheek to his enemy and at the same time his heart would be full of anger and vainglory."[21] Jesus is not asking for a kind of stoicism that leaves the heart unchanged. Rather, the divine Master intends to say that "if any one despises and offends us we must not only repress hatred, but, moreover, be prepared to suffer fresh injuries; without, however, neglecting the obligation of fraternal correction when requisite."[22] Patience. Endurance. Being prepared to suffer fresh injuries, even to the point of reconciling with an enemy. Jesus taught this not only by word, but by example. He continues to turn his other cheek with us: we wound him, but he is prepared to suffer fresh injuries. He doesn't lose patience with us.

Patience, then, is wholly indispensable to the Christian. It requires prayer, such as this one that escaped from de la Colombière's lips.

> My Jesus, let me live in thy Heart and pour all my bitterness into it where it will be utterly consumed. Sheltered in thy Heart I shall not fear impatience. There I will practice silence, resignation to thy will, and constancy. I will thank thee daily for my crosses and ask thy pardon for those who offend me. I will try to acquire patience. I know it is not the work of a day, but it is enough for me to be sure that it can be attained by effort.[23]

One of the signs of *impatience* is losing control of our tongue. "A man full of tongue shall not be directed by God upon the earth," warns Doyle.[24] "Endurance depends much on silence," says Faber, because "power escapes with words. It is only by the help of the grace of silence that the saints carry such heavy crosses.... Silence is the proper atmosphere of the cross, and secrecy its native climate.

21. De Bergamo, *Thoughts and Affections on the Passion of Jesus Christ*, 204.

22. Ibid.

23. Claude de la Colombière, *The Spiritual Direction of Saint Claude de la Colombière* (San Francisco: Ignatius Press, 1998), 28.

24. Francis Doyle, *Principles of Religious Life*, 326.

The best crosses are secret ones, and we may be silent under those that are not secret."[25] We can easily imagine the impatient person being talkative. His subject matter is endless: about why he should be pitied, about why the circumstances are unfair, about why he is justified in acting as he does. We can easily imagine it, because we have frequently done it ourselves. Eymard describes impatience and anger as "fruits of self-love; a severe and sarcastic tone proclaims a soul little dead to self."[26] To the contrary, patience is something practiced with the tongue, and Libermann warns that "if you open your mouth, your patience will escape by that door!"[27]

Where does this impatience come from? To find the answer, we must go way, way back, for Ullathorne detects "the birth of impatience in Satan."[28] To it, Satan joined his malice toward mankind, so Grou offers a stern warning not to give into Satan's malicious temptation to be impatient with God. Whoever you are, "do not imagine that your conversion is impossible, because you have put it off for a great length of time. Do not say; 'I have no longer any favor to expect from God; I have exhausted his goodness; I have tired his patience.' This is a snare of Satan, and the most dangerous snare he can lay for you."[29] Thinking that God has tired of you is the worst insult you can give God. It is worse than atheism. It insults God to say that his goodness has been exhausted, that his wrath over sin overrides the favor he wants to show, that his chastisements come from irritation and not charity, that he is sick of your failures, that he has given up on your redemption. Rather, says Eymard, marvel at divine patience. "God has labored with admirable patience at my conversion. Alas! How could Almighty God endure with so much patience my refusal, my delay to yield to His grace? What father,

25. Frederick Faber, *The Foot of the Cross or, The Sorrows of Mary* (London: Thomas Richardson and Son, 1858), 336.

26. Peter Eymard, *The Divine Eucharist, Third Series: Retreats at the Feet of Jesus Eucharistic* (New York: Fathers of the Blessed Sacrament, 1909), 100.

27. Libermann, *Letters to People in the World*, Spiritan Series 6, vol. 2, 220.

28. Ullathorne, *Christian Patience*, 13.

29. Grou, *Morality, Extracted from the Confessions of Saint Austin*, vol. 2, 141–42. I have added punctuation for clarity.

what mother would not be worn out by such conduct? Ah, God has been as good to me as He is patient!"[30]

Questions of doxology and idolatry are at stake here. We become impatient with God when we sometimes fashion a false god who does not immediately grant our wishes, and sometimes because he does not leave us alone. Jenks identifies all this impatience as proceeding from pride and selfishness, which makes us love our honor better than God and our neighbor. Then "our Blood Rises, our Spirits are Ruffled and Discomposed, our Thoughts are in a Hurry, to lay hold on some Revenge or other . . . these Resentments and Disturbances proceed from *Pride*, and . . . they are all Rooted in *Self-love*. We *Love* our *Honour* because we *Love* our *Selves*."[31]

Jesus said, "By your endurance you will gain your lives" (Lk 21:19). Baker offers this translation: "By patience ye shall keep the possession of your souls."[32] (*Hypomone* can mean perseverance, endurance, patience.) This is the true reason for admiring patience. The greatest happiness anyone can have is to possess his soul, de Sales says, "and the more perfect our patience, the more fully we do so possess our souls. . . . Do not limit your patience to this or that kind of trial, but extend it universally to whatever God may send, or allow to befall you."[33] Faber says we witness this in Mary. "There was no impatience in her manner, no resentment on her countenance, no expostulation on her lips. She possessed her soul perfectly."[34] And de Bergamo says when we examine the Passion closely "are we not forced by our reason to acknowledge Him as God by His patience alone?"[35] And "he loves rather to show Himself to be patient than He does to be deemed innocent!"[36]

Second let us consider Christ's patience on the Cross, since it

30. Eymard, *The Divine Eucharist: Retreats at the Feet of Jesus Eucharistic*, 123–24.

31. Sylvester Jenks, *Practical Discourses Upon the Morality of the Gospel*, vol. 1 (London: s.n., 1699), 192–93. Capitalization is as it appears in this old translation.

32. Baker, *Holy Wisdom*, 273. Vulgate: "*In patientia vestra possidebitis animas vestras.*"

33. De Sales, *Introduction to the Devout Life*, 92.

34. Faber, *The Foot of the Cross*, 268.

35. De Bergamo, *Thoughts and Affections on the Passion of Jesus Christ*, 359.

36. Ibid., 281.

seems supremely important to him. His tormentors mocked him over his patience. They said: If you can rebuild the Temple in three days (Mt 27:40), if you are king (Lk 23:37), if you can save others (Mk 15:32), then come down and we will believe. "Show us your omnipotence if you are God," they seem to say, but de Bergamo says they have it backwards. Jesus "is more solicitous to display His patience than His omnipotence, because it is by patience that He is to work out our salvation."[37] The supreme power, who gave being to the cosmos and life to its inhabitants, refuses to work this one, final miracle. There is something else he prefers to do. "Though He might cause Himself to be acknowledged as God by working this miracle, and coming down from the cross, He prefers rather to teach us patience, than to gain admiration by exercising His power. He would rather be known as God, by dying on the cross and saving our souls, than by descending from it and saving Himself."[38] Is Jesus God? Yes—and the proof is that he did *not* come down from the Cross. He saw it through to the end.

Patience is so important a facet of abnegation that Jesus prefers to teach it to us, rather than to save himself. We are ashamed to be meek and humble, but he is not. There is a long way to go if we are to unite our crosses with his. We have a little spurts of abnegation, but only at certain intervals, and for the briefest moments. De Bergamo observes our tendency to "seek to come down from the cross the very moment that I commence to feel it. Ah, my Jesus! make me love Thee, and love the cross also in imitation of Thee, with a true and persevering love. Of what use is it to begin and not to persevere in virtue, since Thou hast promised Thy glory only to Him who gains it by perseverance?"[39] Patience-Endurance-Perseverance.

The Fathers reminded the heretics that Jesus did not fall from the sky, but instead waited patiently in Mary's womb for his birth. Luke 2:52 says he increased in wisdom and stature, about which Chardon says: "of all the instruments that God used to heighten the anguish of His Son, time was one of the most effective. Jesus ate only when

37. De Bergamo, *Thoughts and Affections on the Passion of Jesus Christ*, 402–3.
38. Ibid., 477.
39. Ibid., 477–78.

He was hungry, drank only when He was thirsty. Though tired, He did not always rest, and did not sleep even during those hours when sleep pressed heavily upon Him."[40] Time is the tool one uses in order to create patience, and Jesus picked up this tool willingly. There is no such thing as "instant endurance"—the terms are contradictory. Patience cannot be had instantaneously. De Chantal knows this from her astute observation of human nature. "My dear Sisters, there are souls that have their passions at rest because nothing crosses them: [they are not to be called virtuous for that] for in fact solid virtue is acquired only in the midst of contradictions. A man cannot say that he is patient when he suffers nothing."[41]

To develop patience requires the passage of time, so Jesus (the eternal son of God) entered time (as the Son of Man). But the most condensed and pressurized instance of patience was the Cross, and by it, Crasset traces the link back to us.

> If I am without a cross,
> I am no disciple of Jesus.
> If I carry not my cross,
> I shall not reign with Jesus...
> When I suffer with patience,
> Jesus suffers with me.
> Jesus reigns in me.
> I am the victim of love.[42]

We see Christ slandered, yet find it hard to endure insults ourselves. We see Christ humiliated, yet find it hard to endure trifling slights without resentment. We see Christ on a literal Cross, yet find it hard to endure the interior crosses designed to crucify sin within. How, then, can we complete our liturgy and become true victims of love?

Olier discovers that Jesus's patience exposes our vices. "Our avarice binds his charity, our anger his mildness, our impatience his

40. Chardon, *The Cross of Jesus*, vol. 1, 67.

41. De Chantal, *Exhortations, Conferences, Instructions*, 161.

42. John Crasset, *Meditations for Every Day in the Year from the Christian Considerations of Father John Crasset, Advent to Pentecost*, transl. and ed. by T.B. Snow (London: R. Washbourne, 1888), 39. These are Snow's selections from *Christian Considerations*, under new translation and put in verse form.

patience, our pride his humility; and thus, by our vices, we chain, and bind, and tear to pieces, as much as we can, our Lord dwelling in us."[43] At the same time, de Bergamo thinks Jesus's patience is the remedy to exactly these vices. "I place against my pride the humility of Jesus; against my impatience, the patience of Jesus; against my anger, the meekness of Jesus; against my aversion and ill-will, the charity and sweetness of Jesus; against my sloth and tepidity, His fervor. . . . Look upon the sacred Humanity of Jesus; this suffices to console me, with the confidence that my iniquities will be pardoned by Thy clemency."[44]

The Cross is an example of indomitable patience. Patience is invincible, unflinching, and impregnable as it protects the charity Jesus has for every person. "What is the patience and long-suffering of God," asks Ullathorne, "but his long-abiding mercy over His wilful and wayward children?"[45] And de Granada is firmly convinced that if those who killed him would have converted, "he was ready to receive them to his grace and favour, even at the very last instant: neyther would hee have shut up the Gates of his Church from any man. . . . What thing in the world can possibly be of greater benignity and patience, then the blood of Christ, that offered life even to them that shed the same blood?"[46] When he asked his Father to forgive them, for they knew not what they did, he was not expressing an idle sentiment: he would have suffered once again for any one of them if it would have helped. The soldier who thrust his spear into Jesus's side did not know it penetrated as deep as the Savior's heart, and released a flood of redemption upon the world.

The story of salvation history recounts the efforts of God to find a place to meet man. Where would it be? On Mount Moriah, with Abraham and Isaac? On Mount Horeb, at a burning bush? On Mount Tabor, with Moses and Elijah? Better still: Mount Calvary,

43. Jean-Jacques Olier, *Catechism of an Interior Life* (Baltimore: Murphy & Co., 1852), 21.

44. De Bergamo, *Thoughts and Affections on the Passion of Jesus Christ*, 390–91.

45. Ullathorne, *The Endowments of Man*, 239.

46. De Granada, *Granada's Meditations Containing Fourteen Devout Exercises*, 399.

with two thieves. "Will you let all your Saviour's toils, sweat and pains be lost to you?" de Granada asks. "What could God have done more, in order to bring men off from sin, than place himself upon a cross betwixt it and them?"[47] Where could God show greater mercy? How could he show greater mercy? The Son of God waited there on Calvary—patiently!—for the human race, which had been in exile since Eden, to come and meet him. How could he better prove his love than waiting on the Cross for us to arrive? He placed himself betwixt humanity and sin, and waited.

The sight of his patience should stir our abnegation, de Bergamo thinks. Look at him: "Oh, how humble and meek is this King of Glory amidst His ignominies! How patient is this Man of Sorrows in His sufferings!" Look at me: "How proud and haughty am I amid my miseries; how much in love with vanities, how anxious for earthly comforts!"[48] It was not only Pilate who said *ecce homo* (behold the man); our Father in heaven says the same to us. "Ah, Eternal Father! since Thou showest me this Man, and commandest me to imitate Him, conquer my malice by Thy grace, that I may blot out in myself all the traces of the old earthly man and reform myself according to the likeness of this divine Man."[49]

Third, consider the patience of God toward us. Patience-Endurance-Perseverance. Divine patience is shown in both creation and redemption. Regarding the former, Ullathorne invites us to consider the action of God moving through creation, and when we do, "we everywhere see the signs of His divine patience, sustaining what is by nature feeble, upholding what left to itself must fall, enduring evil and disorder for the sake of final good, providing for all things according to their needs, and conducting all things to their destinies according to His eternal designs."[50] The entire Trinity has shown patience while the planets established their order, and nature responded to the steady rhythm of night and day, and the rose silently unfolded. Concerning the latter, Eymard invites us to con-

47. De Granada, *The Sinner's Guide*, 39.
48. De Bergamo, *Thoughts and Affections on the Passion of Jesus Christ*, 389.
49. Ibid.
50. Ullathorne, *Christian Patience*, 10.

sider the patience of God in waiting to redeem us. In his longanimity, God may permit the sinner

> to heap up crime upon crime that He may make of him a trophy of His mercy… "God waits to have pity on us." Every hour of that waiting is a new pardon, a new creation of mercy toward us, for justice pressingly urges its claims. It constantly demands our death, which it cannot allow to be deferred. Every moment of our life belongs to God, and would be sufficient for our death. Mercy snatches the sentence from Him, thus perpetually creating for us a new life. Oh, what thanks do we owe the divine mercy! What touches sinners more than all else is that God has waited for them.[51]

The Trinity shows patience with the cosmic establishment, the fall of the angels, the infection of man, the resultant disorder, and the delay of beatitude. The Trinity is even patient with our impatience, which seems to astonish Eymard. "Is not God patience itself toward souls, toward you? Does He become infuriated and violently dash things to pieces? No, He awaits the fruit of His seed years and years. He daily does the little that our cooperation permits Him to do. He recommences what our faults have demolished. He is the grace itself of patience and our model."[52] Bourdaloue also refers to all those "adorable delays, the delays of God, which keep back his anger, suspend his justice, and withhold his vengeance."[53] And in the face of this fact, de Bernières-Louvigny cannot hold back from bursting into prayer:

> O my God, how great is thy patience! how profound and unsearchable! Who but a God of infinite patience could suffer daily such provocations and contradictions from mortals, and yet continue to do them a thousand favours, in hopes of persuading them to amend? O patience of God, how art thou unspeakable;

51. Eymard, *The Divine Eucharist: Fourth Series, the Eucharist and Christian Perfection*, 297–98.

52. Ibid., 651–52.

53. Bourdaloue, *Sermons, and Moral Discourses, on the Important Duties of Christianity, vol.* 2 (Dublin: Published by James Duffy, 1843), 55.

> how art thou unconquerable! . . . O the infinite patience of God towards me! It is to it I owe my preservation or else I had been long since a lost creature for ever![54]

The Cross is a door, and a door has two sides. Man can knock on that door from his side to request grace, peace, and happiness. But God knocks on that door from his side, too! You can hear his knuckles on the other side of the Cross, asking for entrance into our hearts. Amazing—and Segneri can hardly believe it.

> Consider first, who this great Person is Who says: "Behold, I stand." It is the King of Glory. And yet, what is He doing? He is standing at the door of a sinner. . . . God is standing there uninvited; for if He had been invited He would, at least, have found the door open. . . . Such is the unspeakable excess of the love of God in order to gain admittance into the heart even of one who is a rebel against Him.[55]

A proud man would find it disgraceful to be put in such a position, but a patient God, who humbles himself to search for his beloved, approves of it. The reason he knocks is because "it is not His pleasure to take forcible possession."[56]

Saint-Jure is equally astounded. What could be the true reason for God's patient persistence, he wonders.

> O sweetness! O goodness! *I stand at the door* of thy heart. Who is it that speaks thus? It is the King of Kings! The holy and august Trinity at the door of the sinner! *standing*, and not ceasing to knock till the door is opened! . . . Thou ceasest not to knock at the door by Thy graces, Thy lights, Thy inspirations, Thy pious movements, and Thou sayest… *Open to Me, My sister, My spouse, My love, My dove, My beautiful one; immaculate*, not in fact, but in desire to become so; see the state to which I am reduced, My head uncovered as a captive, for I am the captive of thy love.[57]

54. De Bernières-Louvigny, *The Interior Christian*, 101, 102.

55. Segneri, *The Manna of the Soul*, vol. 2, 19–20.

56. Ibid., 21.

57. Saint-Jure, *A Treatise on the Knowledge and Love of Our Lord Jesus Christ*, vol. 1, 360.

The proud man mocks God and says the deity is absent in his life. He looks around at the cosmos and says he cannot find God, but Grou knows that is because God is standing, in divine humility, where the proud man does not see him: at the door of his own heart. "He knocks there, without wearying, for many long years, or rather, we may say, for the whole of our life. His patience in waiting for us is inconceivable; He bears our contempt, our resistance, our obstinacy, with a goodness and a perseverance beyond expression."[58]

De Osuna says someone would be to blame if he left home at the very hour he knew some high dignitaries were about to visit him. "It would appear insulting, and the guests might seek some other dwelling, leaving their indifferent host to himself." This is exactly the position we put God into. "We are certain, and know by the mouth of the Son of God himself that he and the Father and the Holy Spirit will come to dwell with one who loves them and will make their abode with him in no other place but in his soul, which is the dwelling-place of God; but the man himself must be there to receive him."[59] The Trinity will come to make his home in our souls—but *we must be home when God comes*. This is the whole point of liturgical abnegation. Such an easy solution to the problem of divine grace and human works: we do not make God come to us, and we do not make our way to God, but we must be waiting for him when he comes. Being home equals corresponding to grace, a point Challoner drives home by the grammar he uses to explain the parable of the sower. "This seed is heavenly: it is capable of producing fruit a hundred fold: he himself is the sower; and he himself waters with rain from heaven the seed he has sown: and yet three parts in four of this divine seed are lost, *for want of a correspondence in the soil*."[60]

Why would we fail to be home? What possible reason do we have to vacate our souls? Challoner says "we will not keep our souls at home, attentive to that great guest who resides within us" because

58. Grou, *Manual for Interior Souls*, 52.

59. De Osuna, *The Third Spiritual Alphabet*, 168.

60. Richard Challoner, *Considerations*, part I, 66. Italics added.

we "let them continually wander abroad upon vain created amusements.... Turn away my soul, from all these worldly toys which keep thee from God; and return to him thy true and only happiness, and in him repose for ever."[61] A spirit of abnegation is required on our part to give up the trivial distractions that take us away from home at exactly the moment the Trinity comes calling. God will not trespass on an abandoned house, a deserted soul, a vacant heart, where no one is waiting for him to arrive, and no soil corresponds to the gospel seed.

Wait for God; do not let worldly things make you impatient; do not give up on the God who has not given up on you. If Christ saves by his patience on the Cross, then "it is by patience, also, that we ourselves are to cooperate in our eternal salvation,"[62] advises de Bergamo. John of Ávila says that often our contemplation of the Cross does not go far enough. It often happens, he sighs, that people might weep over the Passion in their devotions, but "afterward, when they are offered a very small part of the Lord's sufferings, they have so little patience that it is as if they had learned in prayer not to suffer anything." [63] He wonders how this can be explained.

> I do not know to whom to compare them, except to those who appear in their dreams to do great things, but upon awaking, do everything in reverse. What can be more foolish, after the patience of the Lord in his sufferings has seemed good to me, than not to desire to be patient in my sufferings? Instead, I say to him: "Lord, carry your cross alone, even though it is very heavy, for I do not want to help you, since I am carrying my own cross, even though it is small."[64]

We make plenty of good resolutions to mortify ourselves, to bear patiently with others, to love our neighbor, to forgive our enemies, and so forth, but "unless some one puts them to the test," John con-

61. Richard Challoner, *Think Well On't: or, Reflections on the Great Truths of the Christian Religion, for Every Day in the Month* (Manchester: Printed by R. & W. Dean & Co., 1801), 77.

62. De Bergamo, *Thoughts and Affections on the Passion of Jesus Christ*, 403.

63. John of Ávila, *Audi, Filia*, 219.

64. Ibid.

cludes, "they are dreams rather than realities. Valour must be shown in battle, or else it is but idle boasting."[65] Abnegation is not for theory, it is for practice.

The disciple should be instructed by his master's patience, but instead we are short-tempered. Comparing Jesus to ourselves, Nepveu says "He suffered and He was innocent, yet He did not complain. You suffer and you are guilty, yet you complain."[66] We cannot compare our sufferings to his, but our willingness to suffer could at least begin to approach his if we shared his charity. Christ is the way, the truth, and the life, which means, Jenks concludes, that "when once the *Love of God* has *made the Way Straight*, there's nothing wanting but the *Patience of Christ* to *make it Smooth*," and although we cannot prevent all attacks of self-love and pride, "we can prevent being Surprized by them. . . . This Degree of *Patience* is the surest mark of *true Repentance*."[67]

Carrying one's cross patiently is liturgical abnegation in action. It is a sign, thinks de Granada. "There is no sacrifice more acceptable unto Almighty God, then a troubled and afflicted hart, neither is there any signe more certaine of his love and friendship, then patience in tribulation and affliction."[68] This need not be huge, heroic suffering. That is the privileged vocation of some, but not of all (admirable but maybe not imitable). Nevertheless, even without great opportunities for suffering, we are granted little opportunities "every day, and almost every moment," observes Grou. "Now the smallest vexation borne for God will not go unrewarded. . . . A soul's most ardent desire on earth is to be absolutely assured of loving God. No virtue can supply this assurance more certainly than patience."[69]

In addition to being a mark of repentance, patience is a gift by which we glorify God. That God derives glory from our patience is our motivation for being patient. It is *liturgical patience* because it

65. John of Ávila, *Letters of Blessed John of Ávila*, 85.

66. Nepveu, *Meditations for Every Day in the Month*, 84.

67. Jenks, *Practical Discourses*, vol. 1, 187–88.

68. De Granada, *Granada's Meditations Containing Fourteen Devout Exercises*, 522.

69. Grou, *School of Jesus Christ*, 226.

glorifies God. Suffering for other causes may glorify the ideals of that cause, suffering for the prince may glorify the prince, but the abnegation being considered here should be done to glorify God. Grou is sure that "He is the only Being worthy that men should suffer and sacrifice themselves for Him. He enjoys His own greatness when He sees His creatures acquiescing in His good pleasure, and submitting humbly to His correction, or to the tests to which He puts their love."[70] Arias puts it more flatly: it is part of our deification program. "What glory is so great, as that a man may become like God, in the exercise of *Patience*."[71] Jesus taught us patience not only by word, but by deed; it was a patience whereby he imitated his eternal Father; and since we are members of Christ, it will become us to follow his example.

Liturgy draws its breath from eternity. It does not breathe the noxious air of a fallen world, it inhales eternity. And what could better support patience, Bourdaloue notices. "Eternity is the time of God, and yours is the mortal life. Your time is short, but God's is infinite. Now nothing obliges God to do all things in your time: it is enough that he does them in his own."[72] Wait for God, without impatience. Slow down. Expect crosses where you are, and abandon yourself "to the guidance of the Master," advises Libermann. "Follow Him step by step, never wishing to rush ahead of Him or to anticipate things."[73]

Patience-Endurance-Perseverance. It is the strength required to profit from mortifications, to which we next turn.

70. Ibid.

71. Francis Arias, *A Treatise of Patience* in *English Recusant Literature* 1558–1640 vol. 21 (Menston: The Scolar Press, 1970), 23.

72. Bourdaloue, *Sermons, and Moral Discourses*, vol. 1, 238.

73. Libermann, *Letters to Clergy and Religious*, Spiritan Series 9, vol. 5, 185.

7

Mortification

Let us allow Jesus to set the terms. Horstius writes his book as a dialogue between Christ and the soul, and hears Jesus say this: "First, then, if thou wilt come after me, deny thyself, and take up thy cross and follow me. For, for thy sake it was that I left my throne, put off my majesty, and became partaker of thy lowness, that thou mightst put off the old man and put on the new, which is created according to God, and mightst mortify thy members which are upon the earth."[1] Sounds good in theory; sounds good in Scripture; but sounds hard to put in practice, and the man answers: "I confess, O Lord, that he is worthy of death who refuses to live to thee. Who can give me, O most gracious Jesus, for love of thee, to die to myself and live to thee? But love conquers all things, and what will not thine effect?"[2]

Mortification is another of those hard words used by theologians of abnegation. It is hard in the sense of feeling harsh, and hard in the sense of difficult to understand. Nepveu gets us started by identifying three purposes or aims. "The first aim of Christian mortification is the ordering of our pleasures. . . . The second aim of mortification is to govern a man's whole faculties and powers. . . . The third aim of mortification is to teach us to submit to the cares and troubles, the occupations and responsibilities, and, in fine, all the duties of our position; to bear willingly crosses."[3] Put these together by grouping them under their governing purpose, which is for every Christian, insists Croiset. "'Tis an Error to imagine that Penance is necessary

1. James Merlo Horstius, *The Paradise of the Christian Soul, Delightful for Its Choicest Pleasures of Piety of Every Kind* (London: Burns & Lambert, 1850), 429.

2. Horstius, *The Paradise of the Christian Soul*, 429–30.

3. François Nepveu, *The Hidden Life* (London: J. Masters, 1871), 131–33.

only for great Sinners, and no less an Error to think that Mortification is the Virtue only of the Perfect."[4] Jesus showed us no other way to heaven but by mortification and penance.

I would like to approach mortification as a liturgical reality. At each moment, man is faced with the possibility of liturgizing God or idolizing himself. A choice is demanded, as de Liguori says, because "the heart of man cannot exist without love; it either loves the creature, or loves God."[5] The heart of man is either dead to self and alive to God, or it is alive to itself and dead to God. The heart is programmed to love someone. Christ wants to dwell as King of hearts, but we must remember (says Lebrun) that "He only reigns in those in which sin, the world, and vanity are dead and in which pride, self, and the will are thoroughly subjugated, or at least so enfeebled that they do not prevent Him from being master."[6] Mortification will involve some exterior practices, and for some, these austerities could be practiced intensely: solitude, silence, hunger, vigils, poverty, or bodily severities.

I do not want to overlook the exterior mortifications of passions, but I want to concentrate on their end. Mortification is not an end in itself; it is a means to the end. It is an instrument for dealing a death blow to self-love. Suffering for its own sake would be masochism, not mortification. Interior mortification consists in the denial of your own will, possible to everyone, and Quadrupani identifies it as the most meritorious form. "Those mortifications which are not voluntary, or chosen by ourselves, as sickness, ill success in our business, the envy or insolence of others, when supported with resignation and a cheerful mind, are of all mortifications the most meritorious, because they are sent from God."[7] Croiset agrees that they can seem small yet be meritorious. "The Inconveniences of the Place, of the Season, the Disagreeableness of the Company, Born so that we seem not to mind them, are indeed little Occasions of Mor-

4. John Croiset, *A Spiritual Retreat for One Day in Every Month* (London: Printed by Thomas Hales, 1704), 198.

5. De Liguori, *Preparation for Death* , 64–65.

6. Lebrun, *The Spiritual Teaching of St. John Eudes*, 89.

7. Quadrupani, R.P. [Carlo Giuseppe], *The Christian Instructed: Precepts for Living Christianly in the World* (London: James Burns, 1849), 72.

tification; but the Mortification its self is not little in these small Occasions. It is very meritorious."[8]

Man is created in the image of God, so he should be like a mirror in which God can see himself. God can witness his presence and power at work in the heavens and earth, but man is different. His intellect and will mirrors God more profoundly. The problem, of course, is that the mirror has now been tarnished, or warped, by sin. It is in the condition of a fun house mirror that distorts the image it reflects: the legs look too long, or the head too large. God sees himself, but this does not look right in souls that are warped. What has caused this? De Granada explains that "the sinner is not only the slave of sin; he is also the slave of the principal instigators of sin: the world, the flesh, and the devil. For he who is a servant of the son is likewise a servant of the parents, and these three things are the parents of sin."[9]

Paul identifies this slavery to sin as the state of the *old man*. "We know that our former man was crucified with him so that the sinful body might be destroyed, and we might no longer be enslaved to sin" (Rom 6:6). Die to sin; die to the old self; die to worldliness. Be mortified. The word does not mean simple shame or embarrassment ("I felt mortified by it!"). It means "to make dead." Make the sinful man dead. Mortification puts to death in order to bring to life, laying down chains in order to receive liberty, letting go in order to be taken hold of by God. It is necessary for the perfect love of Jesus. De Granada effectively says, "holiness implies the most perfect imitation of God that is possible, but if a thing cannot *become what it is not* unless it first *ceases to be what it is*, then the first requirement for holiness is that we rid ourselves of all the characteristics of the old man and put on those of the new man, who is fashioned to the image and likeness of God."[10] Mortification is the first step of redemption. First, cease to be what you are; second, become what you are not yet, but desire to be. Redemption (being

8. Croiset, *A Spiritual Retreat for One Day in Every Month*, 204–5.

9. De Granada, *Summa of the Christian Life*, 183.

10. De Granada, *Summa of the Christian Life*, 231. I have added emphasis for clarity.

clothed with Christ) begins with mortification (being stripped of world, flesh and the devil).

Although God was "infinitely happy and glorious in the vision of His own divine beauty," says de Granada, "God is also magnificent and liberal," meaning that he is "diffusive of His goodness. . . . It was as if God did not wish to be alone in His happiness." [11] He created angels in heaven and men on earth who were capable of receiving a share in His glory because they were created in his Image. But just as persons in slovenly and shoddy garments are not admitted to the palaces of kings, so also "sensual and carnal men cannot enter into the heavenly mansion of the King of kings, for they are spiritually shabby and tattered."[12] There is no way around mortification: we cannot put on new virtues if we keep the old vices. It would be like putting a new coat on top of an old, shabby coat: it won't fit.

The death of the old man is God's doing, which makes mortification, itself, already a first kiss of grace. It is the background work of God. While the spiritual gifts are on stage, mortification is backstage, behind the curtain, killing to make alive. Yet our cooperation with this grace must be so willing and voluntary that the tradition speaks about "mortifying oneself." For example, Segneri: "Of your own free choice, you wish to engage in God's service, in preference to that of this vain, transient world, to mortify and subdue yourselves."[13] For example, de Bergamo: "if I will not mortify myself with humility—that is to say, crush my self-love and craving for esteem—I shall be excluded as a follower of Jesus Christ."[14]

To take up our earlier point about crosses, we must *suffer* mortification: permit, allow to occur, submit to. The death of the old man is God's doing, but we must not resist it, which we will be initially tempted to do because our old nature is horrified at the prospect. Mortification rectifies faculties and sets the power of love back in right order. It redirects love from self to God.

11. Ibid., 150.

12. Ibid., 149–50.

13. Paul Segneri, *Lenten Sermons*, vol. 2 (New York: Christian Press Association, 1874), 307.

14. De Bergamo, *Humility of Heart*, 107.

How can something bitter ever taste sweet? Saint-Jure seems to think that love is funny that way. "Here is found true love, which impels the lover to deprive himself of all things for his beloved."[15] Even on the natural plane, true love will impel a lover (spouse, parent, friend) to renounce certain things, and do so happily. Imagine the power of divine love on the supernatural plane. So Saint-Jure considers two ways of purifying our soul and acquiring perfection: by force of blows and by force of fire. "With the hammer of mortification [we give] blows now to one habit, now to another, now to pride, now to envy, and so of the rest; by this means we may, perhaps, accomplish our design, but not so surely or effectually as by the fire of charity which would burn, in a little while, all the bad habits of the field of our soul and render it fertile in holy affections and good works."[16] Mortification may feel like hammer blows at the beginning, but by the end it must come under charity's fire. Massillon says some duties resist, others strengthen; one destroys, the other enlivens. To these two ends, all the duties of the gospel concerning mortification are reduced.

> Some are proposed in order to resist and to weaken that fund of corruption which we bear from our birth; the others in order to perfect that first grace of the Christian which we have received in baptism; that is to say, the one in order to destroy in us the old Adam, the other in order to make Jesus Christ to grow there. Violence, self-denial, and mortification regard the first: prayer, retirement, vigilance, contempt for the world, desire of invisible riches, are comprised in the second: behold the whole Gospel.[17]

Arrival begins with departure. We cannot reach one destination without departing from another. In the practice of baptism in the ancient Church, the candidate would face west (darkness) to renounce Satan, then turn toward the east (the sun) and pledge himself to Christ. Nepveu asks each of us, "what else did all those

15. Saint-Jure, *A Treatise on the Knowledge and Love of Our Lord Jesus Christ*, vol. 1, 262.

16. Ibid., 243.

17. John-Baptist Massillon, *Sermons by John-Baptist Massillon, Bishop of Clermont* (London: Printed for Thomas Tegg, 1839), 408.

baptismal ceremonies mean? . . . Did you not bind yourself to a life of perpetual mortification? Did you not bind yourself at the foot of the altar, before heaven and earth, to renounce the world and its pomps, the flesh and its pleasures, the devil and his works?"[18] If you are baptized, you are bound to a life of mortification. This is not for priest and religious alone. At the font, you promised to mortify anything that impedes your full relationship with the Trinity. God came to your door and knocked at baptism; he continues to knock daily (as we have seen); mortification opens that door a bit wider every day. Why? Because with the crosses that fit in, even more love can fit in. De Sales: "keep your heart very wide to receive in it all sorts of crosses and resignations or abnegations, for the love of him who has received so many of them for us."[19]

One excuse we might offer to avoid mortification is to say we never intended to become saints ourselves. We remember stories from our childhood about the heroic saints, and think those saints are too far above us, too far ahead of us. It is as if we prefer a milder religion, a religion of milder degree, one that will not demand the mortification we associate with the miraculous physical austerities undergone by the saints. But Blosius challenges this. The will is the thing. Look at Mary.

> Thou must not . . . imagine thyself to be remote from God, because, perchance, thou canst not practice great austerity of life, or because thou dost not feel thyself inwardly impelled and attracted towards it. For it is not in this that true perfection and true holiness consist; they consist in the mortification of self-will and of evil inclinations, and in true humility and charity. We do not read that the Blessed Virgin Mary, Mother of God, led so hard a life as did the holy widow Judith; and yet she was by far more perfect than Judith. All the elect walk not outwardly in the same path; but almost surely follow inwardly the same path, namely, the path of humility, and true charity or holy love.[20]

18. Nepveu, *The Hidden Life*, 116–17.

19. De Sales, *Library of St. Francis de Sales: vol. 1, Letters to Persons in the World*, 68.

20. Blosius, *Spiritual Works*, ed. Bowden, 123.

Judith led the more austere life, and Mary was the more perfect. The Mother of God expressed her mortification in her *fiat:* "Let it be to me according to your word." Ask of me what you want; take me where you want; do with me what you want. I will not resist. Renunciation overcomes resistance.

Grou notices a very strange loophole used by the old Adam who will gladly take on pious exercises so long as he does not have to die to himself. The old man is happy to pretend piety so long as it does not cut very deep.

> Enjoin on them as many pious exercises, as many religious practices, even as many austerities as you will: they will fast, and go without sleep, and spend whole days in the churches; but to do violence to their character, to conquer their sensitiveness, to endure contradiction, to give up their own opinion, in a word to mortify their own mind and their own will is what they will not do, and what seems to them not merely difficult, but impossible.[21]

Choosing our own mortification is like choosing our own crosses: we pick one that works mainly on the surface and does not go to the heart. Lacordaire insists that "the most painful mortifications are those which we do not ourselves will, which neither begin nor end where we want them. A man may have been making inward and outward acts of humility for weeks; and yet, when the time comes, a mere want of respect in some one else may upset him."[22]

For some people (maybe for all of us, sometimes), it can be easier to give up chocolate for Lent than to give up our own opinion. It is easier because one can manipulate the world into admiring the mortification. Jesus noticed, which is why he instructed his followers not to let their mortifications be noticeable. He called out the Pharisee who prayed, "God, I thank you that I am not like other men. . . . I fast twice a week, I give tithes of all that I get" (Lk 18:11–12). Instead, Jesus asked his disciples to let their mortifications be secret. "Do not look dismal, like the hypocrites, for they disfigure

21. Grou, *The School of Jesus Christ*, 34.

22. Jean-Baptiste Henri-Dominique Lacordaire, *Letters to Young Men* (London: Art and Book Co., 1902), 86.

their faces that their fasting may be seen by men" (Mt 6:16). Jenks writes such people "are well enough pleased with anything that feeds their pride, and helps them to a false persuasion of their being in the high road of the saints."[23]

I imagine de Sales encouraged by Scupoli's understanding of abnegation. "To conquer and mortify our own appetites, however small they may be, is worthy of greater praise than to storm strong cities, to overcome mighty armies in battle, to work miracles, and to raise the dead."[24] Baker holds the same opinion. "The smallest act of love and service to God, performed with a perfect self-abnegation, is more acceptable and precious in His eyes, than the working of a thousand miracles or the conversion of nations, if in these there are mixed interests of nature."[25] Opportunities abound! what excuse have we for not taking one? Mortification teaches us to endure our crosses "not with patience only but with gratitude," says Nepveu, "rejoicing in that the empire of the flesh is losing its hold over us, the body of sin being destroyed, the old man being crucified, and we ourselves nailed with Jesus Christ upon the Cross. This is what mortification comprises. Hast thou ever practised it?"[26]

"But," we protest, "the great saints lived in deserts and caves, under persecution." A reason I take Fénelon as my favorite theologian of liturgical abnegation is that he did not write his spiritual letters to such persons, but to people with duties in the world (many of whom were members of the court of Louis XIV, the Sun King), encouraging them to serve God in their state of life. One day Fénelon received a letter with just the question we are discussing. The man thought it impossible for him to offer his daily actions to God, since his daily actions consisted of affairs of Court, promenades, visits received and paid, business on behalf of friends and relations, ordering equipment, and so forth. Here is Fénelon's reply.

23. Sylvester Jenks, *The Blind Obedience of an Humble Penitent: The Best Cure for Scruples* (London: Burns Oates and Washbourne, Ltd., 1926), 15.

24. Scupoli, *The Spiritual Combat*, 100.

25. Baker, *Holy Wisdom*, 249.

26. Nepveu, *Hidden Life*, 133.

> ANSWER. The most unimportant acts cease to be so, and become important, directly that they are done with the intention of conformity to God's Will. Indeed, they are often better and purer than what may seem more religious acts; first, because they are less self-chosen, and more according to the order of God's Providence; secondly, because they are simpler, and less exposed to self-complacency; thirdly, because if performed in moderation, and with a right intention of heart, we may find more means of self-abnegation than in actions where excitement or self have a larger part; and lastly, because these trifling matters are continually recurring, and furnish a constant opportunity for unobtrusively serving God.[27]

Mortification will involve exterior austerity, ranging from the martyr suffering, to the monk fasting, to the Christian sacrificing a good he desires. But in each case, it must involve internal control of eye, ear, tongue, sense, and, most of all, the will. Mortification becomes useless if directed by our own will, because it is precisely our own self-will we are trying to put to death. Such is impossible without the grace of God. In all acts of mortification we must have confidence in God's wisdom (faith), in God's goodness (hope), and in God's providence (love). Someone who suffers without obedience would be a false martyr, as John of the Cross makes clear. "Bodily penance, without obedience, is a most imperfect thing; beginners practise it out of a desire for it, and for the pleasure they find in it; and therefore because they herein do their own will, they grow in vice, rather than in virtue."[28] Bodily austerity is required in some degree for all; it is gifted in a high degree to some; in either case, the will is where the real abnegation occurs.

Sometimes a person is called to heroic suffering, but life has miseries and trials enough that we do not have to go in search of them. We have already learned that humility means abiding exactly where God has placed us, not higher and not lower; now we also learn that humility means performing exactly the mortifications God requires

27. Fénelon, *Letters to Men*, 45–46.

28. John of the Cross, *Spiritual Canticle Between the Soul and Christ*, in *The Complete Works*, 376.

of us, no more and no less. Fénelon even says that it may be a mortification to give up a mortification.

> A simple mortification, consisting in nothing more than an unshaken fidelity in providential crosses, is often far more valuable than severe austerities which render the life more marked, and tempt to a vain self-complacency. . . . It is sometimes a very useful mortification to certain fervent souls, to give up their own plans of mortification, and adopt with cheerfulness those which are momentarily revealed in the order of God.[29]

But do not worry, Baker says! God will not forget to give you opportunities for humiliation, patience, and suffering with Christ. "The highest perfection is not to desire to be always suffering, but to be content to suffer all that by God's providence shall befall us. . . . Therefore, let souls never be solicitous, nor set themselves to devise or procure mortifications, as if they thought God had forgotten them."[30] What is the highest perfection? Love. What end does mortification serve? Love. Strive, then, "in order that by means of true mortification of self we may arrive at perfect love of God,"[31] commands Blosius. And who loves God truly? The one for whom "God Himself is 'the One who is': whose taste is for heavenly things, while earthly things are to him worthless: who knows how to restrain his exterior senses, and to free his interior senses from all things, and to apply his powers to God."[32]

Mortification and prayer go together like food and life, so in all discussion of the one, prayer is mentioned frequently. Baker says, "perfection in prayer is accompanied with a proportionate perfection in mortification."[33] Rodríguez calls it an indispensable tool for successful mortification. "Prayer works the same effect upon our heart, which being naturally hard, has a repugnance to mortification and contempt, and feels it very difficult to submit to the will of

29. Fénelon, *Spiritual Progress*, 29.
30. Baker, *Holy Wisdom*, vol. 2, 485.
31. Blosius, *Institutio Spiritualis*, 36–37.
32. Ibid., 37.
33. Baker, *Holy Wisdom*, vol. 1, 206.

another."[34] And Collins thinks neither prayer nor mortification is sufficient alone.

> The spiritual life consists of these two things, and neither of them is sufficient without the other. Yet of the two prayer is the principal and more noble part. For mortification is only of profit, as its practice enables the soul to pray better. Mortification beats down the will of corrupt nature, which is the greatest impediment to perfect prayer. It destroys sensuality, and leaves the soul in freedom for a higher work.[35]

God's two hands are justice and mercy. Sometimes he uses them together; sometimes one before the other; but always both, eventually. We are mistaken when we think mercy cancels justice, or when we prefer God to deal with us mercifully instead of justly. God's justice opposes sin; to idolize anything but God is injustice. Mercy is everything God does to bring us back to loving the Creator, which means mercy restores justice. Mercy does not oppose or contradict justice, it serves it. The justice of God is an act of mercy, thinks Nieremberg. "The more virtuous one is the more he hates sin; the more he hates it, the more he desires its destruction: and therefore God desires more to pardon sin than the penitent himself who begs pardon. God is most accomplished in all goodness, and therefore He of all others most hates sin. . . . Do not then despair, O sinner, by reason of the vastness of thy debt; it is but a trifle in regard of the infinite mercy of God and endless merits of Christ."[36] Abnegation is aligning ourselves with God: what he hates in us, we should hate in ourselves. God's justice is merciful.

Justice and mercy work together. De Caussade says we should accept the pain by which self-love is put to death and humiliation crucifies pride, "not so much because they are the effects of your

34. Alphonsus Rodríguez, *The Practice of Christian and Religious Perfection*, vol. 1 (Dublin: James Duffy, 1861), 269.

35. Henry Collins, *Spiritual Conferences on the Mysteries of Faith, and the Interior Life* (London: R. Washbourne, 1875), 209.

36. John Nieremberg, *Of Adoration in Spirit and Truth* (London: Burns, Oates, and Co., 1871), 24.

justice, but as benefits of your great mercy."[37] With diseased eyes we mistake mercy for justice, when actually they work in tandem and—more amazingly—it is justice that follows mercy. A false treatment imagines that the more mercy God shows, the less justice he exercises, as if justice condemns while mercy lets us off the hook. But a proper understanding knows where to look to find their true relationship, namely, in the Incarnation where Challoner points. See how brightly they shine there! It is just as the Psalmist predicted: "Mercy and truth met each other, justice and peace have kissed" (Ps 85:10).[38] The infinite mercy of God is set out in a clear light by the Incarnation, but the infinite justice is not set aside thereby. Indeed, this justice

> never exerted, nor manifested itself more, than when it insisted upon such a satisfaction for sin, as could not be paid by any lesser or meaner person than a God made man. So that the justice of God has been in effect more evidently demonstrated by the incarnation of the Son of God, coming down here amongst us, to be made a bleeding victim for our sins, than by any other judgments or punishments whatsoever, that either have, or ever could be inflicted by the divine Majesty, either in time or eternity, for the sins of men.[39]

Justice is shown when God is satisfied; mercy satisfies God; mercy fulfills justice; justice desires mercy to act; the merciful, bleeding victim is acting in submission to the Father's justice, for our sake. When our self-denial is made in the court of justice, we accept it happily because it is a benefit of mercy.

That is why Grou thinks we should welcome justice's command of mortification. "How merciful is Thy Justice! in order to satisfy it, to expiate my sins, it does but sentence me to mortify the passions which poison the happiness of my life, to renounce a world whose seduction can only make me unhappy, and to live with Thee only,

37. De Caussade, *Abandonment & Divine Providence*, 106.

38. Quoted in Challoner, *Considerations Upon Christian Truths and Christian Duties*, part II, 275.

39. Challoner, *Considerations Upon Christian Truths and Christian Duties*, part II, 275–76.

and for Thee only, Who art Alone the Source of all consolation."[40] A surprising conclusion: doing mortification for the sake of happiness. The world's vanity no longer fills our eyes, the world's flattery no longer fills our ears, and the happiness we thought the world could give fades, like an oil lamp running out of fuel.

Pride moved Satan; Satan moved Adam and Eve by pride; their children are still moved by pride. Proud of himself, the sinner avoids God as a threat, and this is the worst idolatry. And now there is nothing that cannot be corrupted by pride—even humility, says de Bergamo. "Humility is also so fragile that it is easily tainted by the love of praise, by a word or thought of self-esteem, by vainglory or self-love."[41] Even mortification, says Fénelon: "The hardest of all penances is humiliation of the inner mind; it implies a ceasing to bear and believe in self; it implies a meek submission to God's minister; it is that poverty of spirit which, according to Jesus Christ, makes a man blessed. Without it one can turn even mortification into food for self-love."[42] Even grace, for Fénelon adds: "Our corrupt nature finds a very subtle food in the graces which are most opposed to nature; self-love is fed, not merely by humiliations and austerities, by fervent prayer and mortification, but even by the fullest self-renunciation and utter sacrifice."[43] How odd to become proud of one's humility: the medicine furthers the disease. How odd, too, to become proud of one's mortifications: what should starve self-will feeds it. Fénelon concludes, "we feed our self-love with good works and austerity. We go over our mortifications with ourselves secretly, our victories over our own tastes, our righteous deeds, our patience, humility and detachment. We think we are seeking spiritual consolation in all these things, and we are seeking in them a helpful witness to our own righteousness."[44]

Mortification marks the division—the boundary line—between the Kingdom of God and the kingdom of this world. Jesus walked

40. Jean Grou, *The Practical Science of the Cross in the Use of the Sacraments of Penance and the Eucharist* (London: Joseph Masters, 1871), 54.

41. De Bergamo, *Humility of Heart*, 31.

42. Fénelon, *Letters to Men*, 232.

43. Fénelon, *Letters to Women*, 269.

44. Fénelon, *Christian Perfection*, 48.

that divide in order to show us the difference between the spirit that resides in the one, and the spirit that resides in the other. Here is how Eudes describes that difference. "The spirit of Jesus is a spirit of humility, of modesty, of self-distrust, of mortification and abnegation, of constancy and of firmness. But the spirit of the world is, by contrast, a spirit of pride, presumption, disordered self-love, fickleness and inconstancy."[45] There is danger in doing mortification in the spirit of the world, instead of in the spirit of Jesus.

If we can boast of a mortification to another, after boasting of it to ourselves, then it is not a true mortification. Self-chosen mortifications are more dangerous than those assigned by God, and extraordinary mortifications can be more dangerous than ordinary ones. Many deceive themselves by thinking they would willingly join the grand martyrdoms in the early Church, but they are unwilling to undergo the small mortifications that will work their conversion slowly, day by day. Croiset worries over this attempt at self-control:

> We propose to ourselves certain plans of life which we intend to carry out at certain times; and, as if our conversion and sanctification were secure, we take no further trouble about correcting our imperfections. Though we are convinced that mortification is absolutely necessary if we would be holy, we refuse the crosses that present themselves under the pretext that they are too small. We sigh after greater crosses, only because we see them at a greater distance. We satisfy ourselves in the meantime with these idle imaginations.[46]

A littler mortification actually committed is worth a greater mortification in our fantasy.

This is a theme our authors harp on, as they try to plug up all the holes in the dam through which pride will trickle into a heart. Here are three examples. De la Colombière says, "there is no one to whom, each day, there do not happen a hundred minor things contrary to one's desires and to one's inclinations," so he counsels that

45. Eudes, *The Life and the Kingdom of Jesus in Christian Souls*, 16.
46. Croiset, *Devotion to the Sacred Heart of Jesus*, 68.

instead of waiting for an opportunity of heroic proportions, be on guard "to offer to God all these little annoyances and to accept them as being ordained by Providence."[47] Grou says it is easier to preserve humility in little things because "in them there is nothing for self-love to fix upon as matter for glorification. . . . Therefore, the faithful practice of little things is incomparably safer for us. . . . And if the death of self-love is more gradual, it is none the less sure."[48] And Fénelon urges everyone to mortify their vanity whenever God points it out. "I pray that God may make you gentle, lonely, and childlike, as our manger-born Lord Jesus. Do not seek to be clever, or dogmatic, or keen to the faults of others, or sensitive and touchy, or to be thought better in appearance than you are in reality."[49]

If one wants to build muscle, one does not start with a weight too heavy even to lift. That easily becomes a convenient excuse for giving up the exercise program altogether. In muscle training, this is called doing "repetitions," or "reps;" in training spiritual strength, it is called "a long succession of all kinds of mortifications, trials, and deprivations. . . . This must continue until all things created become as though they did not exist, and God becomes all in all"[50] (de Caussade). Alacoque agrees, and urges "let us not give way to discouragement, dear friend, but take in good part and in a spirit of submission the little mortifications His sweet Providence allows to come to us and try to make good use of them."[51]

Remember that the point of mortification is not to attract flattery, but to produce obedience, resignation, and subservience to God. Guillore concurs when he says great occasions of conquering self are rare, while mundane duties of the Christian life are never-ending.

> Accordingly we find people who have achieved some hard thing giving way weakly under trifles; ready to perform great external

47. Claude de la Colombière, *Sermons vol. 1: Christian Conduct* (DeKalb, IL: NIU Press, 2014), 134.

48. Grou, *Manual for Interior Souls*, 118–19.

49. Fénelon, *Letters to Men*, 38.

50. De Caussade, *Abandonment to Divine Providence*, 50.

51. Alacoque, *The Letters of St. Margaret Mary Alacoque*, Letter 123, Kindle.

> works, but incapable of enduring a life of rule; practising severe bodily austerities, but giving undue license to their tongue; bearing real persecution, but keenly sensitive to a sharp word. Such persons may go bravely through severe temptations, and fall helplessly under some trifling assault; they will dream great things of all they would bear, even to death, for God's sake, thereby fostering vanity and self-conceit; and all the while they cannot put up with a disagreeable remark.[52]

De Ponte outlines the choice for us forcefully when he observes that all actions of religion (piety, prayer, charity, sacrament, etc.) seek to bind us to Almighty God, but in order to be tied to God, one must be untied from self, which is why all religion involves mortification. "All religion is founded upon the mortification of self-will, which if it lives religion dies, and if religion is to live self-will must die."[53] Huby thinks this death-or-life option dates back to the beginning. "The world owes its ruin to self-will, by the disobedience of the first Adam; the world owes its salvation to the obedience of the second Adam."[54]

The point of mortification is not the suffering, and it is certainly not the glory a person might receive from the world. Nicholas Cross realizes that "when once we come to divest ourselves of our selves, that is of Self-love, then all the Terrors of Mortification and Adversity find no Effect; . . . for solid Virtue, like a Rose amidst Thorns, springs not forth, but in the Soil of Afflictions."[55] In the field of mortification, roses bloom. The point of mortification is the glory our suffering might give God, and God is glorified when his law reigns, not our own. "To deny oneself means not to be a law unto oneself but to follow the law of God,"[56] says de Granada, because

52. Guillore, *Self-Renunciation*, 43.

53. Louis de Ponte, *Meditations on the Mysteries of Our Holy Faith*, vol. 1 (London: Richardson and Son, 1852), 299.

54. Vincent Huby, *Spiritual Works of Pere Vincent Huby, S.J.* (London: Burns Oates & Washbourne Ltd., 1930), 114.

55. Nicholas Cross, "Of the Joys of Heaven" in James Ayray et al., *A Select Collection of Catholick Sermons Preached before their Majesties King James II, Mary Queen-Consort, Catherine Queen-Dowager, etc.*, vol. 2 (London: s.n., 1741), 142.

56. De Granada, *Summa of the Christian Life*, 235.

being a law to oneself is precisely what self-will seeks. So he adds, "theologians say that the inordinate love of self is the beginning of all sins. But since the love of God is contrary to the love of self, it follows that charity is the knife that cuts away all sin."[57]

De Sales wrote the following words to a woman during her illness: "Behold a quantity of crosses and mortifications which you have neither chosen nor wished. God has given you them with his holy hand; receive them, kiss them, love them. My God! they are all perfumed with the dignity of the place whence they come."[58] Suffering sickness especially has its quantity of mortifications when that sickness leads to death (as all will eventually do), so we can turn from spiritual death of self-love in this chapter, to the physical death that occurs at the dissolution of body and soul. We shall consider what it means to die well or ill in the next chapter.

57. Ibid., 223.

58. De Sales, *Library of St. Francis de Sales: vol. 1, Letters to Persons in the World*, 217.

8
On Dying Well

Spiritual mortification now encounters literal mortification. The person attached to the temporal takes hope in the idea that the world will remember him after he is dead, but Nieremberg smiles sympathetically at people who want to be remembered, while forgetting that the world they hope remembers them won't last.

> If God, then, should bestow upon thee this life only for a quarter of an hour, and if thou knewest likewise that the world, within an hour after thy death, were also to end, wouldst thou spend that short time in ostentation and setting forth thyself, whereby to raise a fame that might endure that short time after thy life? . . . Know, then, that thou oughtest do the same, although thou wert certain to live a hundred years, and the world to endure a hundred thousand after thee. For *all that has an end is short*, and all time in respect of eternity is but a day, an hour, a moment.[1]

Doyle provided his students a series of succinct definitions of terms in his sermon to them. What is life? "Life is but a dark and wretched passage between time and eternity, and . . . everything in this world is but a means to gain the one thing necessary." What is time? "During the few moments of my mortal life I am borne onwards by time. It is a stream upon which I am floating swiftly, and surely, and inevitably towards eternity." What is the body? "My body is, as it were, the frail vessel in which my soul is embarked." What is death? When "the painted scene of this life will be drawn aside, and you will behold that real world for which you were created." "It is the gate through which the soul must pass to the embraces of her God."[2]

1. John Nieremberg, *The Difference Between Temporal and Eternal* (Dublin: James Duffy and Co., Ltd., 1884), 69. Italics added.

2. Francis Doyle, *Lectures for Boys*, vol. 1 (London: R. Washbourne, 1896), 89–90, 150.

King David says, "I am about to go the way of all the earth" (1 Kings 2:2), and Nicholas Cross agrees. "When he summons, we must go; for death has no eyes to be dazled at the splendor and majesty of great ones; nor ears to be moved with the howlings of the miserable: Ah what pleasure then can it be to enjoy that which in a moment may be snatched from us, or we from it."[3] Just as we placed creation against nothingness in an earlier chapter, we now place life against eternity. The vanity of placing all one's confidence in what shall end is expressed by de Estella's definition of a vain thing as "that which filleth not the place where it is."[4] This world cannot fill the soul that lives in it.

When we were children we understood the events affecting us against a few years of life; when we got older we could see a pattern unfold when measured against a few decades of life; at the end, we must measure this life against eternity. That is the only justification of divine providence, says de Segur. "*It is by the measure of eternity that we must judge all that happens to us in this world.* In any other way it is, we repeat, impossible that we should understand any of the designs of God."[5] You cannot understand what is being done to you by Providence against any earthly horizon, only against an eternal horizon (an eternal horizon we glimpse in liturgy, which is why liturgy is so important for understanding life).

This life is sufficient time to prepare for everlasting life, which is why when theologians of abnegation look at death, they speak of it more as a beginning than an end. The birth of a baby is the end of nine months in the womb, true, but it is also the beginning of ninety years in the world. The death of a man is the end of ninety years in this world, true, but it is also the beginning of an eternity. Nicholas Cross thus sees death as that which will "put an end to our pilgrimage here, be the upshot of our misery, a return from our

3. Nicolas of the Holy Cross, *Pious Reflections*, 146.

4. Diego de Estella, *The Contempt of the World and the Vanities Thereof* (S. Omers: for John Heigham, 1622), 357.

5. Louis Gaston de Segur, *Familiar Instructions and Evening Lectures on All the Truths of Religion*, vol. 1 (London: Burns & Oates, 1878), 25.

banishment, and an entrance into our eternal happiness,"[6] and therefore we should submit to the sentence of mortality God has spoken.

This leads de Lehen to ask what difference there is if one person dies twenty years before another?

> Both have been dead a long time. The separation which then seemed so long and so hard, now appears to them as nothing; and it was in reality only a very short one. Soon shall the separated be reunited. The memory of their brief parting will scarcely remain. We act as if we were to live hundreds of years—yes, even forever. What foolishness! How quickly the dying follow the dead! He who sets out only two days after his friend upon the same journey, finds that the distance between them is not so great. Life flows on like a stream. The past is only a dream; the present is flying at the very moment in which we think to hold it, and is buried in the abyss of the past. The future will follow in its train; and it, too, will vanish rapidly.[7]

If two people were to walk a hundred miles, what would it matter if one left on Wednesday and the other on Friday? We all have people (fathers, mothers, grandparents, perhaps siblings, maybe friends) who have stepped off first, but every one of us will soon follow. De Sales thinks God knows when to harvest his souls. "We gather the strawberries and the cherries before the bergamot pears; but it is because their season requires it. Let us allow God to gather what He has planted in His orchard: He takes everything in its season."[8] The fruits will ripen in July, August, and September; we will die in our sixties, seventies, or eighties. Let the Master Gardener decide.

But there is a special perspective on dying that our spiritual theologians bring up on which I would like to concentrate in this chapter. They speak of death as an act, an achievement, the doing of a deed, which is serious because eternal happiness or misery rests upon it. Instead of treating death like closing the curtain after the

6. Nicolas of the Holy Cross, *Pious Reflections*, 168.

7. Edouard de Lehen, *The Way of Interior Peace* (New York: Benziger Brothers, 1888), 78–79.

8. De Sales, *The Consoling Thoughts of Saint Francis de Sales*, ed. Huguet, 284.

play has finished, they treat death as a final action in the final act of the play. It is a task assigned to each person, and more consequential than any other moment in the play. An athlete trains to run a race, a musician rehearses to perform a concert, and a person lives to prepare for death. The race, the concert, the death-act is the thing. A good death is one in which a person does what he is supposed to do in death. And what is that?

De Sales knows the answer indubitably: the dying person should imitate Christ's death, as he has striven to imitate Christ in everything else. "As the Christian life is only an imitation and expression of the life which Jesus Christ led for us, so the Christian death ought to be only an imitation and expression of the death which Jesus Christ endured for us."[9] To make a good death, we should do with ours what Jesus did with his, which is possible because he has united our two deaths together.

Life has been given for the purpose of preparing for its climax. A consummation is a perfection and death is a moment for perfection. If proof of our love of God is resignation to his will in the trials we endure, then Segneri asks

> how much more must this be the case in regard to that special trial of our death, from which, beyond all others, we naturally shrink? . . . Get the mastery over it, and make a sacrifice of your self-will by cheerfully accepting death at whatever time it may please God to appoint it to you. Be assured that an act such as this will more conduce to your perfection than any other act of your whole former life.[10]

A great reversal has taken place. These authors do not think of death as the interruption of a *good life*, they rather think of a *good death* as the capstone of a whole life. They do not see a good life lived in denial of death, but life as a preparation for a good death; not death confounding life, but death providing the reason for life; death is not the ceasing of activity, it is the final act, which finalizes a life; death is not a whimper, it is life's zenith. Every mortal creature

9. De Sales, *The Consoling Thoughts of Saint Francis de Sales*, ed. Huguet, 340.
10. Segneri, *Lenten Sermons*, vol. 2, 197.

is given existence with the intention of being brought up to this gate. Jenks calls it being "upon the borders of eternity; when we are, as it were, betwixt two worlds, the end of this and the beginning of the next."[11] No wonder Segneri says we here find life's purpose. "What is the end for which God keeps us in this world? Is it to study how to take our pleasure here, to follow our fancy, to let nature have its way? Most surely not. We are kept in this world that we may prepare for death, for that passage on which depends an eternity of reward or punishment."[12]

Man's occupation of time makes his life different from the existence of the angels. Angelic acts have a *permanence of nature*, which made their fall irreparable in a way Faber says made "the act of rebellion and the lightning from the face of God seem to be but one act, so closely the one followed on the other."[13] Men live with a *permanence of time*, making actions irrevocable, and this is what Faber says death puts securely in place. "Our eternity depends on the state in which we are when we die—death fixes it—bad life with good death is secure—good life with bad death is perdition."[14] During life we are given the opportunity for do-overs: we can promise not to commit a fault again; we can ask lovers and friends for second chances. But there is no opportunity to repair a wicked death, because its fault is without remedy.

Happiness will depend upon how far the theological virtues infiltrate us. Do we concur with divine grace in faith, comply with divine providence in hope, and conform to divine nature in charity? Death sums the whole, which is why Faber says we may only discover the whole at the end. Be ready to be surprised.

> The significance of a whole life often comes uppermost only in the preparation for death. Our destiny only begins to be fulfilled, after it appears to have been worked out. Who knows what he is

11. Jenks, *A Contrite and Humble Heart* (Dublin: P. Wogan, 1779), 50.

12. Segneri, *The Manna of the Soul*, vol. 1, 276.

13. Frederick Faber, *The Blessed Sacrament: or, The Works and Ways of God* (London: Burns Oates & Washbourne Ltd., 1861), 95.

14. Frederick Faber, *Notes on Doctrinal and Spiritual Subjects: The Faith and the Spiritual Life*, vol. 2 (London: Thomas Richardson and Son, 1866), 362.

> intended for? What we have dreamed was our mission is of all things the least likely to have been such. For missions are divine things, and therefore generally hidden, generally unconsciously fulfilled. If there are some who seem to have done their work early, and then live on we know not why, there are far more who do their real work late on, and not a few who only do it in the act of dying.[15]

Gallwey repeats the thought in one of his funeral sermons when he says, "Death is a tell-tale," and rarely are we lucky enough to know things a man has held in secret with God. "A prayer is discovered penned by his own hand, carefully studied, and apparently much used. It was not meant for the eyes of men. It was to be known to his own soul and to his Father in Heaven."[16] "Death sets many things to rights, corrects many a false estimate of men and things."[17]

One can die ill or well, poorly or successfully, wrongly or rightly, wickedly or righteously, so a wise student prepares for it. "What higher science can you attain?" asks Crasset, and for what else should one spend a life that was given expressly for the purpose of preparing for it?

> Every one studies that pursuit on which depends his success in life. It should be the business of all men to learn how to be saved. It is not necessary to study in order to die. But it is necessary both to think and act, in order to die well. It is impossible to perform well that which one has done only once. . . . Is life too long to prepare for death? Is time at your disposal, that you banish all thoughts of eternity? . . . Are your accounts ready?[18]

Chronos is brought to a high pitch in this moment of *kairos*. The act of death takes a person out of time: it is the doorstep between time and eternity. So Saint-Jure calls it "the consummation of our work, the end of our voyage, the harbor where we cast anchor or are irre-

15. Faber, *Bethlehem*, 231.

16. Peter Gallwey, *Salvage From the Wreck: A Few Memories of Friends Departed, Preserved in Funeral Discourses* (London: Burns & Oates, 1889), 178.

17. Ibid., 202.

18. Crasset, *Christian Considerations*, 12–13.

trievably wrecked."[19] And de Granada describes it as if one were "to launch out from the mouth of the harbour and to sail into the open sea. . . . In the space of a few hours will be given me, either Life eternal, or death for evermore."[20]

We should say something about deathbed conversions.

On the one hand, this possibility is immensely hopeful. Death caps life so powerfully that Faber marvels over even the most reprobate who is able to find his sins cancelled at this moment. "Because God is such a God as we know Him well to be, we boldly claim all that unknown land of catholic deathbeds for the simple sovereignty of the divine compassion. That hour may explain many inexplicable salvations."[21] Or, again,

> The hour of death is very spacious. It gives God room. It turns minutes into years. It redoubles and redoubles the swift processes of the mind just on the eve of its ejection from the body. It is an hour of truth, and an hour of truth is longer than a century of falsehood. . . . It is God's last chance with His creature, and divine wisdom must know well how to use its chances. A man is freed from many laws, when time and space are visibly melting away in the white light of eternity, or rather he is being brought under wider and larger laws. He can live many lives within the compass of His agony. We know very little of what goes on then.[22]

When a life is placed on the scale, there may be some hidden weights which only God knows about, and we do not. Gallwey points to Tobit 4:10, which he reads as "Almsdeeds will not suffer the soul to go into darkness."

> So then, even if in the last hour all looked hopeless, and the dying sinner seemed hardened and impenitent, and if now the drops of

19. Jean Baptiste Saint-Jure, *A Treatise on the Knowledge and Love of Our Lord Jesus Christ*, vol. 3 (New York: P. O'Shea, 1875), 325.

20. Luis de Granada, *Considerations on the Mysteries of the Faith* (London: Joseph Masters, 1862), 74–75.

21. Frederick Faber, *The Creator and the Creature, or, The Wonders of Divine Love* (London: Thomas Richardson and Son, 1857), 347.

22. Ibid., 345–46.

> sweat are on the forehead, and the doctor whispers that he is powerless, and the friends have commenced their tears and sobbing, and the spirits of darkness are waiting impatient and sure of their prey; yet, I say, that even in this extreme case, were such a case possible, if the dying man has really done his duty well in almsgiving, his works of mercy will never suffer his soul to go into darkness. Before it is too late, while life still lasts, a grace will come into his heart like the grace given to the Good Thief on Calvary.[23]

On the other hand, Crasset is right when he says "it is a perilous thing to avoid all thoughts of death until your last hour is at hand! How can you prepare for judgment at the moment when you approach the tribunal of your judge?"[24] All spiritual writers warn that life is a continual warfare which must be waged actively right up to, and into the moment of death. We are promised that God will forgive, we are not promised that we will be given tomorrow to repent. This is tersely presented by de Liguori as being crucially important:

> The Lord assures us that death is certain, that we may prepare for it; but, on the other hand, he leaves us uncertain as to the time of our death, that we may be always prepared for it—two points of the utmost importance.
>
> First Point. It is certain that we shall die.
> Second Point. It is uncertain when we shall die.[25]

Therefore, Nicholas Cross observes, only "to those who make it the subject of their daily meditation and daily expectation, its arrival do no harm."[26] We will only do death once, but we will most certainly do it. We can be certain of the fact, but not the timing—and this is by God's design. These two truths are like the twin pincers of a forceps by which God extracts us out from this life and delivers our

23. Gallwey, *Salvage from the Wreck*, 381–82.
24. Crasset, *Christian Considerations*, 12.
25. De Liguori, Sermon 33 in "Sermons for All the Sundays in the Year" in *Saint Alphonsus de Liguori Collection: 20 Books* (Aeterna Press, Kindle edition, 2016), 951.
26. Nicolas of the Holy Cross, *Pious Reflections*, 159.

birth into eternal life. What God will do in that hour can make us glad or miserable, but in either case, there will be no second chances. Pay attention to what you will be glad to have done for you, and to you, when the hour of death comes. There will not be time to repent when there is no more time.

Boudon presents a warning "that many have persevered for a long time in the love of the hidden life, entertaining a holy contempt for the esteem and affection of creatures, caring only to be known of God alone—who in the end have fallen into a state of great relaxation."[27] A rope may have been taut for many years, holding fast its weight, but if it goes limp at the last moment, it fails. The theological virtues must remain in play not only up to the edge of death, they must remain in force into this moment, especially. Segneri identifies three errors in relying on a deathbed conversion.

> Every sinner who puts off making a good confession till the time of his death takes for granted three things which are false and fallacious. The first is, that he will have it in his power to make his confession; the second, that the confession he makes will be a good one; the third, that when he has made a good confession he is sure to be saved. But what a tissue of error all this is! No wonder that the devil keeps some sinners so tightly bound by it that he never loses his hold over them.[28]

Our authors take a sage view of human nature. De Liguori writes, "he will never have these holy feelings in death, who has not practised them in life.... That which is not done during life is very difficult to be done in death."[29]

Knowing that each moment contributes to the final person, one ought to be careful about each moment. "But they are so many! And they come so fast," we exclaim. It is difficult to remain vigilant during the flow. That is why an awareness of their cessation helps to

27. Henri-Marie Boudon, *The Hidden Life of Jesus* (London: Burns, Oates, & Co., 1869), 154.

28. Segneri, *The Manna of the Soul*, vol. 1, 466.

29. De Liguori, *Considerations* in *Saint Alphonsus de Liguori Selection* (Kindle Book, Aeterna Press, 2016), 78.

evaluate their significance, in total and individually. Von Cochem advises all to not postpone preparation for something that happens only once. "There is no greater, no more important art upon earth than the art of dying a good death. Upon this thy whole eternity depends; an eternity of surpassing felicity or of unutterable torment. Only one trial is accorded thee; if thou dost not stand this one trial, all is lost, an eternity of misery is before thee."[30] If one does not commence the practice now, how can the performance be accomplished upon the deathbed? One would be unskilled, unpracticed, unrehearsed. By that time, the mind might be clouded and the heart set, de Liguori warns. "It is not to be denied that such a man may be converted at his death and obtain salvation; but the mind obscured, the heart hardened, the bad habits formed, the passions predominant, render it morally impossible for him to die happily. An extraordinary grace will be necessary for him; but does God reserve such a grace to bestow it upon one who has continued ungrateful to him even until the moment of death?"[31] Deathbed conversions can happen, but under extraordinary grace, and Segneri wants to know "on what ground, however, do you rest your pretensions of being so highly favored? Have you received any extraordinary promise to this effect? or any special revelation?" [32] What you think shows respect toward God, might be showing him an insult.

What one should beg for is perseverance. This is the capstone of patience, and a gift of grace directed by God's providential design for each individual soul. The Christian does not desire not to die—rather, the Christian prays God not to depart from him as he dies. So Segneri recommends repeating the words of the Psalmist when one sees death approaching. "These words should ever be on thy lips, accompanied by the reflection that death is very near thee, for these words were spoken by the Psalmist as one about to die. 'Thou art my God, depart not from me; for tribulation is very near, for

30. Martin von Cochem, *The Four Last Things: Death. Judgment. Hell. Heaven.* (New York: Benziger Brothers, 1899), 31.

31. Alphonsus de Liguori, *The Way of Salvation and of Perfection*, vol. 2 of *The Complete Works of Saint Alphonsus de Liguori, The Ascetical Works* (New York: Benziger Brothers, 1886), 51.

32. Segneri, *Lenten Sermons*, vol. 1, 122.

there is none to help me.' [Ps 22:11] What more pressing need hast thou than that the Lord should not depart from thee in thy last moments? Remember that on them depends an eternity of reward or punishment."[33] One cannot fail to notice that he is pointing us to a Psalm that Jesus referenced on the Cross.

Give Bellarmine a chance to summarize what we have been saying so far. "All our happiness or unhappiness depends on a good or bad death. And so who but someone clearly stupid and without the least judgment will dare to pass from this life by death without first having used all his diligence to learn to die well and to prepare himself to meet death?"[34] If passing the course depended upon this one exam, if a career depended upon this one assignment, if receiving the part depended on this one audition, then one would prepare well for it. But who prepares for death in such a way? A death is not good (a *euthanasia*) when one leaves this world according to one's wishes, it is good when one enters eternity according to God's wishes. Our happiness is contingent on facing God's countenance, our misery is contingent on our turning our back on him. We will be left facing the direction we were facing at death because it ends our opportunity for conversion (turning around one last time).

A number of our authors make use of a forestry example from Ecclesiastes 11:3. "If a tree falls to the south or to the north, in the place where the tree falls, there it will lie." Our choices in life incline our soul, so to speak, and Saint-Jure is certain that at death the soul will fall in the direction it leans. "It is with the death of a man as with the fall of a tree: the tree always falls in the direction to which it inclines, to which it naturally gravitates; so man falls in death where the works of his life make him incline, being drawn down by their weight."[35] Since the inclination cannot be repaired after death, therefore correct it now, because the step from our world to the next is only made once. Segneri is certain that if "once you make a false one, 'tis never to be recovered. Either the Tree falls to the

33. Segneri, *The Manna of the Soul*, vol. 1, 116.

34. Bellarmine, *The Art of Dying Well*, 206.

35. Saint-Jure, *A Treatise on the Knowledge and Love of Our Lord Jesus Christ*, vol. 3, 327.

South, or to the North; *Where-ever it falls*, says our Savior, *there will it lie for ever*. What Care therefore ought all Christians to take."[36]

Though difficult for us to digest, the favors of God include ordaining the kind of death most convenient for someone's salvation: with pains or without, slowly or suddenly, in youth or old age. De Sales writes these words about the death of his younger sister.

> I know well that you would fain ask me: "And you, how did you bear it?"... I will always take the side of Divine Providence; it does every thing well, and disposes of all things for the best. What a happiness for the child, to have been *taken away from the world, that iniquity might not alter her understanding*, and to have left this miry place before being defiled by it! We gather the strawberries and the cherries before the bergamot pears; but it is because their season requires it. Let us allow God to gather what He has planted in His orchard: He takes every thing in its season.[37]

In a collection of funeral discourses, Gallwey addresses the questions of "why now?" or "why so young?" He also gives answers difficult for us to digest unless we have been on a diet of liturgical abnegation. To the first, he says "let us remember that what we call life here on earth must be, in the eyes of those who have reached their home in Heaven, a [dreary] banishment," and these days in the valley of tears "are no more the true life for which man was created, than the nine months before his birth were."[38] To the second, he says that even the dying and dead have a witness to give about the Kingdom of God. "His death is sudden. Yes! but is it therefore unblessed? . . . Oftentimes in His charity and His yearning that the sinner may not perish, but be converted and live, our Father in Heaven suddenly and most unexpectedly snaps 'the silver cord' of one who is innocent and well prepared, in order that the warning may reach the hearts of survivors who are neither innocent nor well

36. Paul Segnery [sic] (Segneri), *True Wisdom, or Considerations for Every Day of the Week* (s.l., s.n., 1716), 58–59.

37. De Sales, *The Consoling Thoughts of Saint Francis de Sales*, 283–84.

38. Gallwey, *Salvage from the Wreck*, 103.

prepared for death."[39] While we focus on the death of one, God has his eyes on the salvation of many.

In one way, it's ironic to talk about dying well as "an art" because an art is a skill at doing a specified thing, *typically acquired through practice.* "In other arts," says Horstius, "if a fault is committed the first time through carelessness or ignorance, it is easily corrected the second; but in this, if there be made but one mistake, repentance afterwards will be useless and too late."[40] What happens one time, and only one time, cannot be trained for by repetition. "If we could die twice, the risk would not be so great, for should we happen to die in sin the first time, we need not therefore be eternally lost, we could repair our error by dying in the state of grace the next time; but we can die only once, and on death depends irrevocably our eternal happiness or misery."[41] Death is a person's final performance, his coda, and it cannot be repeated, repaired, reconstructed, or refurbished. Death is the final examination, which every student must take, for which every student should prepare, but which no student may retake. As such, death is a stern pedagogue. Success in hard things can be helped by prudence and forethought, but the hard thing itself can only be done once. Challoner agrees it is natural to hope we could repeat an ill death! How welcome this would be to the sinner because then

> he might repair the fault, by taking more care a second time. But, alas! we can die but once; and when once we have set our foot within the gates of eternity there is no coming back; and if it be a miserable eternity into which we have stepped, there is no redemption. . . . O, how hard it is to do that well which we can do but once, and can never try or practise beforehand! O my soul, see, then, thou take care to study well this important lesson by a continual preparation for death.[42]

39. Ibid., 177.

40. Horstius, *The Paradise of the Christian Soul*, 534.

41. Saint-Jure, *A Treatise on the Knowledge and Love of Our Lord Jesus Christ*, vol. 3, 325.

42. Challoner, *Considerations Upon Christian Truths and Christian Duties*, part II, 11.

Study well, prepare constantly, pray fervently. Those who live in a state of pride may be led at death into great fears, and those in a state of despair may receive at death great consolations.

Death is not only final in the sense of being last (the letter Z in the alphabet), but also in the sense of being settled (something never-to-be-repeated), and its unrepeatability raises the stakes of its execution. Its finality means everything depends upon doing it well. Faber says that although no two deaths are quite alike (they can be "sudden, lingering, violent, quiet, or amidst temptations"[43]) yet all possess the same two features of *inevitability* and *unrepeatability*.

> It comes to all. There is no escape. There are no exceptions.... Moreover, it is an act of which we have no experience, because it is done only once.... It has to be done but once. Everything depends upon the doing of it well.... Once over, all discussion, deliberation, retrospect, discovery of mistakes, fresh plans, are out of the question. It was one, absolute, final, immutable act; and now that it is done, it must be left as it is, helplessly fertile of eternal consequences.[44]

Procrastination gives a feeling of postponement, but this is a fantasy. We know this on one level, but deny it on another, because the acknowledgement comes with a cost. De Castañiza fears "worldlings hear not willingly this doctrine, because it interrupts them in the career of their pleasure, which they follow with overmuch passion and affection, and consequently leave it not without great grief and affliction."[45] They prefer not to make death familiar to their thoughts under the fancy that there will be a time later—a time before, or a time after—to deal with it. Time seems abundant now, but the judgment comes, Segneri says, because "just as there can be no judgment formed of a statue till the sculptor's work is done, nor of a book till it has been read through, so neither can man, who changes every hour, be judged till his thread of life is spun out."[46] If

43. Frederick Faber, *Spiritual Conferences* (New York: Benziger Brothers, 1870), 67–74.

44. Faber, *Spiritual Conferences*, 60–61.

45. De Castañiza, *The Spiritual Conflict and Conquest*, 135–36.

46. Segneri, *The Manna of the Soul*, vol. 1, 373.

one wants to know the identity of a person, one must wait until that person is finished. An identity accumulates over time, made through a series of transitions. First a child, then a young adult, then an employee; first single, then married, then a parent; first contentious, then tried, then compassionate; first distracted, then stricken, then introspective. Our point of view only sees a life in pieces, from one day to the next, or one year to the next; from one satisfaction to the next disappointment; from one happiness, to a misery, and back to happiness again. But God's viewpoint looks upon an entire life—the final statue, the entire volume—and only death can offer a completed product up to his gaze.

All religions have had some kind of last ritual surrounding death because all religions recognize it is a sacred moment. Although someone can pretend his life is his own while he lives it, that pretense must be dropped at death because he no longer can control (continue) life by his own power. Contact is made with God's world, and the light of the supernatural infiltrates the natural. The Christian religion has last rites at death because the Church has been gifted with sacraments for just such a moment. In the words of the Catechism, "the Church for the last time speaks Christ's words of pardon and absolution over the dying Christian, seals him for the last time with a strengthening anointing, and gives him Christ in viaticum as nourishment for the journey."[47] Holy moments are occasions for prayer, which is why Eudes observes it is a holy practice, when present at a deathbed,

> to kneel down at the moment the person dies, to adore the advent of the Son of God, who comes to judge that soul right there in the body, where it remains until it is consigned elsewhere by His judgment. [And] if it is beneficial to adore the Son of God in the exercise of His judgment upon others at the hour of death, how much more should you adore Him in His coming for you and His judgment at the hour of your death.[48]

47. Catechism of the Catholic Church, paragraph 1020.

48. John Eudes, *The Life and Kingdom of Jesus in Christian Souls* (New York: P. J. Kenedy & Sons, 1946), 329.

Death is a moment wherein the most intense adoration of an entire lifetime can be practiced, so perhaps the best way to describe the connection between a good death after a good life is to describe the death as a *crowning* of a life. It is the ultimate existential moment, casting meaning backward. Such deaths are aided by the grace that comes from Christ, through the Holy Spirit, by the Virgin Mary. Faber thinks a life of abnegation, that has borne its crosses, is the likeliest of all things to bring Mary to our bedsides at death, because "a cross-bearing life is forever meeting Mary. . . . However long the agony has been, however troubled in spirit the poor passing soul, blessed above all the dead are those, whose eyes Mary herself has closed!"[49]

When Horstius records a dialogue between Christ and man about dying well, he puts these words in Christ's mouth: "Nothing concerns thee so much, as to know how to die well, because, according as thou chance to die, so wilt thou be happy or miserable to all eternity. But, to die well, nothing is so necessary as to live well; and it was that thou mightst do both that I gave for thee my life as well as my death."[50] Christ lived and died so we might live well and die well. He is the exemplar and empowerer of the good life and the good death. And as his obedient death glories the Father, so our death—if it becomes an icon of his—can become a liturgical act of sacrifice, says Crasset:

> Of all the good that man can desire the greatest is to die well; death is not frightful to him who has lived well, it is rather the consummation of his desires, because it is the end of his combats, the crown of his merits, the entrance into the glory which awaits him, and the passage to a better life. Fear not, God will not abandon in death those who have been his faithful servants in life. He fortifies them with his grace; He lets them lean on his bosom; He dispels their fears, and orders his angels to console, defend and receive their souls, and bear them to heaven.
>
> Oh *the death of his saints is precious in the sight of the Lord*. The sacrifice is glorious; the victim is acceptable.[51]

49. Faber, *The Foot of the Cross*, 340–41.
50. Horstius, *The Paradise of the Christian Soul*, 558–59.
51. Crasset, *Christian Considerations*, 431.

De Bergamo thinks we can use our biological death to the advantage of our spiritual death. "Our self-love is wounded at the thought that we must soon die, and when we least expect it, and that with death everything comes to an end for us in this world; but at the same time this reflection weakens and humbles our self-love."[52] The mortification of chapter 7, practiced at death in chapter 8, takes us to the weakening and humbling of self-love in chapter 9. Christ's obedient death glorified the Father, because he sought always to do the Father's will, not his own. If our death can become an icon of his, then our life must follow the pattern he commanded when he said "deny yourself"—that is, deny your self-will and self-love. We turn now to these.

52. De Bergamo, *Humility of Heart*, 70.

9

Self-Will and Self-Love

"Ah! self-will, it is time for you to die, since I no longer desire to live but in the will of my God"[1] (de Sales).

Self-love and self-will are connected, as de Fonseca explains with an illustration. "We say oft-times, that a man stands in his own light, which makes him that he cannot see . . . and if a man puts his hand upon his eyes, [it is] no marvel if he cannot see either the object or his hand: All this and more doth self-love to the eye of the soul's reason; for it presents nothing to reason, but what it self desires, and reason seeing nothing else, it offer nothing else to be desired and sought by the will, but that which self-love affecteth."[2] We get in our own way, and in God's way. Self-love is a mutiny over our faculties which are designed to serve God.

Here we have our pair, then: (a) the perfection of obedience to God is the mortification of self-will, and (b) the perfection of the love of God is mortification of self-love. Self-love sways the will, and is its moving spring. Fastening our love and will on something in a way that excludes God, or omits God, or opposes God is called sin, and when we analyze sin, we discover both self-love and self-will at work. De Granada focuses on the former: "all sins originally proceed from self-love, for they are all committed through a desire of some particular good this self-love makes us covet."[3] Saint-Jure focuses on the latter: "after all the definitions given to sin, by theologians, to explain its nature, it must be said, that it is the effect of self-will."[4]

1. De Sales, in Jane Chantal, *Meditations for Retreats, taken from the Writings of St. Francis de Sales* (New York: Benziger Brothers, 1900), 168.

2. Christopher de Fonseca, *Theion Enotikon: A Discourse of Holy Love, by which the Soul is United Unto God* (London: Printed by J. Flesher, 1652), 118.

3. De Granada, *The Sinner's Guide*, 282.

4. Saint-Jure, *The Religious*, vol. 1, 577.

Self-Will and Self-Love

Is sin the result of self-love or self-will? Yes.

We must start by noticing that all these authors realize there is a right way and a wrong way to do self-love. Jenks works himself all the way back to the point of creation. "Our *Personal Being* is it not made to the Image of God himself? . . . He, who made us, planted Self-love in the Center of our Nature."[5] We can also turn to the New Testament for evidence of an acceptable kind of self-love. Saint-Jure points to the kind of self-love Jesus meant when he commanded us to love our neighbor as ourselves. "It is evident that He supposes we love ourselves, and with a good and reasonable love, since He gives it to us as the rule and the measure of that which we ought to bear towards our neighbor."[6] Camus agrees. "By the love of self I mean a natural, just, and legitimate love, so legitimate indeed as to be commanded by the law of God which bids us love our neighbors as ourselves. . . . Nevertheless, this love of ourselves, however just and reasonable it may be, turns only too easily, and too imperceptibly, into a self-love."[7]

So all the theologians of abnegation suppose a distinction between a good and bad kind of self-love. The problem is that good, natural, and legitimate love can become bad, unnatural, and unjust, and here are three examples of names our theologians give when distinguishing legitimate and illegitimate self-love. Saint-Jure calls them *virtuous and vicious*. "Man can love himself with a good and laudable love, which consists in loving himself for eternity, which is, to love God. . . . [But] there is a love of self which is vicious, having its source in sin; this is commonly called self-love." [8] Fénelon calls them *innocent and selfish*, "The simple desire of our own happiness, kept in due subordination, is innocent. This desire is natural to us; and is properly denominated the principle of self-love. When the principle of self-love passes its appropriate limit, it

5. Sylvester Jenks, *An Essay Upon the Art of Love, Containing an Exact Anatomy of Love and all the Other Passions which Attend it* (London: s.n., 1702), 26–27.

6. Saint-Jure, *The Religious*, vol. 1, 564.

7. Camus, *The Spirit of St. Francis de Sales*, 277–78.

8. Saint-Jure, *A Treatise on the Knowledge and Love of Our Lord Jesus Christ*, vol. 3, 151.

becomes selfishness. Self-love is innocent; selfishness is wrong."[9] And Grou calls them *well-directed and dishonest.* "It is well-directed love that makes me desire my happiness, and that seeks it in God," but "the sin of self-love consists in viewing nothing honestly, neither happiness nor even God Himself, except in relation to self."[10]

I am not going to give time to the virtuous, innocent, and well-directed self-love, I only wanted to acknowledge that it exists. Rather, I am going to talk about the vicious, selfish, and dishonest kind of self-love that derives from original sin, because that is the problematic kind requiring abnegation. What does it look like? Here are some of its signs, tersely worded, to get us oriented.

- "One of the most dangerous fruits of self-love is confidence in oneself and presumption"[11] (Libermann).
- "What is more delicious to a delicate self-love, than to hear itself applauded for not being self-love?"[12] (Fénelon).
- "Self-love intensely dreads obscurity, it is tenacious of being seen, known, and esteemed"[13] (Grou).
- "Discouragement is a mark of excessive love of self and of zeal unaccompanied by knowledge"[14] (De Sales).
- "Complain as little as possible of your wrongs… self-love always magnifies our injuries"[15] (De Sales).

The key problem of self-love is that it can only be cured from outside itself, because how can self-love annihilate itself when it loves itself?

9. François Fénelon, *Maxims of the Saints, www.ccel.org/ccel/fenelon/maxims/maxims.htm*, https://www.ccel.org/ccel/ Bernières-/maxims/maxims.htm, article 16.

10. Grou, *Meditations Upon the Love of God*, 16.

11. Libermann, *Letters to Clergy and Religious*, Spiritan Series 7, Vol. 3, 294.

12. Fénelon, *Spiritual Progress*, 31.

13. Grou, *The Spiritual Maxims*, 180.

14. Camus, *The Spirit of St. Francis de Sales*, 443.

15. De Sales, *Introduction to the Devout Life*, 93–94.

Augustine called sin "being curved in upon oneself" (*incurvatus in se*). Our love was designed to beam toward God (even if passing through creatures on the way), and our will was designed to submit to God (even if exercising dominion over creation in the meantime). But something feels wrong with both redirecting the beam of love upon ourselves, and putting ourselves under our own governance. Consider the effect of putting the prefix "self-" on almost any word: *self-love, self-will, self-esteem, self-centeredness, self-display, self-sufficiency, self-interest, self-satisfaction, self-pleasing, self-seeking, self-glorification, self-judgment, self-indulgence, self-conceit,* or *self-flattery.* Once again, I remind you that there is a proper form for each of these words. A child must grow into a self-sufficient and self-reliant adult. But there is an improper form, as well, and that is the problem we are diagnosing. Grou warns that the devil's ultimate goal is "to usurp the place of God in the heart and to induce us to transfer from our Creator to himself our adoration and allegiance."[16] And if this involves adoration and allegiance, we know we are facing a liturgical issue.

Self-love even ruins the therapy designed to cure it. Piety, grace, virtue, humility—these can all be twisted in our own favor by self-love, as Grou regretfully notices.

> Self-love finds food in everything it contemplates, and admires itself in every attempt I make to conquer a fault or acquire a virtue; it drinks up the praise bestowed upon me, it takes pride even in what I mean to be acts of self-humiliation. It forcibly appropriates what is God's work only, and would fain take His glory for itself. There is no hope save in Him; and He must fight for me. My self-love is His enemy too. He must subdue, crush, destroy it in me, or I can never get the victory. Blessed and All-powerful Lord, I give myself up to Thee, deal with me as Thou wilt.[17]

The catastrophe of original sin has injected pride into our reactions, our plans, and even our religion. Homage, obedience, esteem, praise, and all sorts of other ingredients of religion have been redi-

16. Grou, *The Interior of Jesus and Mary,* vol. 1, 161–62.
17. Grou, *The Hidden Life of the Soul,* 179–80.

rected from God to self. "What has ungrateful man done?" Eudes asks. "He has become separated from God and devoted his interests to self. Instead of employing his love for God, he has devoted it to himself and developed self-love. . . . Instead of referring to God all the blessings of nature and grace, man appropriates them to himself by complacency and self-esteem, as if they came from himself, who is only nothingness."[18] That is why the problem can be classified as liturgical: it asks, "Who is sovereign?" The failure is liturgical, because the stream of affection man should return to God in thanksgiving is redirected toward himself. Abnegation is about straightening out love, and mortification is the crowbar that bends it back into shape.

How serious is this problem? After all, when a doctor makes a diagnosis, he wants to know the seriousness of the disease. Eudes does not mince words. "We should treat self-will as a beast of prey, a ravening wolf, a ferocious lioness, the source of hell, for without it there would be no hell. It is the mother of all the abominations of the earth. Self-will is a venomous serpent, a detestable homicide that kills body and soul at the same time, an execrable deicide that kills God insofar as it is able."[19] If it were possible to kill God (deicide), this would do it. It does go so far as to kill the life God wants to share with us and live in us. We usurp his kingdom, de Sales says. "We wish to serve God in one way, while He desires to be served in another; we wish *what* He wishes, but not *as* He wishes it. We do not submit ourselves wholly and as we should do to His will."[20] So it would seem, concludes Baker, that the choice between heaven and hell can be made now, here, already. "In a word, the difference between heaven and hell is, that hell is full of nothing but self-love and propriety; whereas there is not the least degree of either in heaven, nor anything but the fulfilling of God's will and seeking of His glory."[21]

Because the soul loves herself, she loves her own will, and finds that submission to God stings. Because self-love makes a sinner seek

18. Eudes, *Meditations on Various Subjects*, 120.
19. Ibid., 217.
20. Camus, *The Spirit of St. Francis de Sales*, 251.
21. Baker, *Holy Wisdom*, 249.

his own will over God's, Grou recommends our abnegation therapy to begin with self-love. "In proportion as self-love is weakened, and we give up our own judgment and bend our own will to the will of God, which is His own glory and His own good pleasure, so will our difficulties be overcome, our conflicts will cease, our troubles will vanish, and peace and calm will be established in our hearts."[22] The only thing that keeps a soul from the embrace of the heavenly Spouse, says Blosius, "is the preposterous love with which thou seekest thyself, reflectest on thyself, and delightest not in God, but in thyself."[23]

Here are some challenging words that de Caussade writes in a letter of spiritual direction about self-will being a presumptuousness that comes from self-love. The director is blunt with his student.

> It seems to me that no one has ever offered so much resistance as you. This proceeds from a very strongly rooted self-love, from a secret great presumption and confidence in yourself that, possibly, you may never have found out; for, mark well, that directly you are spoken to about this total abandonment to God you feel a certain interior commotion as though all were lost, and as if you had been told to throw yourself, with your eyes shut, into an abyss. It seems a trifle, yet it is very much the contrary, for the greatest assurance of salvation in this life can only be obtained in this total abandonment.[24]

In briefer words (those of de Sales), "our one aim must be to make the love of God reign supreme over self-love."[25]

Satan lays a trap that John of Ávila describes as "the devil [sitting] like a king on his throne, and from there he gives orders to everyone."[26]

> He exalts us with vanity and lies, and afterward knocks us down in a truly miserable fall. He puffs us up with thoughts that incline us

22. Grou, *Manual for Interior Souls*, 303.
23. Blosius, *Spiritual Works*, 26.
24. De Caussade, *Abandonment to Divine Providence*, 190–91.
25. De Sales, *Library of St. Francis de Sales: vol. 5, The Spiritual Conferences*, 278.
26. John of Ávila, *Audi, Filia*, 285.

> to high self-esteem in something, and thus makes us fall into pride. He knows through experience that this evil was enough to change him from an angel into a demon. So he works with all his might to make us like him in pride so that we may be like him in his torments.[27]

To escape the trap, we should let God occupy the throne in the deepest part of our heart, with love and will as courtiers in attendance at that royal court. We can't stop loving (this is hardwired into our nature). But we can redirect self-love toward divine love—the sort of love that the persons of the Trinity share. We can't stop willing (that belongs to human nature, too). Rather, we exchange self-will for full obedience—the sort the Son showed to the Father eternally and incarnately.

On the one hand, we are victims. On the other, we give permission. Self-love moves us toward pride, boasting, untruth, and malice, which are "the spirit of the devil, who is the ruler of this world," says Libermann. "This spirit inspires the worldings with the desire for display, for self-esteem, for self-love, a spirit that attributes everything to self, instead of directing all things to the love of God alone. It makes them seek their own interest, and not the interest of *God alone*, as Our Lord did and taught."[28] This is more than a matter of selfishness. Curing that would be a moral accomplishment, like teaching someone to be polite. This is a matter of idolatry, and fixing it will require stabilizing our capsized liturgy. Grou says self-love is nothing but a contest with God. "Nothing better marks the character of self-love, or should make it more hateful to us, than this title: Rival of the love of God. . . . We can bestow our whole love on but one only of two objects: God or self. To set God above all things, and refer all to Him, is to be actuated by charity. . . . To refer all things to self, is to be filled with self-love."[29] The quarrel of Lucifer with God at the start of creation, and the seduction of our first parents by Lucifer in the garden, is played out daily, in every soul. Who is Lord?

27. Ibid., 75.
28. Libermann, *Letters to People in the World*, Spiritan Series 6, vol. 2, 40.
29. Grou, *The Spiritual Maxims*, 169.

What is frightening, Grou observes, is that "this self-love intrudes even into spiritual things, when we love virtue, and the gifts of God, and the holiness of God, and God Himself, only for our own sakes.... In one word, when we set up our own selves as the centre and object of our affections."[30] Just as we saw pride under the surface of a feigned humility, so we can now find self-love just under the surface of a spiritual piety, if the cure has been superficial. Do you want to know why your prayer life is so feeble? Here is Grou's explanation.

> You repeat a great number of prayers, but your mind is not attending to them and the prayers do not come from your heart. You are praying only with a view to your own interests, and you forget that nothing serves your interests better than loving God well. You ask Him for everything except love, which is the thing you should ask for most of all. You perform good works, but self-love plays a large part in them; you have worldly motives or you have a personal interest in the matter, and although the works are many there is hardly one that is done simply for God's sake.[31]

Surin thinks a sign of a proud soul mingling self-love with piety and religion is when that person is left weary and dissatisfied. "This was caused, and is almost invariably caused, by a secret self-seeking. We think we have the best intention possible; we could swear that in the undertaking we have in hand, we regard God Alone; and yet we are sad, and feel a certain distaste which troubles our peace of mind. This is to be attributed only to this unregulated self-love."[32]

If the incision does not go deep enough, some cancer is left. If abnegation does not go deep enough, the self is left even in our devotion. Self-love is sneaky that way; it hides itself behind excuses. Fénelon says "we are sharp, oversensitive, difficult, hard to get along with. It is self-interest which causes all this, but the self-interest screens itself with a hundred fine reasons."[33] Self-love hides itself for

30. Grou, *Manual for Interior Souls*, 328.
31. Grou, *The School of Jesus Christ*, 64.
32. Surin, *The Foundations of the Spiritual Life*, 78.
33. Fénelon, *Christian Perfection*, 60.

the very same reason that Adam and Eve hid themselves after eating the forbidden fruit. Hearing God walking in the garden, their self-love hid them among the trees of the garden (Gen 3:8), not only because self-love cannot bear being seen by God, but also because it cannot bear to see itself. We are constantly in the state our forebearers were in one minute after they sinned. Fénelon writes:

> the sight would overwhelm it with shame and vexation; and if it catches an accidental glimpse, it seeks some false light which may soften and condone what is so hideous. And thus we always keep up some illusion so long as we retain any self-love. To see ourselves perfectly, self-love must be rooted up, and the love of God reign solely in us, and then the same light which shows our faults would remove them.[34]

When self-love hides itself in darkness, that same darkness obscures other truths—truths about God, self, and reality. Surin understands that "one who thinks only of himself, who loves himself alone, is always in darkness, and cannot, in this state, perceive the truth, because he sees all things in the false colours with which self-love depicts them to his imagination, as when we look through a blackened glass, all that we see appears dark."[35] Self-love is like a pair of glasses with the wrong prescription, through which we cannot see the world as it is, or ourselves as we are, or the commandments we should obey. Such has been the state of mankind since its exile from Eden, almost as if the serpent chased after mankind in their exile. This is probably why de Caussade describes wretched self-love as something that "turns and twists like a serpent, and is only too successful in preserving its life in the midst of the most fearful deaths."[36]

The situation is dire, but have hope! God is eager to lend us a hand, as Drane knows. "I suppose one day or other we have all said, 'There is only one thing I care for, and that is to love God.' Then God takes us at our word, and tries to help us by digging out self-love. That hurts us, and so we cry out, but there is no other way. So

34. Fénelon, *Letters to Men*, 113.
35. Surin, *The Foundations of the Spiritual Life*, 77–78.
36. De Caussade, *Abandonment to Divine Providence*, 183.

we let Him dig, and we will dig with Him; and, when all the rubbish is cleared away, and a nice empty space made, He will pour in the beautiful wine out of His wine-cellar, and we shall have our heart's desire."[37] We cannot, of our own strength, dislodge Satan from the throne he has usurped, but Grou says "as a Christian really gives himself to God and to His service, divine love takes possession of his heart, sets up its throne within it, and forthwith proceeds to drive out self-love."[38] Christ will dislodge the devil by a grace that will renovate the heart when it empowers abnegation. Then our self-love and self-will can be restored back to what they were in Paradise. No, more. Our love and will shall be further perfected, and not just returned to an original natural state. When our faculties are unified with Jesus, then our will shall conform to his obedience to the Father, and our love shall conform to his love for the Father.

Maladies are cured by their contraries: pride by humility, avarice by alms-giving, lust by chastity, et cetera. Self-love and self-will are cured by their contraries, and when they see them approaching, they are petrified at the prospect. Self-love fears its mortification, and self-will fears losing its control. They are scared to death. Good! Mortification begins bitter, but turns sweet when the lover discovers he is annihilating something inferior in order to be blessed with something much more superior. Camus says someone can be fed with "so full a taste of the Manna of the blessed Eternitie, that things possessed in *Tyme* may become loathsome unto them."[39] The world is good—it is simply not sufficient to satisfy the appetite of those creatures who have been stamped with the image of the infinite God. If a staircase is constructed for the purpose of ascending from earth to heaven, each step on it may be good, but evil results if we stop climbing and sit like squatters on a particular step. Even Eden should not have satisfied Adam and Eve; that they hoped it would was the problem.

We have all had even a natural sense of foreboding at some future sacrifice, only to discover when we get near it that the good on the

37. Drane, *A Memoir of Mother Francis Raphael*, 186–87.
38. Grou, *The Spiritual Maxims*, 170.
39. Camus, *A Draught of Eternitie*, 69.

other side makes the trial on this side to be as nothing. De Granada describes it this way:

> The happiness that will be ours when we possess God will be greater beyond compare than any happiness in created goods. Nor should we marvel at this, for if the sun is better able to enlighten the world than all the stars together, and if the light of the stars is lost in the brilliance of the sun, why should it seem remarkable that the Creator alone should be sufficient to satisfy the human heart and that He gives greater happiness than all created good together?[40]

The brilliance of the sun hides the light of the dimmer stars. The brilliance of eternity overpowers the dim light of the temporal, the brilliance of the Creator overpowers the dim light of creatures, the brilliance of the final good overpowers the dim joy received from temporal (temporary) goods.

What makes renunciation easy is that we are sure it is done for our welfare, and not for our injury. This translates as confidence in the providential goodness of God. De Sales likes to point this out, and often uses images of the gardener pruning the vine.

> To renounce ourselves is simply to purify ourselves from everything that is done through the instinct of self-love, which, so long as we are in this mortal life, will not fail to produce off-shoots, which should be immediately cut away, just as we do with the vine.
>
> And as it is not sufficient to trim the vine once a year, but it must be cut at one time and at another stripped of its leaves, so that the vine-dresser must have the pruning-hook continually ready to cut off the useless shoots; in the same way we must deal with our imperfections.[41]

And how long will self-love and self-will require this pruning hook? Until the grave, we must admit. It can be mortified in us, says de Sales, "but still it never dies; indeed, from time to time and on different occasions, it produces shoots in us, which show that though

40. De Granada, *Summa of the Christian Life*, 221.
41. De Sales, *Mystical Flora*, 18.

cut off it is not rooted out."[42] But you should remain hopeful so long as God is willing to persevere, so Grou finds solace in realizing that "He must fight for me. My self-love is His enemy too. He must subdue, crush, destroy it in me, or I can never get the victory. Blessed and All-powerful Lord, I give myself up to Thee, deal with me as Thou wilt."[43]

The defeat of self-love does not come through argument, says Alacoque. "We must not reason with [self-love], for it feeds and grows fat on arguments."[44] With this, Fénelon agrees. "Try to discuss little, but to do a great deal. If one does not take care, one's whole life slips away in theorising, and we want a second career for practice. There is always a risk lest we fancy ourselves to have advanced in proportion to our theories about perfection; whereas all such grand ideas, so far from really promoting self-mortification, do but tend to foster the old Adam in us through self-confidence."[45] Neither does the defeat of self-will come through the efforts of our will, because then self is in control again. Irritation against self-will can come from, or add to, pride. It can only be defeated by surrender.

Denying yourself is surrender to Providence, and, according to de Sales, such a person strives "patiently, gently, humbly, and calmly, looking for deliverance rather to God's Goodness and Providence than to his own industry or efforts."[46] "What we want is a quiet, steady, firm displeasure at our own faults."[47] Perhaps you have met some quiet saints like this. If so, you might also recognize what Libermann sees in a person of true piety. "The state of true perfection is always one of peace. Troubles come usually, nay always, from a source that is not God. . . . When God acts in our souls, and we follow His divine impulses without intruding our faults and natural

42. De Sales, *Library of St. Francis de Sales:* vol. 1, *Letters to Persons in the World,* 345.

43. Grou, *The Hidden Life of the Soul,* 180.

44. Alacoque, *The Letters of St. Margaret Mary Alacoque,* Letter 90, Kindle.

45. Fénelon, *Letters to Men,* 35.

46. De Sales, *Introduction to the Devout Life,* 202.

47. Ibid., 111–12.

ideas, He always acts with peace, and it is this peace that enables us to recognize His divine presence."[48]

God chooses to raise us up to happiness because it serves his glory. A condition for entering heaven is abnegation, since "heaven is closed against self-love; all motives of self-interest are banished from it,"[49] as Grou notes. "Heaven would be no longer Heaven if self-love could find entrance there."[50] "The sole love which can exist there is the pure love of God."[51] God has opened the gates, and his providence marks out the pathway for every person, different for every set of life circumstances. The potter shapes each clay according to his design—and what is the part of the clay? If salvation is God's work, what is man's part? Grou wants to know. "He can give himself up simply to God; he can leave God to work the destruction of that self-love, he can second the dealings of God's loving jealousy, he can lie still under the Hand which strips and chastens him in seeming severity."[52]

The first step in the Christian life is not us taking a step, but rather letting God take his. Let him enter, let him act, let him direct, as Surin recommends. "Wear a blindfold where self-love and human wisdom are concerned, and spread out all the sails of your heart, in order to catch the winds of the Holy Spirit, abandoning your power to divine love. If you act through that love, you will find a marvelous strength for everything, in order to collect all the Holy Spirit's gusts."[53] So here is the key to abnegation language: we cannot be our own physician because self-love is too touchy. Fénelon says "sickly self-love cannot be touched without screaming; the mere tip of a finger seems to scarify it."[54] Therefore, annihilation of self is simply another way of saying grace alone, just as nothingness

48. Libermann, *Letters to Religious Sisters and Aspirants*, Spiritan Series 5, vol. 1, 6.

49. Grou, *Meditations Upon the Love of God*, 131.

50. Grou, *The Hidden Life of the Soul*, 89.

51. Grou, *Manual for Interior Souls*, 326.

52. Grou, *The Hidden Life of the Soul*, 89.

53. Jean-Joseph Surin, *Into the Dark Night and Back: The Mystical Writings of Jean-Joseph Surin* (Leiden: Brill, 2019), 490.

54. Fénelon, *Letters to Women*, 72.

is another way of saying God alone. Abnegation means laying down one's self-will and letting God do something to us. De Granada finds obedience to be "the greatest sacrifice that God exacts of man and the greatest gift that man can give to God, because in this he gives himself."[55] And this, adds Olier, "is why our Lord put abnegation in his gospel as the first step we must take in the Christian life! . . . Because self-centeredness, being filled with the self, blocks Jesus Christ and the fullness of his divine life from entering us."[56]

How is this possible? Only through a Mediator who stands at the midpoint, opening heaven to earth, and earth to heaven. How is self-love overcome by humiliation and subjection and mortification? How is self-will overcome by renunciation and submission and obedience? Surin answers:

> It is done by casting one's eyes on Jesus Christ, who was given to us as a model and whom all predestined persons ought to resemble. We see that he, the Son of God, the chief and the king of all men, who guides us by divine wisdom and by zeal for the glory of his Father and for our salvation, chose a type of life where he fought unto death against self-love, living in abjection, in poverty, in suffering. He took on human lowliness, scorn, rejection, contradictions, in order to give us courage, and he acquired for us a treasure and a fund of grace by dying for us.[57]

The instructions de Liguori gives to priests about their dignity and duties are applicable to every Christian when it comes to interior mortification to combat self-will. The means of conquering self-will are (1) prayer, (2) doing violence to self with determined will, (3) making examen on the passion that most molests us, (4) to not have strong commitment to a multitude of desires, and (5) to practice mortification even in small things.[58]

Abnegation goes forth in full strides of liturgy, indifferent to the

55. De Granada, *Summa of the Christian Life*, 322.

56. Olier, *Introduction to the Christian Life and Virtues*, in *Bérulle and the French School*, 262–63.

57. Surin, *Into the Dark Night and Back*, 497.

58. Alphonsus de Liguori, *Dignity and Duties of the Priest* (New York: Benziger Brothers, 1889), 360.

distraction of creatures, diffident about our own autonomous powers, detached from our own self-love and self-will. Liturgizing involves abnegation because putting our eyes upon Jesus, we take our eyes off ourselves, our self, our selfishness, our self-love, our self-will, our self-esteem. This liturgical state is the reign of God's will in our hearts, where self-will is expunged by submission to his will. At that point, John of the Cross can see that "the Bridegroom whom thou lovest is 'the treasure hidden in the field' of thy soul, for which the wise merchant gave all that he had, so thou, if thou will find Him, must forget all that is thine, withdraw from all created things, and hide thyself in the secret retreat of the spirit, shutting the door upon thyself—that is, denying thy will in all things—and praying to thy Father in secret."[59] Liturgy is the discovery of the pearl of great price; liturgical abnegation is the denial of all else in order to purchase that field and obtain that pearl.

But how can we embrace Jesus when he lived so long ago? Grou says Our Lord had an ingenious, inventive idea. The flow of blood coming from his side (grace) cannot be stopped, just as you cannot prevent a water leak from going everywhere.

> Jesus[,] not contented with a passing sacrifice, the memory of which would soon be effaced from the minds of men, has willed to render the Sacrifice of His Cross ever-abiding in His Church: He willed to find in the contrivances of His Love effectual means to apply its merits to His members in every place and every age: He willed, so to speak, to found His Cross in the Eucharist, and to change it into an inexhaustible Fount, whence the merits of His Precious Blood should be shed abroad everywhere, to vivify, to sanctify His members.[60]

After feeding upon Christ himself at the altar, there is no pain or melancholy felt when denying the world and self. Hatred of self-will leads to obedience; hatred of self-esteem leads to humility; hatred of self-indulgence leads to renunciation; hatred of pride leads to

59. John of the Cross, *Spiritual Canticle Between the Soul and Christ*, in *The Complete Works*, 17.

60. Grou, *The Practical Science of the Cross*, 79.

meekness; hatred of self-love leads us to abandon ourselves and become true servants of God. And to this Eucharist we turn in the next chapter, and to Communion in it we turn in the last.

10

The Miracle of the Eucharist

This sacrament of love is all about union. De Bérulle describes it as "a second union" that Jesus willed to have with us after, and in honor of, the first union he accomplished in the Incarnation. "O greatness! O power of our mysteries!—during these moments we are really and substantially united with him as one single substance. That is, the body and blood of Jesus Christ are in both God and us."[1] God sought union with his sons and daughters by various means in salvation history, but when the time had fully come, God sent his Son, born of a woman, and the hypostatic union was an unexpected, miraculous, gracious, and astounding union of divine nature and human nature. The Incarnation stands in the background of the Eucharist as a sacrament of union. Eymard is not shy to imagine Our Lord quitting the tabernacle and coming to us to say:

> I am going to be incarnated in this person. I am going to unite Myself sacramentally to her, in order that My Personality may take the place of hers. I want to be her principle, and to elevate her being and her actions to the divine Unity. I shall think and will in her soul. I shall live in her body, love in her heart, glorify My Father in her as I glorified Him on earth in My Sacred Humanity [.] I am going to continue for the glory of My Father, for His love, and for the honor of this creature, My meriting and suffering life. I shall give to her actions a supernatural and divine value, and I shall be the centre of her affections and the principle of a new life, which will be the reproduction of My own life.[2]

1. Pierre de Bérulle, *Discourses on the State and Grandeurs of Jesus: The Ineffable Union of the Deity with Humanity* (Washington, DC: Catholic University of America Press, 2023), 123–24.

2. Eymard, *The Divine Eucharist: Fourth Series, the Eucharist and Christian Perfection*, 571.

Grou says that at the Eucharist, Jesus fastens "to my heart the same Body which Thy Love fastened to the Cross. . . . Thy Love makes Thee in some sort die therein again, and my soul becomes the sepulchre where my Savior buries Himself, and where He wills to bury me with Him."[3] If Christ did not fear being buried in a stone sepulchre, he will not fear being buried in our soul; if he rose from the tomb, he will raise us up when he sanctifies us; if we have love for the cross in our heart, we will join Jesus on his, and he will join us on ours. *Jesus's love* fastened him to the Cross, and *our love* fastens us to the same place, so de Condren concludes that "as it is by the sacrifice of the Cross that Jesus Christ has redeemed us, so it is by His Resurrection, and by the Eucharistic Sacrifice and communion which correspond to it, that He sanctifies us."[4]

At the altar you can witness the lengths to which God has gone to captivate your love, and de Liguori says this sight should stir your affection. "Make me hunger to be continually in Thy presence in the Blessed Sacrament, to receive Thee into myself, and to keep Thee company. I should be indeed ungrateful did I not accept so sweet and gracious an invitation."[5] He adds that when the soul sits down across the altar-table from God, she will fall more deeply in love with him and therefore accept her self-abnegation. "Yes, I do renounce all other love, and choose for myself Thy sweet love, my God, my all. Begone, ye creatures! what do you want with me? Go and enjoy the love of those who seek you. I wish only for my God; for God alone will I keep all my heart and all my affections."[6] The Eucharist should stir the soul. Huby wonders "can we then carry a furnace of love in our bosom, and feel no heat?"[7] He asks, "O amorous heart of my Jesus, O burning furnace of divine love, how is it

3. Grou, *The Practical Science of the Cross*, 105–6.

4. Charles de Condren, *The Eternal Sacrifice* (London: Thomas Baker, 1906), 118.

5. Alphonsus de Liguori, *Visits to the Blessed Sacrament and to the Blessed Virgin*, in *The Holy Eucharist*, vol. 6 of *The Ascetical Works* (New York: Benziger Brothers, 1887), 179.

6. De Liguori, *The Sacrifice of Jesus Christ* in *The Holy Eucharist*, vol. 6 of *The Ascetical Works*, 90.

7. Huby, *The Spiritual Retreat of the Reverend Father Vincent Huby*, 139–40.

possible thou shouldst not melt our icy hearts?"[8] That furnace of love sets a liturgy of abnegation ablaze.

There is a sense in which abnegation is preparation for the Eucharist, and another sense in which abnegation is a consequence of the Eucharist. Nieremberg speaks of spiritual abnegation as *completing* the Eucharist. "Jesus does not want to be offered alone. The Mass is the sacrifice of Christ, but it is also the sacrifice of Christ's mystical members, of the Church. It involves essentially the offering of Christ's mystical members, immolated with Him in the same sacrifice and in the same sentiments of self-abandonment and complete submission. . . . That union of thought, heart, and prayer with the sacrifice of Christ through the liturgy must be completed by the union with it of the actions of our daily life."[9] De la Bouillerie speaks of it as *reviving* and *reproducing* Jesus in us.

> When Jesus Christ appeared in this world, He manifested Himself by His exterior form, by His words, and by His actions; these, then, are the things we must revive in us.
>
> First, the exterior form of the Saviour, so amiable, so meek, that to express the Incarnation the Apostle employed this simple word, "Goodness appeared." [Tit 3:4]. . . .
>
> Who will give us to reproduce in ourselves the meek and gentle exterior of Jesus Christ, so that the world seeing us may say, Goodness has appeared—*Benignitas apparuit?*[10]

The Eucharist requires abnegation, and it causes abnegation.

When we sense God's Presence, we run after him, which means denying whatever slows, or delays, or impedes us from doing so. In preparation to receive any human guest, we clean our houses, observes Jacob Blake.

8. Ibid., 130.

9. John Nieremberg, *The Marvels of Divine Grace: Meditations Based on the "Glories of Divine Grace" original treatise by Fr. Nieremberg*, ed. Alice Lady Lovat (London: R. & T. Washbourne, Ltd., 1917), 160–61.

10. M. L'Abbe de la Bouillerie, *Hours Before the Altar; or, Meditations on the Holy Eucharist* (London: Richardson and Son, 1858), 124–25.

> Is it not more due to God, that a Christian should cleanse his Heart, and empty it of all Indecency, when it is about to entertain the divine Majesty; casting out all domineering Passions, that *Christ* alone might have the chief Command and Sovereignty therein? . . . He gives not to God a Lodging that pleases him, unless he empties himself even of himself. . . . Even Man himself is not to abide with himself, that so the little Lodging (which of it self is too narrow) may become somewhat more capacious.[11]

And in consequence of the Eucharist, de Liguori hears the soul say to the world:

> Creatures, depart from me; go out altogether from my heart. I loved you once, because I was blind; now I love you not, nor can I ever love you again. I have found another good, infinitely more delightful than you; I have found in myself my Jesus, who has enamoured me by his beauty; to this love I have given myself entirely. He has already accepted me, so that I am no longer my own. Creatures, farewell: I am not, nor shall I ever again be yours; but I am and shall be always Christ's.[12]

When God draws us to himself, he simultaneously draws us away from anything we might substitute for him.

By the shedding of his precious blood, Jesus enrolls us as citizens in what Frederick Faber calls "the empire of the Precious Blood," which has royal rights over creation. One can hear Faber being overwhelmed at the thought.

> It is one of the most excellent inventions of His wisdom. It is the principal feeder of His glory. It is the repose of His purity. It is the delight of His mercy. It is the participation of His power. It is the display of His magnificence. It is the covenant of His patience. It is the reparation of His honour. It is the tranquility of His anger. It is the imitation of His fruitfulness. It is the adornment of His sanctity. It is the expression of His love. But, above all, it ministers to

11. James Blake, "On the Blessed Sacrament," in *A Select Collection of Catholick Sermons*, vol. 2, 412 and 413.

12. De Liguori, *The Sacrifice of Jesus Christ*, in *The Holy Eucharist, vol. 6 of The Ascetical Works*, 98.

> the dominion of God. . . . It humbles the rebellious, and brings home the exiles, and reclaims the aliens. It pacifies; it builds up; it gives laws; it restores old things; it inaugurates new things. It grants amnesties; and dispenses pardons.[13]

The blood with which a Christian was marked at baptism, like the lintels in Egypt, is the same blood given for drink at the Eucharist. No wonder the devil thinks that when he "has succeeded in driving away a soul from Holy Communion he has gained his ends, and Jesus weeps"[14] (Thérèse of Lisieux). The very last place Satan wants to find his prey is worshiping at the altar of the Lord.

When the soul is inebriated with the glad drink of the Spirit, Bona hears her sing the song of the bridal chamber. "Full of love, [she] melts away, losing herself, and being, as it were, brought to nothing, she falls fainting into the bottomless deep of eternal love. There, dead to herself, she lives in God. She knows nothing, she feels nothing but love. She loses herself in the divine darkness, but such losing is a true finding."[15] (The experience of nothingness is experienced at the altar.) Catholic spirituality is a love song: that is why the Song of Solomon is in the Bible. If the soul's final end is union with the eternal Trinity, why would she settle for communion with things of the temporal world? Thus Christianity includes abnegation. De Bernières-Louvigny calls it "the *law of Christianity* that we ought to love abjection, Jesus having loved it by his Father's order: and he is the grand example we must imitate."[16] And "the more a soul participates of the spirit and interior of the Son of God the more she esteems and loves the cross, and, consequently, does the more glorify God the Father."[17] Abnegation happens because the soul wants to follow Jesus when he calls.

Theologians have traditionally identified two purposes or causes

13. Frederick Faber, *The Precious Blood; or, The Price of Our Salvation* (London: Burns & Oates, Ltd., 1860), 77–78.

14. Thérèse Lisieux, *Thoughts of the Servant of God Thérèse of the Child Jesus* (New York: P.J. Kenedy & Sons, 1915), 160.

15. Bona, The *Easy Way to God*, 26.

16. De Bernières-Louvigny, *The Interior Christian*, 35. Emphasis added.

17. Ibid., 47.

of liturgy. (1) The glorification of God, and (2) the sanctification of man. Does this not make obvious that the Cross was Jesus's liturgy? He was crucified to glorify his Father in heaven by sanctifying sinners. His liturgy has now moved forward from history into a mystical and sacramental reality. Eymard is bold enough to say that in the Eucharist his Incarnation is recommenced.

> Our Lord who has assumed the state of all the virtues in the Blessed Sacrament, having entered into His glory, can no longer make meritorious acts of them. Nevertheless, He ardently desires to practise them for the glory of His Father. He wishes to live again, to find a soul capable of meriting, with faculties that can truly love, labor, and sacrifice. It is for this that He unites Himself to His Faithful, who become His members. He is their Chief, their Head, their moral and supernatural Heart. He pours into them His grace, His divine sap, moving them, making them act and labor. Then He performs in them meritorious and satisfactory works. He takes on again His life of *viator*, His Incarnation is recommenced. The Father sees Him again poor, chaste, obedient, meek, and humble as in the days of His mortal life. He lives again in us.[18]

Crasset uses the same language. "The sacrament of communion is a new incarnation. When you go to holy communion, you go to conceive in your hearts the Son of God and of Mary. . . . The Holy Ghost attends you to accomplish the great mystery of the work of the Most High, and to cover you with the shadow of faith, without which it is impossible to conceive Jesus Christ."[19] Are you astonished he descended to enter her womb? But she was the purest of virgins and conceived without sin. More astonishing is that he descends into a heart so soiled by impurity and disorder as yours. "Supply by your humility all that is wanting in you of purity."[20]

I therefore imagine four altars: the wood altar of Calvary, the mystical stone altar of the Church, the spiritual altar of our hearts,

18. Peter Eymard, *The Divine Eucharist*, vol. 4, *The Eucharist and Christian Perfection* (New York: Fathers of the Blessed Sacrament, 1912), 122–23.

19. Crasset, *Christian Considerations*, 337–38.

20. Ibid., 338.

and the celestial altar in heaven. Christ is at work upon them all; the Cross is connected to them all; and Jesus appears as one single victim on them all, even though one is bloody, one is sacramental, one is interior, and one is supernal. The reason for multiple altars is the restless outreach of charity. Jesus could just not let it rest! Huby marvels:

> In order to content the immense desire he has of remaining with us, his love multiplies him and communicates him to every country of the world, to every church of the same town.
>
> Perhaps Jesus imparts himself to us for some years, for some ages only? No, again. The bonds of love which hold Jesus captive under the sacred species, will detain him on our altars as long as there shall be one single man on earth.[21]

The sacrifice would be offered but once on the *historical* altar, but the whole point of the *ecclesial* altar is its perpetuity. Grou identifies this as the advantage the Eucharist has over the Cross. Jesus's divine ingenuity "found a wondrous means to make it reign in the world until the end of time; He has mysteriously enclosed it in a sacrament of love, where it is made visible, not to our senses, but to our faith.... We behold in the Eucharist Jesus Christ crucified as they saw Him upon Calvary nailed to the Cross."[22] About the Last Supper Nicholas Cross says "it is usual at the parting of friends for the spirits to fall into commotion ... this evidences the great affection God had for man, that being to return to his Eternal father he contrived a means to be always with us, I say such a contrivance that nothing but love could have found out: a contrivance that sets out his love even beyond our Creation, or redemption."[23] No wonder we are amazed. God exceeds our expectations. As de Bérulle says,

> when God wants his Incarnate Word to be present in many places in his new nature, he employs his power to create a new masterwork and a new mystery, in which he multiplies the presence and

21. Huby, *The Spiritual Retreat of the Reverend Father Vincent Huby*, 135.
22. Grou, *The Practical Science of the Cross*, 59.
23. Nicolas of the Holy Cross, *Pious Reflections*, 126–27.

> not the essence of this his nature. We see this in the most holy mystery of the Eucharist. . . . A remarkable miracle! For it is performed so many times and in so many places. A perpetual miracle! For it will endure to the end of the world. A miracle of Jesus Christ and of Jesus Christ upon himself![24]

Libermann identifies three objects our Savior had in view when he instituted the holy Eucharist. First, it was to unite us with his liturgical abnegation. "It is a life of separation from all creatures and of total surrender into the hands of His heavenly Father. He does not seek to be honored, loved and esteemed by creatures; He does not pursue the pleasures and enjoyments of the earth; He turns aside from them."[25] Second, it was to make a share for us in his union with his Father. "It is His will that we seek nothing, desire, love and will nothing but His heavenly Father. We may, therefore, be assured that every movement of our soul that does not tend directed toward God, is not from Jesus living in us."[26] And third, it was to dispose us to live his life. "If we wish to prepare for Holy Communion, we must be disposed to live only the life of our Divine Savior. We should, therefore, purify our souls from every earthly affection, and rid ourselves of every natural movement and desire."[27] One can see the Holy Spirit's governance of the life of abnegation in each of these activities.

In feeding his disciples (then and now) with his own life, Christ empowers love for God until it is pure. Grou says this is precisely the spiritual transformation the Holy Spirit intends for us, as "little by little, we are transformed into the image of Jesus Christ, and each good Communion adds some more perfect strokes to this transformation."[28] As his life on earth was coming to an end Jesus offered up an intercession. "*Rogo, Pater, ut sint unum*: I ask of thee, O Father! that they may be made partakers of the union that is between us," and de Bernières-Louvigny says this prayer is finally answered: "the

24. De Bérulle, *Discourses on the State and Grandeurs of Jesus*, 103.
25. Libermann, *Letters to Clergy and Religious*, Spiritan Series 8, vol. 4, 88–89.
26. Ibid.
27. Ibid.
28. Grou, *Manual for Interior Souls*, 360.

union he enjoys with God the Father is the model of that which he desires we should contract with him by means of this divine sacrament."[29]

Every Eucharist is well-received if it leads to greater abnegation, because that is an increased imitation of Christ's Cross. Bruyère understands that "our Lord's Eucharistic life is one of total abnegation, silence, poverty, obedience, absolute isolation and tranquil self-surrender which seem to be the ideal of what the soul's life will be when it has become perfectly united with God."[30] If the food the body takes in does not empower the body's movement, what good is it? If the spiritual food the soul imbibes does not empower spiritual movement, what good is it?

The gratuitous grace of God must receive our correspondence, and this is worked out at the altar of the Eucharist more precisely than anywhere else. Abnegation is not a condition we must fulfill before God will approach us, but it is a condition for receiving God. The sacraments work *ex opere operato*, of course. ("By the very fact of the action's being performed."[31]) But the *fruitfulness* of the sacraments requires our being disposed for that grace. If not, we bring back less with us, for the same reason that Grou notices one who goes to the river with a thimble will bring back less water than the one who goes with a bucket. "Jesus Christ sheds the grace of His Sacrament in all hearts according to their dispositions.... He fills that which each brings to Him."[32] Quadrupani finds this image going back to Augustine, who said the sea "contains immense waters, and we obtain a greater or lesser quantity of these waters, according to the size of the vessel with which we draw them up. Those immense waters collected in the ocean are a type of the immense merits of Jesus Christ collected in the Mass; the greater or lesser vase is the greater or lesser devotion of those who assist at the sacrifice."[33] So de Granada applies the illustration by saying "the

29. De Bernières-Louvigny, *The Interior Christian*, 194.
30. Bruyère, *Spiritual Life and Prayer*, 64.
31. Catechism of the Catholic Church, paragraph 1128.
32. Grou, *The Practical Science of the Cross*, 160–61.
33. Quadrupani, *The Christian Instructed*, 14.

better the preparation for Communion, the more the grace that is conferred. One who goes to get water from the sea will get as much water as the size of his vessel can hold. As far as the ocean is concerned, there will never be a lack of water, but there will be less water received on account of the smallness of the container. The same happens with those who approach the Eucharist, which is a sea of divine grace."[34]

Saint-Jure acknowledges the Catholic teaching that says sacraments operate grace of themselves, in virtue of their institution, but still he adds that "they do this in a manner proportioned to the dispositions of those who receive them; so that he who is but little disposed receives but little grace. The Sacrament of the Eucharist, then, gives very little when we receive it negligently."[35] Why don't we receive the grace the sacrament is supposed to bring? In a word, "it is for want of due preparation," which de Sales says consists of three elements: "the first preparation is purity of intention; the second is attention; the third is humility."[36] Altogether, he summarizes, these preparations join together in the chief disposition, which is "total abandonment of ourselves to the mercy of God, the submission of our will and all our affections, without reserve, to His dominion."[37] Purity of intention, humility, self-denial, and submission to God are the very footprints of abnegation that we have been tracking.

Love will produce a desire to annihilate whatever hinders the growth of love. So we should not be surprised that the sacrament of love (a name for the Eucharist) will enkindle a willingness to abnegate prideful self, and flattering honor, and worldly vanity. Liturgy uses instruments from the tool chest of abnegation to purify the love we give, and the love we are capable of receiving. A person whose liturgy runs so rough needs a Divine Mechanic to tune it, and his first recommendation to perfect this person's liturgy will be mortification, renunciation, surrender, and abnegation. Everyone

34. De Granada, *Summa of the Christian Life*, 498.

35. Saint-Jure, *A Treatise on the Knowledge and Love of Our Lord Jesus Christ*, vol. 1, 646–47.

36. De Sales, *Library of St. Francis de Sales: vol. 5, The Spiritual Conferences*, 348.

37. Ibid., 350.

believes in humility theoretically, but de Bergamo wants to know whether "in your preparation for that divine Sacrament and in your thanksgiving, do you make due acts of humility?"[38] Everyone believes in rejecting vainglory, but Blosius wants to know whether we still find it difficult to admit unworthiness. "When thou art about to receive the most holy Eucharist, see that thou art not present unworthily at that tremendous and heavenly Table. Keep thyself low, hide thyself in the valley of profound humiliation; confess—yea, confess thyself to be wholly a sinner."[39]

Essentially, the dispositions that make the Eucharist be fruitful in us are the very standards of abnegation. Here are four examples of the claim.

- Libermann identifies them as sacrifice, self-denial, and self-annihilation:

  > Our Lord wanted us to share in His spirit of sacrifice, for the Most Holy Eucharist is a sacrifice. . . . This shows that our first preparation for Holy Communion should be a spirit of renunciation.[40]

- Croiset identifies them as poverty, humility, and spiritual hunger:

  > The general dispositions which we ought to bring to Communion are: profound humility and a sincere acknowledgment of our poverty; a certain spiritual hunger, which indicates, at the same time, the need we have of this food, and our good dispositions to profit by it; a great purity of heart, an ardent love of Jesus Christ, or at least an ardent desire of loving Him, and of accomplishing the design which He had in giving Himself to us in the Eucharist—namely, to unite us intimately to Him by a perfect conformity of heart and mind. Those who, at Communion, have no sentiment of devotion, no fervour, no tenderness, are certainly without some of these dispositions.[41]

- De Castañiza identifies them as withdrawing from the deceits of the world, and from self-pleasing vainglory.

38. De Bergamo, *Humility of Heart*, 153–54.
39. Blosius, *The Manual of the Spiritual Life*, 60–61.
40. Libermann, *Letters to Clergy and Religious*, Spiritan Series 8, vol. 4, 49–50.
41. Croiset, *Devotion to the Sacred Heart of Jesus*, 153.

> The remedy of all this, O dear souls, is unfeigned *humility.* Cast one glance of your soul's eye upwards upon your Creator's might and mercy; all your perfections come out of His treasury, and are lent you to be improved for His service, not to be proud of for your own satisfaction. And look down with your other eye upon your bottomless nothing; see there your own base indignity and brutish ingratitude, your great impurity and gross impiety, and be ashamed to desire any temporal esteem, who so truly deserve eternal damnation.[42]

• And Eudes finds the Eucharist to be a master class in abnegation when he considers the manner under which Jesus still comes to us.

> Our Lord Jesus Christ comes to you in the Blessed Eucharist, with the greatest humility, abasing Himself so far as to take the form and appearance of bread, to give Himself to you, and with the most ardent love that impels Him to give you, in this Sacrament, all the greatest, most dear, and most precious things He has. You also should receive Him in this same Sacrament with the deepest humility and the greatest love. These are the two principal dispositions you should have when you go to Holy Communion.[43]

No one should be discouraged, though. De la Colombière is convinced that no matter how faltering our attempts, Christ still rashly comes with mercy. "What is our purity? What care do we take to prepare our soul? . . . We commit faults on the eve, on the day, in the very action itself. And yet He comes! What goodness! We go to Him. What rashness!"[44] And Crasset almost suggests that Jesus stammers when expressing his eagerness to come to us.

> Daughters of Jerusalem, say to my spouse, to my well-beloved that I wait and languish with love. Say to her that I have descended from heaven to discourse with her, and remain on earth to enter

42. Juan de Castañiza, *The Spiritual Conflict and Conquest*, ed. Jerome Vaughan (London: Burns & Oates, Ltd., 1903), 224–25. This volume contains two titles: "Spiritual Conflict" and "Spiritual Conquest." Scupoli's version does not have the latter title, from which this quote comes.

43. Eudes, *The Life and the Kingdom of Jesus in Christian Souls*, 132.

44. De la Colombière, *Faithful Servant*, 64.

> into the sanctuary of her heart; I have taken the form of bread to nourish her, and all my pleasure is in conversing with and abiding with her, that I wish to espouse her in the face of the Church, and to contract with her an alliance so perfect that we may be as one person and one spirit, like the union which exists between my Father and I. Why, then, does she fly from me? Why despise and neglect me?[45]

There is a well-known passage in Philippians about Christ's humility. "Have this mind among yourselves, which was in Christ Jesus, who, though he was in the form of God, did not count equality with God a thing to be grasped, but emptied himself, taking the form of a servant" (Phil 2:5–7). The Greek word for "emptying" is *kenosis*, and theologians speak of the Incarnation as a mystery of divine *kenosis*. This seems to be how God operates on this side of the Last Judgment: he comes among his people by self-emptying, humiliation, poverty, and abandonment. Grou does not therefore find it surprising to notice traces of this *kenosis* in the Eucharist. What the Word did at the Incarnation, he will do again at the altar. "Already to unite Thyself to human nature, Thou hast emptied Thyself, in the Incarnation, of the Majesty of Thy Divine Being; once more Thou dost will to annihilate Thyself in the Eucharist, that Thou mayest unite Thyself to me."[46] Neither does Chardon find *kenosis* absent at altar, Communion, or tabernacle. "The Eucharistic Christ does not disdain either the cabins of the poor or the huts of the lepers. He does not prefer the dwellings of princes or the magnificent palaces of monarchs. Cancerous lips touch His mouth, as well as lips that rival the roses in their color and sweetness. Nothing can daunt His loving inclination to give Himself."[47]

Christ's *kenosis* inspires our abnegation. We have not a glory like his to deny, but we do have a will to deny, which we must do if we want to follow his example of having no desire except for his Father. The content of our denials is different, of course. His was denial of

45. Crasset, *Christian Considerations*, 352

46. Grou, *The Practical Science of the Cross*, 101.

47. Chardon, *Cross of Jesus*, vol. 1, 104.

a glory that was rightfully his; ours is a denial (abnegation) of vainglory over a status we have wrongfully stolen. Christ emptied himself, taking the form of a servant; we are to empty ourselves of pride and vainglory, taking on the form of his children. What Christ does, we should do reciprocally, in our own way and at our own capacity. We should annihilate ourselves when communicating in the Blessed Sacrament, as Our Lord annihilated himself in order to communicate himself to us in it. Saint-Jure therefore thinks Jesus's eucharistic *kenosis* can be a model for our abnegation.

> At the simple word of a priest, He descends from heaven to earth; . . . He hides His greatness and infinite Majesty under the species of bread and wine; He hides therein the noblest union the divine wisdom could form, the hypostatic union of the Divine Word with human nature; . . . He annihilates Himself in some manner for love of us; . . . He obeys, He humbles Himself, He exposes Himself to outrages and elevates Himself above nature for love of us. Urged by a reciprocal love, we will practice, especially to-day, obedience, humility, mortification, we will stifle within us all the movements of corrupt nature, and do all in our power to prepare worthily for His visit.[48]

Our self-love makes for disobedience, but Christ acts in an opposite way. He was obedient to his Father in heaven, obedient to Mary and Joseph, obedient to the authorities who sentenced him to crucifixion, and now he is obedient to the words of a priest, as Saint-Jure observes. "In order to come to us [in the Mass], He deigns to obey the voice of a man, to abase Himself, to make Himself little, to lead a hidden life in the general mortifications of His senses. . . . So, to go to Him, we ought to practise heroic acts of obedience, humility, recollection and mortification; to separate things most closely united, that is, to separate ourselves from attachment to our honor, our convenience, our judgment, and all that is imperfect in us."[49] His arrival is gratuitous, and we will never make ourselves worthy of the

48. Saint-Jure, *A Treatise on the Knowledge and Love of Our Lord Jesus Christ*, vol. 1, 677, 679.

49. Ibid., 671.

King's visit. But we should go out to him with the same dispositions with which he came to us: obedience, humility, and self-denial. If we annihilate ourselves, Vianney says it is only "after the example of His profound annihilation in the Sacrament of the Eucharist."[50]

This is a boundless marvel, Boudon thinks, on par with Creation, the Incarnation, and the Resurrection. "O infinite wonder! abiding with us on this earth of ours in the Divine Eucharist, He appears therein no more than if He were absent altogether. He remains hidden there under the appearance of bread and wine, under the appearance of a crumb of bread and a drop of wine! Can He, I would ask, conceal Himself more perfectly? Assuredly it must be confessed that the love of this God-Man for the hidden life is most intense and most amazing."[51] Did you think the Word of God was well-hidden in the manger of Bethlehem? For thirty-three years in Galilee? Between the two thieves? Consider now the Eucharist. The Word seems to have such a love for the hidden life (for *kenosis*) that Eymard is not surprised to find him continuing it in the Blessed Sacrament. "I can without fear approach Him, contemplate Him, and speak to Him. If His glory shone around, who would dare speak to Him[?].... A mother lisps with her little one, and puts herself within its reach to raise it in her arms; and so does Jesus make Himself little with the little in order to raise them to Himself and up to God.... Behold how Jesus veiled encourages our weakness! What greater proof of love than this Eucharistic veil?"[52]

Scaramelli says the heavenly food of the Eucharist fills the soul with delights proper to the spirit, so this sacrament "has the special property of giving a delight.... Saint Cyprian adds that the pleasure which the soul receives from this Bread of Angels is so intense as to alienate and detach it from all worldly gratifications."[53] Once the eyebeam has a glint of heaven in it, the corruptible world no longer feeds the soul. Adam's appetite was ruined by his diet of for-

50. Vianney, *The Little Catechism of the Curé of Ars*, 33.

51. Boudon, *The Hidden Life of Jesus*, 64–65.

52. Peter Eymard, *The Divine Eucharist, First Series: The Real Presence* (New York: Fathers of the Blessed Sacrament, 1907), 120–21.

53. Scaramelli, *Directorium Asceticum; Or, Guide to the Spiritual Life*, vol. 1, 614.

bidden fruit, and he gorged himself upon the world with the passions of avarice (i.e., cupidity). But our healed appetite ruins our taste for vainglory, and avarice, and envy, and ire, and replaces it with a hunger for the second Adam, who gives us a totally different food to eat. His "holy and virginal Flesh," Grou says, "has the virtue of deadening in our hearts the fire of cupidity, of extinguishing the ardour of our passions, of purifying our thoughts, of regulating our desires, of repressing the revolt of our senses, and of submitting the flesh to the spirit."[54]

Our diet is changed in the Eucharist, and it gives strength in the ways of abnegation. When Christ feeds us, it is not to empower us to fulfill our own designs, but to fulfill his. He feeds us the flesh with which he obeyed his Father, in order to create the same obedience in us. He feeds us the flesh with which he made acts of mercy, in order to create such mercy in us. He feeds us with the flesh that lived under poverty and meekness and humility, in order to create powers of abnegation in us. The Eucharist does exist for the sake of empowerment, then, but so that communicants can become soldiers of Christ. Nouet approaches the divine Eucharist in precisely this way: as "an arsenal, whence we procure arms for combating our invisible enemies."[55] The Son of God

> took arms in the womb of the most pure of Virgins, with which to combat death.... The arms which He took, were the weakness of our human flesh, which He clothed with the power of His Divinity.... Under this weak appearance, the Divinity was a hidden hook, which pierced the dragon with a mortal stroke. In this respect, the altar resembles the womb of the Blessed Virgin; it is the tower of David, in which we find every sort of weapon, offensive and defensive.[56]

By the Eucharist, Christ is building an army, and this spiritual army will attack hell, and its gates will not prevail against the onrush. The

54. Grou, *The Practical Science of the Cross*, 171.

55. Jacques Nouet, *Octave Corpus Christi; or, the Mystical Life of our Lord in the Blessed Sacrament* (London: Thomas Richardson and Son, 1847), 57.

56. Ibid., 57–58.

Resurrection holds the key to liturgical abnegation, because the reason why Christ feeds us with his death is so he might raise us, with himself, to eternal life. When this mystery takes hold of a person, he can come from Communion with the words of Simeon on our lips: "It is time, O Lord; now permit my soul to depart in peace, and to quit this mortal life, because I receive within me the spring and source of immortality."[57]

Do we like the idea of being conformed to a Savior who lived long ago, because we think he will not disturb us now? The gospel suddenly becomes more real and practical when he shows up at the Eucharist. He walks out of the pages of history to be enthroned before us on the altar where, Saint-Jure says, he "assures us that whoever eats Him will live by Him, as He lives by His Father, that is . . . He will communicate Himself to him, imprint on him the traits of His perfections, enable him to lead a holy and divine life, and render him as a god on earth."[58] Put simply, Jesus ought to form Jesus in us.

The Apostle Paul has already warned us that exterior actions alone do not make an acceptable sacrifice to God. Giving goods to the poor, the practice of fasting, even giving up one's body to be burned, is as nothing if charity does not reign in us (1 Cor 13:3). The sacrifice most pleasing and acceptable to God is to give our will over to him, and Bona says this is what God asks of us in the Mass. "We can offer to God nothing more pleasing, no victim better and more acceptable, than our own will; intirely [sic] to resign that to God, and desire that in all things it may be subject and conformable to his blessed will, is that living and holy sacrifice wherein God delights . . . [this is] the highest act of Religion we can perform on Earth."[59] See how evidently liturgy and abnegation connect. The most pleasing sacrifice we can make is to deny our own will in favor of God's.

57. De Bernières-Louvigny, *The Interior Christian*, 201.

58. Saint-Jure, *A Treatise on the Knowledge and Love of Our Lord Jesus Christ*, vol. 1, 634.

59. Bona, *Precepts and Practical Rules*, part II, 83.

This life is a time of probation (trial, testing, growth), and that changes one's perception of the afflictions that one (temporarily) undergoes, because birth pangs are different from the pangs of death. The humiliations, adversities, afflictions, and sufferings all change in meaning once they are understood to be steps on a pathway leading to love—the very love that gives the name "sacrament of love" to the Eucharist. At that point, de la Colombière says, we can make a trustful surrender to Providence.

> If you would be convinced that in all He allows and in all that happens to you God has no other end in view but your real advantage and your eternal happiness, reflect a moment on all He has done for you; you are now suffering, but remember that the author of this suffering is He who chose to spend His life suffering to save you from everlasting suffering, whose angel is always at your side guarding your body and soul by His order, who sacrifices Himself daily on the altar to expiate your sins and appease His Father's anger, who comes lovingly to you in the Holy Eucharist and whose greatest pleasure is to be united to you. We must be very ungrateful to mistrust Him after He has shown such proofs of His love and to imagine that He can intend us harm. [60]

We hesitate; we balk; we say the blow is too hard. But "what have you to fear from a hand that was pierced and nailed to the cross for you?"[61]

When God sends us trials, the Eucharist should convince us that they are for our real advantage and eternal happiness. So de la Colombière admits

> the path I have to tread is full of thorns . . . [but] is there a thorn in it that He has not reddened with His own blood?—The chalice He offers you is a bitter one. But remember that it is your Redeemer who offers it. Loving you as He does, could He bring Himself to treat you so severely if the need were not urgent, the

60. Claude de la Colombière in Jean Saint-Jure and Claude de la Colombière, *Trustful Surrender to Divine Providence* (Charlotte, NC: TAN Books and Publishers, 1983), 43.

61. Ibid.

> gain not worthwhile? Can we dare to refuse the chalice He has prepared for us Himself? [62]

The crucified Lord of the Eucharist is the gate through which to enter a theology of abnegation, which happens when the miracle of the Eucharist on the altar becomes the miracle of Communion in our hearts. This is our final chapter.

62. Ibid., 43–44.

11

The Miracle of Communion

If one thinks that these theologians of abnegation have forgotten the importance of Communion, one would be wrong.

- "Do not regulate your Communions by your life, but your life by your frequent Communions"[1] (Fénelon).
- "Some saints have been made saints by one thing. One Communion is enough to make a saint"[2] (Faber).
- "Salvation depends sometimes upon one Communion. How do you know whether this Communion may not be the one you omit?"[3] (de Sales).
- "A single good Communion is enough to make a Saint"[4] (Croiset).
- "One good communion will make a saint, and to render it good it is necessary to have good will and perfect contrition"[5] (Crasset).

These comments require explanation, of course, and an attached warning. Crasset, for example, goes on to say "*One* good communion would suffice to make a saint. How many have you made? Are you any better? Have you corrected *one defect?* Have you acquired one virtue? What account will you render?"[6] Saint-Jure acknowledges that a single Communion would be enough to make you holy if you were excellently disposed, but "you have received him so many times, yet no such results have appeared! So many journeys that he

1. Fénelon, *Letters to Men*, 221.
2. Faber, *Spiritual Conferences*, 225.
3. De Sales and Crasset, *The Secret of Sanctity*, 73.
4. Croiset, *Devotion to the Sacred Heart of Jesus*, 152.
5. Crasset, *Christian Considerations*, 115.
6. Ibid., 418.

has made from heaven to earth for you, so many miracles that he has worked in himself and in nature, have produced nothing in you!"[7] But these warnings must be balanced with grace's invitation, lest we be afraid to approach the table the King of Heaven has set. Crasset tells us to see whence our permission comes. "If we measure our unworthiness in the excellence of this holy sacrament, we will never communicate. If we measure it by our poverty, we will communicate every day. Jesus is not in this sacrament to make us fear Him, but to make us love Him."[8] "Fear is good, but love is still better."[9]

De Liguori recounts how Jesus appeared one day to Sister Paula Maresca and "showed her two vessels, one of gold and another of silver, and said to her, that in the former he preserved her sacramental communions, and in the latter her spiritual communions."[10] In meditating on the miracle of Communion, we will consider both ways of communing.

Sacramental Communion

De Sales tells his spiritual daughter how she can communicate fearlessly by explaining what abnegation is really all about. *Annihilate me* really means *establish Thyself in me.*

> Tell her . . . to communicate fearlessly, calmly, yet with all humility, in order to correspond with the action of that Spouse who in order to unite Himself with us annihilated Himself. . . . Oh! my daughter, those who communicate according to the spirit of the Heavenly Bridegroom, annihilate themselves and say to our Lord: feed on me, change me, annihilate me, convert me into Thyself. . . . What ought not we to do in order that He may possess us, that He may feed on us, that He may make us what He pleases?[11]

And Mother Françoise-Madeleine de Chaugy connects the fruits of Communion to liturgical abnegation in a similar fashion:

7. Saint-Jure, *Union with our Lord*, 379.

8. Crasset, *Christian Considerations*, 115–16.

9. Ibid., 354.

10. Alphonsus de Liguori, *The True Spouse of Jesus Christ, or, The Nun Sanctified by the Virtues of Her State* (New York: Benziger Brothers, 1899), 371–72.

11. Camus, *The Spirit of St. Francis de Sales*, 395–96.

> The whole fruit of a good reception of the Holy Eucharist… [consists] in a complete change of life, and a real transformation of our inclinations and desires into those of Jesus Christ, to whom we have the honour of being united by this Sacrament of love; and Who exacts from our hearts, as an homage to this divine union, an entire separation from all worldly love and intercourse. For it is impossible to be united at the same time to the world and to Jesus Christ.[12]

I proposed from the start that liturgy should not be isolated from our spiritual life because a union should be forged between the altar of the Cross, the sacramental altar, and the spiritual altar of our heart. De Bernières-Louvigny reveals that "sometimes, when communicating, I picture to myself that my heart is an altar, and that Jesus Christ comes to remain upon it in the same manner as on the altar where Holy Mass is celebrated. Wherefore my heart received him lovingly and simply; and united itself to all his divine operations relating both to his heavenly Father, and to creatures."[13] On each altar, Jesus is still offering himself in sacrificial oblation to the Father, the full glory of which is only seen at the celestial altar in heaven. That is why Grou finds Jesus uniting and consummating his sacrifice with ours, joining our self-abnegation to his self-annihilation.. "He makes of us and of Himself one selfsame living Victim, spiritual, acceptable to the Divine Majesty. It is by this that He renders us crucified members with Him, that in feeding us with His death, He makes us die to the world and to sin, in order to make us live with Him in God alone, and for God alone."[14]

What a joy it would be if the vainglorious revolts in our hearts could be conquered. Happiness before, happiness after, happiness on both sides of Communion. First, Doyle says, "what a happiness will it be for you if, each time you go to Communion, you can say to Him: 'My dear Jesus! I have during the past week, by the assistance of Thy grace, gained several victories over Thy enemies, by not

12. De Chaugy, *Life of Mother Marie Jacqueline Favre*, 101.
13. De Bernières-Louvigny, *The Interior Christian*, 180–81.
14. Grou, *The Practical Science of the Cross*, 168.

yielding to their suggestions.'"[15] Second, de Sales famously said, "Oh my God! how happy should I be, if one day, after Holy Communion, I should find my own wretched heart gone from my breast, and the Heart of my Saviour in its place."[16] Have we any task in cooperating with this heart transplant surgery? Eudes answers the question by saying "it should be your desire, your care and your chief occupation to form Jesus in you, to make Him live and reign in you together with His spirit, His devotion, His virtues, His sentiments, His inclinations and dispositions. . . . God places this task in your hands, for you to work at it without interruption."[17] Communion with Christ at the altar requires communication with Christ in the heart, which is why liturgy has an abnegation component. Whenever we approach the Eucharist with self-love, we impair its fruits in us. Grou tackles the problem head on.

> Many persons think themselves saints, because they communicate weekly, or daily, who yet never dream of correcting their faults; and who perhaps do not even know them, because they are so blinded by self-love; they are impatient, harsh, censorious, full of self-esteem and contempt of their neighbour, proud of the multitude of their external observances, and destitute of the slightest idea of internal mortification.
>
> All the fruit they derive from their Communions and other pious exercises, consists in spiritual vanity, secret pride, and all the subtle vices engendered by devotion grafted on self-seeking.[18]

The body of Christ on which we feed should empower us to run the race, and instead, we seem to be running in place. Where is our advance in holiness? Saint-Jure notices that there are pious persons who communicate often "without advancing in virtue, and who, after fifty or a hundred communions, are as proud, as vain, as sub-

15. Doyle, *Lectures for Boys*, vol. 1, 76.

16. De Sales, quoted in de Chantal, *I. The Mystical Explanation of the Canticle of Canticles by St. Francis de Sales; II. The Depositions of St. Jane Frances de Chantal in the Cause of the Canonisation of St. Francis de Sales* in *Library of St. Francis de Sales*, vol. 6 (London: Burns & Oates, 1908), 89.

17. Eudes, *The Life and Kingdom of Jesus in Christian Souls*, 79.

18. Grou, *The Spiritual Maxims*, 51.

ject to anger, as deceitful, as full of themselves, and as void of God, as if they had never communicated."[19] The one who enters is Jesus, the omnipotent God, who can deliver a person from vices and make him virtuous and perfect. He has done it for others; Saint-Jure thinks Jesus is willing to produce in everyone the same effects, in some degree, if we were disposed for it.

Do not abandon the sacrament, instead, add the collaboration of spiritual warfare to your sacramental life. Croiset takes a long view when speaking to priests about devotion to the Sacred Heart.

> For a year, for ten years perhaps, you have said Mass every day. You have received the Body and Blood of Jesus Christ more than three thousand times in your life; and yet, for a year, for ten years, you have been fighting against some imagination, some fancy, you say, which hinders you from belonging entirely to God. . . . Are we therefore to leave off Communion? Must we give up saying Mass daily? No; but we must regulate our life and free ourselves from the vices and failings that hinder us from profiting by it.[20]

To communicate fruitfully, join abnegation to the Mass. Grou says we must receive the Body and Blood of Jesus with the express desire that he will produce in us his love of the Cross: "let us judge by our love of the cross of the fruit of our Communions."[21] Do you want to make better Communions? Then "come with a special desire that you may thereby grow in love for His Cross, that is for humiliation and suffering, self-renunciation, and self-oblation. Let this be the test of your Communions. Do not hold them to be good, because you have been kindled with warm glowing feelings, but rather if you have come away with fresh courage to conquer self, to fight against your own will, to bear whatever God may lay upon you."[22]

We can know food is healthy if it strengthens and nourishes us. (Otherwise, it is called junk food.) How does food become part of our body? John of the Angels remembers that we need teeth to

19. Saint-Jure, *A Treatise on the Knowledge and Love of Our Lord Jesus Christ*, vol. 1, 630.

20. Croiset, *Devotion to the Sacred Heart of Jesus*, 94–95.

21. Grou, *Manual for Interior Souls*, 365.

22. Grou, *The Hidden Life of the Soul*, 109.

break it, molars to crumble it, warmth in the stomach to dissolve it. But "we shall need to go through more twists and turns than these do to become worthy of God's nourishment in Communion! We shall first have to be crushed and broken with abnegation and contrition, emaciated with penance and consumed with the fire of love and devotion in order to be commensurate with Christ who, crushed, emaciated and broken with the immensity of his love for us, offered himself to the Father on a Cross."[23] Is the body of Christ nourishing us in Communion? Grou thinks we can know if it increases our strength to overcome self, namely,

> our natural inclinations and dislikes, our sloth, our weakness, our inconsistency, the horror we have of all contradiction, restraint and humiliation; in short all that resists God's Grace within us. If this strength increases with each Communion, if we acquire self-control, if we are less self-indulgent, more devoted, more patient, more stedfast in our resolutions, more indifferent to the world's praise and blame, more docile to the leadings of grace, we may rest satisfied that our Communions are good.[24]

You become what you eat. If you eat Jesus, you should become loving as he loved, ready to suffer as he suffered, obedient as he obeyed. The Eucharist is the sacrament of love, after all, and not only does the love of God descend to us, our love must also ascend to him. The two loves rendezvous on the Cross. It is a signpost, like an X, marking the center point between heaven and earth. To meet us at this cynosure, Christ emptied himself (kenosis) and came from heaven to earth. For us to meet Christ at the altar, we must take leave of ourselves (abnegate), and rise up to meet him, says John of the Angels.

> It is a bold, perhaps perplexing thing for me to say, I know, that when we receive Holy Communion properly, we take leave of ourselves. But I consider this to be most true. Just as the humble serf will take leave of his lodgings upon the king setting foot in them so, when we receiving [sic] Communion worthily, we *come out of*

23. De los Angeles, *The Loving Struggle*, 172.
24. Grou, *The Hidden Life of the Soul*, 110–11.

> *ourselves* as God enters in. Now, what do I mean, exactly, *coming out of oneself, taking leave of oneself?* I mean surrender, I mean renunciation and self-denial, I mean extricating self-love from our hearts so that only God may live and reign there. I mean saying "no" to our egotistical "yes," and "yes" to our bull-headed "no." I mean shedding one's old life and receiving the new. I mean ridding our soul of all sin because, for as long as it is there, neither are we in God nor God in us.[25]

The altar is a trysting place. "To tryst": to agree, as between lovers, to meet at a certain time and place. The sacrament of love is where we have a tryst with God.

God has imposed an obligation on anyone who would be saved, which we can summarize as keeping the commandments, renouncing self-love, denying our own will in favor of keeping God's, and warfare against the corrupt inclinations of our hearts. This abnegation is interior sacrifice, just as Jesus's perpetual sacrifice was his interior submission to the divine will. Grou therefore concludes that "the perpetual Sacrifice which He exacts from His members must be wholly interior, as is His own in the Divine Eucharist; it must be still more the Sacrifice of their souls than of their bodies, the Sacrifice of their natural inclinations and of their earthly desires than of the goods of the earth, the Sacrifice of their will ever submissive to the Will of God; ever annihilated, as that of Jesus Christ in the Will of God."[26]

Our Good Shepherd has given his sheep a divine fare capable of feeding abnegation, deep love, daily sacrifice, constant companionship, and spiritual reformation. The reason the grass is good for the sheep is not because it tastes sweet, but because it nourishes their sanctification. Grou says "the further we advance in mortification of self, the more we are weaned from all sweetnesses. If the heavenly food is then less delicious, it is more strengthening. The soul, in its trials, needs consolation less than strength, which latter is abundantly bestowed in those Communions in which nothing seems

25. De los Angeles, *The Loving Struggle*, 164.
26. Grou, *The Practical Science of the Cross*, 188.

to be imparted."[27] This is why so many of our theologians warn us against expecting sensible consolations, as does, for example, Camus. "The union of a meek and faithful soul to God, is much firmer and much closer in the still small voice of humble piety, than in sensible consolation, or great fervor of devotion. . . . The bees which make most wax, are precisely those which make least honey."[28] Or Bona, who calls sensible consolations a sort of "spiritual gluttony." Such persons "make every effort, not that they may worship God present, but that they may elicit some sense of sweetness. . . . As a rule, these are lukewarm, addicted to their own will, and enemies of mortification and self-denial."[29] Our liturgy is often improved by some time spent in the dark nights of the senses and of the soul. Let us think our Communions good and fruitful when we approach God with naked faith, and love him purely for himself alone. We should go to the table of life with the same disposition Christ had.

Jesus is the supernatural woodworker who cut down Eden's tree so it could do no more harm, shaped it into the wood of his Cross, which sprouted growth as a new tree of life, that he could then carve as an altar for us and a tabernacle for himself in our churches. If our human worship is to be engrafted by the Holy Spirit into the liturgy the Son gave to the Father, then the Father must have our full attention. Attend to him, not yourself. Our reception of the Eucharist is right and just when it produces a liturgical power of abnegation through which we can rise to new life. For Grou, the infallible proof of the goodness of our Communions is "if we acquire more mastery over ourselves, if we are less delicate and sensitive, more generous in undertaking, more patient in suffering, more faithful to our good resolutions, more indifferent to the esteem or contempt of men, more obedient to all the impulses of Divine grace, more ready for all the sacrifices God asks of us."[30]

27. Grou, *The Spiritual Maxims*, 62–63.

28. Camus, *The Beauties of St. Francis de Sales* (London: Longman, Rees, Orme, Brown, and Green, 1829), 70.

29. Bona, *A Treatise of Spiritual Life*, 175–76.

30. Grou, *Manual for Interior Souls*, 367.

This may be a difficult lesson for persons of a certain piety. Like the Pharisee among the Jews, the Pharisee among the Christians will thank God he is not like other men. When this person's Communion has "wrung forth a few tears," then Grou imagines that his "soul fancies itself lifted altogether above this world, and gifted with eagles' wings for the loftiest of flights." This subtle temptation is difficult to avoid "if God does not give a helping hand, by raising up some matter for humiliation, or by withdrawing His misused consolations."[31] God is only too happy to stand by with trials and humiliations, ready to combat spiritual pride! Therefore Quadrupani warns, "be careful that your fasts and your abstinence do not serve to provoke your vanity, or that they are not the effect of your love of your own will. If they are not the effect of obedience they are repudiated by God."[32] And if your neighbor seems wanting in consolation, "beware of presumption by despising [him] because he is without them," cautions John of Ávila, "for, very possibly, he is holier and more dear to God than you are."[33] John of the Cross knew by experience that "God frequently withholds these sensible favours from men, that they may fix the eyes of faith upon Himself."[34] The aridity felt in the dark night of the soul can also be felt at the communion altar rail, and for the same reason: namely, for our final good.

Consolations can soon fade, but the spiritual fruits of abnegation in spiritual warfare should continue even upon one's return home. This warfare is an aftershock of Communion. Here are some signs Grou recognizes:

> You should return to your own homes on leaving the Holy Altar, with more love than you carried thither with you; and so with the desire and the determination to be more firmly and closely united to God, to be more attentive and more faithful to grace; more

31. Grou, *The Spiritual Maxims*, 200.
32. Quadrupani, *The Christian Instructed*, 72.
33. John of Ávila, *Letters of Blessed John of Ávila*, 31.
34. John of the Cross, *The Obscure Night of the Soul*, in *The Complete Works of Saint John of the Cross*, vol. 1 (London: Longman, Green, Longman, Roberts & Green, 1864), 342.

> watchful over yourselves; more courageous to fight and to do violence to yourselves; more charitable towards your neighbour, more gentle and patient in bearing with him; more careful in fulfilling the duties of your station; more generous in giving to God; stronger in suffering all those crosses which may come into your way.[35]

Sacramental graces, and the gifts of the Holy Spirit, should increase after each Communion, and Lallemant wants to know why we do not always perceive them. "Whence comes this? From our unmortified passions, our attachments and disorderly affections, and our habitual faults. We allow these vicious principles to have more dominion over us than sacramental graces and the gifts of the Holy Spirit."[36] When liturgy soaks as far as the interior life of the spirit, it is liturgical spirituality.

The whole purpose of spiritual warfare consists of being set free from slavery to Satan, in order to become a slave to Christ (Eph 6:6). We are not enrolled in the Kingdom of God if grace does not enter deeply enough to discover our disorders and correct them, which is the mission of grace with which we are asked to correspond. Place yourself in spirit with the Blessed Virgin. She contemplated the Lamb's Passover sacrifice on the Cross, and we should contemplate the same Lamb, mystically renewing the same sacrifice in our heart. The person at Communion should fix his eye on the altar, as Mary's eye was fixed on her son crucified. Love aims the eye at the beloved, and cloaks all else.

When both sacramental Communions and spiritual communions feast upon Christ, then the presence of his Cross becomes joyful, Saint-Jure thinks. "When you have communicated you are filled with Jesus Christ entire, because you possess his body, his soul, his divinity, and all that he is. Being thus filled with Jesus Christ, this divine plenitude should spread over your soul, your body, and your senses, to impress upon them a disposition of conformity to him, and to communicate to them his virtues."[37] But this joy has a cost (the cost which has been the subject of this book). This perfect sat-

35. Grou, *Meditations Upon the Love of God*, 120.
36. Lallemant, in de Sales and Crasset, *Secret of Sanctity*, 245.
37. Saint-Jure, *Union with our Lord*, 368.

isfaction is only, says Surin, "for those who, by complete self-abnegation, and a general renunciation of all that is not God, and that does not tend to God, have perfectly emptied themselves of all creatures. It is to them that our Lord communicates himself, He honours them with His familiar converse."[38]

When we discover our nothingness by pouring ourselves out entirely to God, when our humility positions our prayer, when we replace self-will with God's will, when we overcome self-love with divine love, when the creation delights only because it illuminates the Creator, when we are no longer tricked by the devil and the deceits of the world, then—and only then—do we receive the gift of joy in Communion, and as a result, de Sales says we shall "go to Holy Communion boldly; we shall gradually become accustomed to this heavenly food and learn to digest it to our profit."[39] If Christ gives us all—namely, himself—then why would we keep back anything of ourselves? And if Christ gives us all—namely, himself—then why would we seek anything more? "If you sincerely believe that Christ comes in Holy Communion to dwell within you, what better safety can you find than in committing all that concerns you unreservedly to Him?"[40] Saint-Jure asks. And he adds that some saints experience extraordinary effects, but the ordinary effect of Communion for most of us will be an increase of charity, which "blunts the sting of sin which is within us, and thus hinders the disorderly movements of appetite, or moderates them when they appear, extinguishes the fire of concupiscence, and renders the flesh pure and submissive to the spirit."[41]

The Eucharist girds our liturgical abnegation. The gift is personal (between persons), and not automatic (accomplished without wills). God gives, and we respond. After his act comes our task, in de Ravignan's eyes. "God gives, what has He not given? He gives His very Self, He identifies Himself with us by every means of union,

38. Surin, *The Foundations of the Spiritual Life*, 108.

39. De Sales, *Maxims and Counsels* , 125.

40. Grou, *The Hidden Life of the Soul*, 106.

41. Saint-Jure, *A Treatise on the Knowledge and Love of Our Lord Jesus Christ*, vol. 1, 618.

especially in the Blessed Eucharist and in prayer. . . . And what else must I do? I must also give up everything—organs, memory, intelligence, affections, will, sufferings, in a word, everything appertaining to self. I shall give myself up and sacrifice myself, and this oblation I shall make through obedience."[42] These are the twin blades of liturgical abnegation: all is given, all is asked for. We give in response to what God has given. Mortification is both preparation and consequence because it is proportioned to the grace being communicated. Liturgical abnegation is the exchange of tattered garments for royal robes. Abnegation is liturgical because it stems from the "therefore"—*since* Christ graces us, *therefore* we deny world, self, vanity. "Should a woman of mean condition be married to a king, she would soon leave that state of poverty which environed her, to appear in the equipage of a queen,"[43] observes Granada. "Give me a share of thy banquet," we ask, but Jesus also asks us for a share of a banquet. Nouet says, "as Jesus Christ invites us to his heavenly table, we should also prepare a banquet of these *fruits that are sweet to his palate;* these are charity, peace, meekness, liberality, patience, joy in in the Holy Ghost, and all other virtues, which are the effects of a worthy communion."[44]

Grou thinks that God intends to penetrate more deeply than we might have expected when we felt his first touch. We fear it, but we desire it, too. "The perpetual Sacrifice of Jesus Christ in the Holy Eucharist is wholly interior; it is the sacrifice of a spiritual and living Victim; ours must be so likewise. Contempt for vanities of this world, detachment from the fleeting goods of earth, mortification of the senses; all this is easy to him who has no other will than that of God . . . to him who is quickened by the Spirit of Jesus Christ."[45] God is jealous for our souls and hearts.

Jealousy is not a vice when it is a desire for something that legitimately belongs to a person. In this case, God is jealous for our

42. De Ravignan, *Ravignan's Last Retreat*, 183–84.

43. Luis de Granada, *A Memorial of a Christian Life* (New York: The Catholic Publication Society, 1870), 293.

44. Jacques Nouet, *Meditations on the Life of Our Lord* (Dublin: Browne & Nolan, Ltd., 1956), 225.

45. Grou, *The Practical Science of the Cross*, 190.

souls—because he possessed them in the first place, because they are legitimately his. God's jealousy is a holy love, pressed by his justice. God's jealousy is a zeal for our greater good, pressed by his mercy. When God takes back his property (not a bad definition of exorcism), then the soul in liberty has a taste of the Supreme Good. John of the Angels finds jealousy arising from a very, very deep love. When the Spouse says in the Canticle to "seal me upon your heart," the reasons for the command

> are the same a lover most deeply in love would give: because *love is as powerful as death.* As if he had said: if you love me as I love you, you will love nothing else, for true love admits of no shared company. Your love for me will be as death is to other men, a death absolute and irrevocable, as if life had never been. My love shall be death to all your other passions; my love shall be a knife to your carnal desires, for I will suffer no other loves in the house where I dwell. I love you and my love for you is jealous, most jealous, and my jealousy is as rigorous and tormenting as hell. I shall tolerate no competition.[46]

Love is as powerful as death. The Sacrament of Love is powerful enough to cause mortification.

Abnegation does not despise the world; it runs out of the world, and out of self, in order to run after God, and into God. Its feet are made fleet by the savoriness of the Eucharist still on the lips. Therefore, the contempt Bona is talking about is a holy contempt, not a haughty one. Holy contempt is a sort of scorn; scorn is mockery or derision; derision is ridicule and laughter; and what does the person of liturgical abnegation ridicule? Satan—when he tells us the world (soon ending) is the final abode for a soul (which will not end). The flesh—when it tells us that a corruptible good is as gratifying as the Supreme Good. The flattery of the world—when it tells us that our best happiness is around us now, and not ahead of us in heaven. When the devil tells us such things, we can barely stifle our laughter and we hold him in contempt.

Sacramental manna is a wilderness food, a viaticum for our time

46. De los Angeles, *The Loving Struggle*, 34.

in the desert, which is the time of purification. Be amazed, says Vianney, at the fare God offers us during that time: himself!

> To sustain the soul in the pilgrimage of life, God looked over creation, and found nothing that was worthy of it. He then turned to Himself, and resolved to give Himself. O my soul, how great you are, since nothing less than God can satisfy thee! The food of the soul is the Body and Blood of God! . . . How happy are the pure souls that have the happiness of being united to Our Lord by Communion! They will shine like beautiful diamonds in Heaven, because God will be seen in them.[47]

It is a tribute to the soul's value that God feeds her with himself, because nothing less than himself can satisfy her. All this talk of abnegation in Catholic spirituality concerns the *perfection of the soul.* "What must we do in that case?" de Chantal asks her Visitation daughters.

> We must crush those thoughts of complacency and vain satisfaction, humble ourselves and seek humiliation, give God glory for all, and recognize that of ourselves we can do nothing. In one word, we must be FAITHFULLY FAITHFUL and HUMBLY HUMBLE; the meaning of which is, we must in all things seek only the glory of God, and do nothing but to please Him.[48]

Spiritual Communion

Sacramental Communion is a miracle, but there is another miracle, that of spiritual communion. It can be (and should be) part of preparing for receiving sacramental Communion in the Mass. Saint-Jure counsels, "after the *Pater*, we must prepare for spiritual Communion, which is one of the most excellent exercises of the interior life."[49] De Liguori urges "as often as you hear mass, to make a spiritual communion during the communion of the priest."[50] "When

47. Vianney, *The Little Catechism of the Curé of Ars*, 43.

48. De Chantal, *Exhortations, Conferences, Instructions*, 167. The capitalization is in her original text.

49. Saint-Jure, *A Treatise on the Knowledge and Love of Our Lord Jesus Christ*, vol. 2, 41–42.

50. De Liguori, *The True Spouse of Jesus Christ*, 373.

the priest communicates, make the spiritual Communion thus: 'My Jesus, I love Thee, and I long for Thee in my soul; I embrace Thee, and wish nevermore to be separated from Thee.'"[51] His other version has attained widespread use:

> My Jesus, I believe that Thou art truly present in the Most Blessed Sacrament. I love Thee above all things, and I desire to possess Thee within my soul. Since I am unable now to receive Thee sacramentally, come at least spiritually into my heart. I embrace Thee as being already there, and unite myself wholly to Thee; never permit me to be separated from Thee.[52]

But spiritual communion also names spiritual reception of communion when one does not assist at the sacrament. It is communion from a distance. Von Cochem compares receiving spiritual communion to these sorts of gospel miracles Jesus performed. "Even as Christ when on earth both healed many sick persons by laying upon them His sacred hands, and also restored many to health at a distance . . . so, while He imparts great graces to those who receive Him worthily in the Adorable Sacrament of the Altar, He is none the less generous towards those who only receive Him in desire."[53] The keystone for this spiritual communion is desire. Everyone cites Thomas on this score. For example, de Liguori: "A spiritual communion, as St. Thomas says (3 p. q. 30, a. 1, ad. 3,) consists in an ardent desire of receiving Jesus Christ in the holy sacrament."[54] For example, Boudon: "It consists, according to St. Thomas, in an ardent desire to receive Jesus Christ in the Most Holy Sacrament and in affectionate sentiments, as if He had really been received."[55] Gallwey connects it to the baptism by desire. "There is, as we know, a baptism of desire, through which men can enter the

51. De Liguori, *The Way of Salvation and of Perfection*, 505.

52. De Liguori, *The Holy Eucharist, vol. 6 of The Ascetical Works*, 124.

53. Martin Von Cochem, *Cochem's Explanation of the Holy Sacrifice of the Mass* (New York: Benziger Brothers, 1896), 254–55.

54. De Liguori, *The True Spouse of Jesus Christ*, 371–72.

55. Henri-Marie Boudon, *The Book of Perpetual Adoration; or The Love of Jesus in the Most Holy Sacrament* (London: R. Washbourne, 1873), 76.

Kingdom of God even though the water has not been poured nor the sacred word pronounced. And as a fervent spiritual communion may bring great grace to the soul which hungers for the Body of the Lord but cannot have It, so, too, can our Lord by graces unseen supply the place of other sacraments."[56]

The emphasis here is upon the burning desire to receive Jesus in Communion, even if not sacramentally, as Vianney says.

> If we are deprived of Sacramental Communion, let us replace it, as far as we can, by spiritual communion, which we can make every moment; for we ought to have always a burning desire to receive the good God.... When we cannot come to church, let us turn towards the tabernacle: a wall cannot separate us from the good God.... We can receive the good God only once a day; a soul on fire with love supplies for this by the desire to receive Him every moment. O man, how great thou art! fed with the Body and Blood of a God! Oh, how sweet a life is this life of union with the good God![57]

Rodríguez mentions the same advantage: that one can "oftener perform it. For sacramental communion can be received once a-week, or at most only once a-day; but spiritual communion may be made several times a-day."[58]

How often? we are driven to ask, and you may find the numbers astonishing. Leonard of Port Maurice says "morning, evening, or night, in church or in your room, and even without asking permission of your confessor."[59] De Liguori says "make during the day many spiritual Communions; at least three."[60] Scupoli reminds that Communion can be practiced in two ways "sacramentally once a day, and spiritually every hour and every moment; [and] thou shouldest not to neglect to take It very frequently in the second

56. Gallwey, *Salvage from the Wreck*, 268.

57. Vianney, *The Little Catechism of the Curé of Ars*, 49.

58. Rodríguez, *The Practice of Christian and Religious Perfection*, vol. 2, 473.

59. Leonard of Port Maurice, *The Hidden Treasure; or, the Value of Excellence of the Holy Sacrifice of the Mass* (Dublin: James Duffy and Co., 1895), 76.

60. Alphonsus de Liguori, *Mental Prayer and the Exercises of a Retreat*, in *Saint Alphonsus de Liguori Selection* (Aeterna Books: s.l., 2016), Kindle 2136.

way."[61] Scaramelli goes further: "these spiritual Communions may be frequently repeated, even a hundred times a day."[62]

How often? We ask again. Persons in Religion are enflamed to such a degree that Faber recalls "the Blessed Agatha of the Cross so pined with love of the Blessed Sacrament that it is said that she would have died if her confessor had not taught her the practice of spiritual communion, and then she used to make two hundred spiritual communions every day."[63] And de Liguori recalls that "Blessed Angela of the Cross, a Dominican nun, went so far as to say: 'If my confessor had not taught me this method of communicating I could scarcely live.' Hence, she used to make a hundred spiritual communions every day, and a hundred more every night. But how, you will ask, could she make so many? St. Augustine answers: 'Give me a lover, and he understands what I say.'"[64]

How often? Until it is a rhythm of life. Mother Drane says Sister Maria de Santiago's "love of the Blessed Sacrament was such that she had at last come to make a spiritual communion at almost every breath she drew."[65] And Faber recalls that Maria Scolastica Muratori "tried to make a spiritual communion every time she raised her eyes or drew her breath, so that, as she said, Were I to die suddenly, I should die as it were inhaling my God"[66] (Faber).

But forget the arithmetic. Here is the point, from Challoner. Spiritual communion is not tied to place or time. It overflows the ritual liturgy, and, building upon the sacramental Communion, the spiritual takes residence in our hearts.

> A spiritual communion may be made, with fruit to the soul, not only as often as we assist at the sacrifice of the altar, but also at any other hour we please, either of the day or night; and this by sigh-

61. Scupoli, *The Spiritual Conflict*, 134.

62. Scaramelli, *Directorium Asceticum*, vol. 1, 657–58.

63. Faber, *The Blessed Sacrament*, 515.

64. De Liguori, *True Spouse of Jesus Christ*, 372.

65. Mother Frances Raphael (Augusta Theodosia Drane), *The Spirit of the Dominican Order, Illustrated from the Lives of Its Saints*, (London: R. & T. Washbourne, Ltd., 1910), 157.

66. Faber, *The Blessed Sacrament*, 519.

> ing after Jesus Christ, by inviting him into our souls, by offering our whole souls to him, by embracing him, and loving him, with all our power. For he loves all them that love him, he is quickly found by all that seek him, and gives himself to all that give themselves to him. . . . This kind of communion is not tied to time or place, but will bring thy God to thee whenever thou pleasest.[67]

Liturgy desires God's glory (theolatry); sin desires one's own glory (autolatry); abnegation combats wrong-headed worship so a person liturgizes the correct God. (To be perfectly clear, I mean liturgize him, and not myself.) That's why this kind of abnegation is liturgical: it arises from grace and leads to glory. Jesus feeds us with his own victimized flesh, Christ empowers his followers to rise with him from their deadened state and challenge their pride of life, the lust of the flesh, and the lust of the eyes (1 Jn 2:16–17).

Satan smirks: "Can a sinner ascend to heaven?" Jesus smiles, and replies: "Yes, over my dead body."

67. Challoner, *Considerations Upon Christian Truths and Christian Duties* part I, 278–79.

Postscript

Labor then directed by the hand of this divine Master, and when you shall be worn out and the Master lets you fall to take another younger, stronger, more apt than you, quietly retire and disappear without murmur to be unknown and forgotten.

Are you not happy to have served God?

Oh! if the pen, the instrument of the loving heart of St. Francis of Sales, had life as I have, how it would have thanked him for having used it and worn it out writing those beautiful pages of the Treatise on the Love of God.

Enviable pen, what has become of thee?
Who knows thee? Who thinks of thee?

But I know that Thou my God, Thou wilt be ever mindful of Thy little instrument, particularly when she shall have become worn and completely useless in Thy service! Oh, grant me to be forgotten, unknown by all and loved by Thee alone, my God!

Adrien Sylvain
Gold Sands

Dates of the Lives of Authors

Alacoque, Margaret Mary. 1647–1690. French Visitation Nun.
Baker, Augustine. 1575–1641. English Benedictine Congregation.
Barbanson, Constantine. 1581–1631. Belgian Capuchin.
Blosius (Louis of Blois). 1506–1566. Flemish Benedictine.
Bona, Giovanni. 1609–1674. Italian Cistercian, cardinal.
Bossuet, Jacques-Bénigne. 1627–1704. French bishop.
Boudon, Henri-Marie. 1624–1702. French abbot.
Bourdaloue, Louis. 1632–1704. French Jesuit preacher.
Boutauld, Michel. 1652–1688. French Jesuit Preacher.
Bruyère, Cécile. 1845–1909. French Benedictine.
Camus, Jean Pierre. 1584–1652. French bishop of Belley.
Canfield, Benedict (William of Filoh). 1564–1610. English theologian, Catholic convert.
Challoner, Richard. 1691–1781. English bishop.
Chardon, Louis. 1595–1651. French Dominican priest.
Collins, Henry. 1827–1919. English Catholic priest.
Crasset, John (Jean). 1618–1692. French Jesuit.
Croiset, John. 1656–1738. French Jesuit.
Cross, Nicolas (also Nicolas of the holy Cross). English Franciscan 1616–1698.
De Bergamo, Gaetano Maria. 1672–1753. Italian Capuchin.
De Bernières-Louvigny, Jean. 1602–1659. French contemplative.
De Bérulle, Pierre. 1575–1629. French cardinal, founder French Oratory.
De Castañiza, Juan. 1555–1599. Spanish Benedictine.
De Caussade, Jean Pierre. 1675–1751. French Jesuit.
De Chantal, Jane Francis. 1572–1641. French Order of the Visitation of Holy Mary.
De Chaugy, Françoise-Madeleine. 1611–1680. French Order of the Visitation of Holy Mary.
De Condren, Charles. 1588–1641. French Oratory.
De Estella, Diego. 1524–1578. Spanish Franciscan.

De Fonseca, Christopher (Cristobal). 1550–1621. Spanish Augustinian.

De Granada, Luis. 1504–1588. Spanish Dominican.

De la Bouillerie, M. L'Abbe. 1810–1882. French Bishop.

De la Colombière, Claude. 1641–1682. French Jesuit.

De Lehen, Edouard. 1807–1867. French Jesuit.

De Liguori, Alphonsus. 1696–1787. Italian Redemptorist.

De Lombez, Ambrose. 1708–1778. French Capuchin.

De Montfort, Louis-Marie Grignion. 1673–1716. French priest.

De Osuna, Francisco. 1492–1540. Spanish Franciscan.

De Paul, Vincent. 1581–1660. French Priest, founder of the Confraternities of Charity.

De Ponte, Louis (Luis de la Puente). 1554–1624. Spanish Jesuit.

De Ravignan, Gustave François Xavier. 1795–1858. French Jesuit.

De Sales, Francis. 1567–1622. French Bishop of Geneva.

De Segur, Louis Gaston. 1820–1881. French prelate and apologist.

Doyle, Francis Cuthbert. 1842–1932. Prefect College of St Edmund's, Douai.

Drane, Augusta Theodosia (Mother Francis Raphael). 1823–1894. English Dominican.

Elizabeth of the Trinity. 1880–1906. French Discalced Carmelite.

Eudes, John. 1601–1680. French founder of The Eudists.

Eymard, Peter. 1811–1868. French Priest.

Faber, Frederick. 1814–1863. English Oratorian.

Fénelon, François. 1651–1715. French Archbishop of Cambrai.

Froget, Barthelemy. 1843–1905. Dominican.

Gertrude, Teresa. 1832–1889. English Carmelite.

Grou, Jean. 1731–1803, French Jesuit.

Guillore, François. 1615–1684. French Jesuit.

Horstius, Jacob Merlo. 1597–1644. Catholic priest.

Huby, Vincent. 1608–1693. French Jesuit.

Huguet, Jean-Joseph. 1812–1884. French Priest.

Jenks, Sylvester. 1656–1714. English priest.

John Evangelist of Boisleduc (Balduke). d. 1637. Dutch Capuchin.

John of Ávila. 1499–1569. Spanish priest, saint, doctor.

John of the Cross. 1542–1591. Spanish Carmelite.

Lacordaire, Jean-Baptiste Henri-Dominique. 1802–1861. French

Dominican.
Lallemant, Louis. 1588–1635. French Jesuit.
Languet de Gergy, Jean-Joseph. 1677–1753. French. Bishop of Soissons, archbishop of Sens.
Lebrun, Charles. 1619–1690. French Eudist.
Leen, Edward. 1885–1944. Irish, Congregation of the Holy Ghost.
Libermann, Francis. 1802–1852. French Spiritan.
Lopez, Gregory. 1542–1596. Spanish, first hermit of New Spain (Mexico).
Malaval, François. 1627–1719. French mystic, blind from birth.
Marie of the Incarnation. 1599–1672. French Ursuline nun in Quebec.
Nepveu, François. 1639–1708. French Jesuit.
Nieremberg, John. 1595–1658. Spanish Jesuit (born Madrid to German parents).
Olier, Jean-Jacques. 1608–1657. French founder of the Sulpicians.
Pollien, François. 1853–1936. French Carthusian.
Quadrupani, Carlo Giuseppe 1740–1806. Italian Barnabite.
Rigoleuc, Jean. 1596–1658. French Jesuit.
Rodriguez, Alphonsus (Alfonso). 1538–1616. Spanish Jesuit priest.
Rogacci, Benedict. 1646–1719. Italian Jesuit.
Saint-Jure, Jean Baptiste. 1588–1657. French Jesuit.
Scaramelli, John Baptist. 1687–1752. Italian Jesuit.
Scupoli, Lorenzo. 1530–1610. Italian priest.
Segneri, Paul. 1624–1694. Italian Jesuit.
Surin, John-Joseph. 1600–1665. French Jesuit.
Teresa of Ávila. 1515–1582. Spanish Discalced Carmelite.
Thérèse of Lisieux. 1873–1897. French Carmelite.
Tronson, Louis. 1622–1700. French Sulpician.
Ullathorne, William Bernard. 1806–1889. Bishop of Birmingham.
Vianney, Jean Baptiste. 1786–1859. French parish priest.

Bibliography

I have not attempted to make an exhaustive bibliography. These are all the authors who have been whispering to me, whether or not they speak aloud as a quotation in the text.

Abelly, Louis. *The Life of the Venerable Servant of God: Vincent de Paul*, vol. 1. New York: New City Press, Vincentian Studies Institute, 1993.

_______. *The Life of the Venerable Servant of God: Vincent de Paul*, vol. 2. New York: New City Press, Vincentian Studies Institute, 1993.

_______. *The Life of the Venerable Servant of God: Vincent de Paul*, vol. 3. New York: New City Press, Vincentian Studies Institute, 1993.

Acarie, Barbe. https://www.madame-acarie.org/en/home-english/

_______. *A Gracious Life. Being the Life of Barbara Acarie*, by Emily Bowles. London: Burns and Oates, 1879.

_______. *Barbe Acarie: Wife and Mystic*, by Lancelot Sheppard. London: Burns and Oates, 1953.

Alacoque, Margaret Mary. *The Autobiography of Saint Margaret Mary.* Charlotte, NC: TAN Books, 2012. Kindle edition.

_______. *The Letters of St. Margaret Mary Alacoque*. Charlotte, NC: TAN Books, 2012. Kindle edition.

Anonymous. *Meditations for Every Day in the Year, Collected from Different Spiritual Writers, and Suited for the Practice Called "'Quarter of an Hour's Solitude.'"* Translated by Edward Mico. New York: Benziger Brothers, 1884.

Anonymous. *The Life of the Venerable F. Louis de Ponte of the Society of Jesus*. London: Thomas Richardson and Son, 1882.

Anonymous. *The Redeemer's Call to Consecrated Souls*. Tarpon Springs, FL: Logos Institute Press, 2012.

Arias, Francis. *The Charity of Jesus Christ*. London: Burns and Oates, 1880.

_______. *An Exhortation to Spirituall Profit*, adjoined to Antonio de Molina, *A Treatise of Mental Prayer*. s.l., Permissu Superiorum, 1617.

_______. *The Little Memorial: Concerning the Good and Fruitful Use of the Sacraments*. Menston: The Scolar Press, 1972.

_______. *A Treatise of Benignity*. English Recusant Literature, v. 339. s.l.: The Scolar Press, 1977

_______. *A Treatise of Patience.* English Recusant Literature, v. 21. s.l: The Scolar Press, 1970.

_______. *The Virtues of Mary, Mother of God.* London: Burns and Oates, 1890.

Ayray, James, John Betham, Angel Bix, et al. *A Select Collection of Catholick [sic] Sermons Preached before their Majesties King James II, Mary Queen-Consort, Catherine Queen-Dowager, etc.*, vol. 1. London: s.n., 1741.

_______. *A Select Collection of Catholick [sic] Sermons Preached before their Majesties King James II, Mary Queen-Consort, Catherine Queen-Dowager, etc.*, vol. 2. London: s.n., 1741.

Baker, Augustine. *Confessions of Venerable Augustine Baker.* London: Burns Oates & Washbourne Ltd., 1922.

_______. *The Fall and Restitution of Man.* Salzburg: Analecta Cartusiana, 2013.

_______. *Holy Wisdom, Or Directions for the Prayer of Contemplation Extracted out of more than Forty Treatises*, ed. R.F. Serenus Cressy. New York: Burns & Oates, 1911.

_______. *The Inner Life of Dame Gertrude More*, vol. 1. London: R.&T. Washbourne, Ltd., 1911.

_______. *The Inner Life and the Writings of Dame Gertrude More*, vol. 2. London: R.&T. Washbourne, Ltd., 1911.

Barbanson, Constantine. *The Secret Paths of Divine Love.* London: Burns Oates & Washbourne Ltd., 1928.

Bellarmine, Robert. *The Autobiography of St. Robert Bellarmine.* The Woodstock Letters, vol. 84, Issue 1, 3–30.

_______. *Saint Robert Bellarmine Collection.* Aeterna Press, s.l., 2016.

_______. *A Short Catechism, or Christian Doctrine.* 1677.

_______. *The Soul's Ascension to God by the Steps of Creation.* London: for Robert Gibson, 1703.

_______. *Spiritual Writings.* New York: Paulist Press, 1989.

Bellecius, Aloysius. *Solid Virtue, or A Treatise on the Obstacles to Solid Virtue, the Means of Acquiring, and Motives for Practicing It.* London: R.&T. Washbourne, Ltd., 1914.

_______. [Bellecio] *Spiritual Exercises According to the Method of Saint Ignatius of Loyola.* London: Burns & Oates, 1876.

Berthier. Jean-Baptiste. *States of the Christian Life and Vocation, According to the Doctors and Theologians of the Church.* New York: P. O'Shea, 1879.

Binet, Etienne. *Divine Favors Granted to Saint Joseph.* Rockford, IL: TAN Books, 1983.

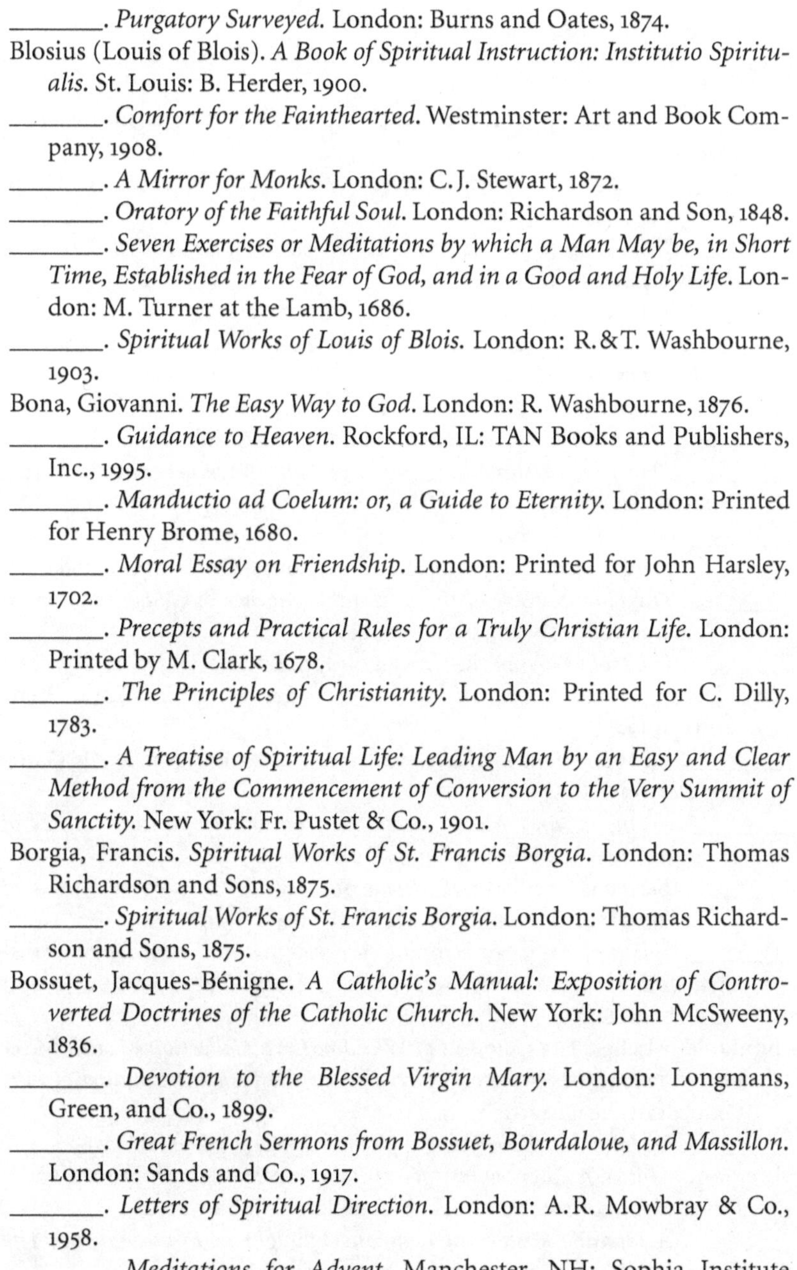

_______. *Purgatory Surveyed.* London: Burns and Oates, 1874.

Blosius (Louis of Blois). *A Book of Spiritual Instruction: Institutio Spiritualis.* St. Louis: B. Herder, 1900.

_______. *Comfort for the Fainthearted.* Westminster: Art and Book Company, 1908.

_______. *A Mirror for Monks.* London: C.J. Stewart, 1872.

_______. *Oratory of the Faithful Soul.* London: Richardson and Son, 1848.

_______. *Seven Exercises or Meditations by which a Man May be, in Short Time, Established in the Fear of God, and in a Good and Holy Life.* London: M. Turner at the Lamb, 1686.

_______. *Spiritual Works of Louis of Blois.* London: R.&T. Washbourne, 1903.

Bona, Giovanni. *The Easy Way to God.* London: R. Washbourne, 1876.

_______. *Guidance to Heaven.* Rockford, IL: TAN Books and Publishers, Inc., 1995.

_______. *Manductio ad Coelum: or, a Guide to Eternity.* London: Printed for Henry Brome, 1680.

_______. *Moral Essay on Friendship.* London: Printed for John Harsley, 1702.

_______. *Precepts and Practical Rules for a Truly Christian Life.* London: Printed by M. Clark, 1678.

_______. *The Principles of Christianity.* London: Printed for C. Dilly, 1783.

_______. *A Treatise of Spiritual Life: Leading Man by an Easy and Clear Method from the Commencement of Conversion to the Very Summit of Sanctity.* New York: Fr. Pustet & Co., 1901.

Borgia, Francis. *Spiritual Works of St. Francis Borgia.* London: Thomas Richardson and Sons, 1875.

_______. *Spiritual Works of St. Francis Borgia.* London: Thomas Richardson and Sons, 1875.

Bossuet, Jacques-Bénigne. *A Catholic's Manual: Exposition of Controverted Doctrines of the Catholic Church.* New York: John McSweeny, 1836.

_______. *Devotion to the Blessed Virgin Mary.* London: Longmans, Green, and Co., 1899.

_______. *Great French Sermons from Bossuet, Bourdaloue, and Massillon.* London: Sands and Co., 1917.

_______. *Letters of Spiritual Direction.* London: A.R. Mowbray & Co., 1958.

_______. *Meditations for Advent.* Manchester, NH: Sophia Institute

Press, 2012.

_______. *Meditations on Mary.* Manchester, NH: Sophia Institute Press, 2015.

_______. *Meditations for Lent.* Manchester, NH: Sophia Institute Press, 2013.

_______. *Selections from Meditations on the Gospels*, vol. 1. Chicago: Henry Regnery Co., 1962.

_______. *Selections from Meditations on the Gospels*, vol. 2. Chicago: Henry Regnery Co., 1962.

_______. *Select Sermons.* London: W. Clarke, 1800.

_______. *A Treatise of Communion Under Both Species.* Paris: Sebastian Marks Cramoisy, 1685.

Boudon, Henri-Marie. *The Book of Perpetual Adoration; or The Love of Jesus in the Most Holy Sacrament.* London: R. Washbourne, 1873.

_______. *Devotion to the Nine Choirs of Holy Angels.* London: Burns, Oates, & Co., 1869.

_______. *God is Everywhere Present.* London, JP Coghlan

_______. *The Hidden Life of Jesus.* London: Burns, Oates, & Co., 1869.

_______. *The Holy Slavery of the Admirable Mother of God.* CreateSpace Independent Publishing Platform, 2013.

_______. *The Holy Ways of the Cross.* London: Burnes, Oates, & Co., 1875.

Bourdaloue, Louis. *Bourdalou* [sic] *at Versailles*, 1670. New York: Brentano's, 1919.

_______. *Eight Sermons for Holy Week and Easter.* London: Wells Gardner, Darton & Co., 1844.

_______. *Sermons, and Moral Discourses, on the Important Duties of Christianity*, vol. 1. Dublin: James Duffy, 1843.

_______. *Sermons, and Moral Discourses, on the Important Duties of Christianity*, vol. 2. Dublin: James Duffy, 1843,

_______. *Spiritual Exercises: Readings for a Retreat of Seven Days. Translated and Abridged from the French of Bourdaloue.* London: Joseph Masters, 1868.

Boutauld, Michel. *The Counsels of Wisdom: Or a Collection of such Maxims of Solomon as are most Necessary for the Prudent Conduct of Life.* Oxford: At the Theatre, 1736.

_______. *A Method of Conversing with God.* Liege: H. Dessain, 1789.

Bremond, Henri. *A Literary History of Religious Thought in France, vol. 1: Devout Humanism.* New York: Macmillan Company, 1928.

_______. *A Literary History of Religious Thought in France*, vol. 2: *The Coming of Mysticism.* New York: Macmillan Company, 1930.

_______. *A Literary History of Religious Thought in France,* vol. 3: *The Triumph of Mysticism.* New York: Macmillan Company, 1935.

Brother Lawrence (Nicholas Herman). *The Practice of the Presence of God the Best Rule of a Holy Life.* New York: Fleming H. Revell Co., 1895.

_______. *The Great Advantages that Arise to a Christian, by Preserving in His Mind a Constant Sense of the Divine Presence; Set Forth in the Life of Nicolas Herman.* Edinburgh: printed for Mr. W. Monro and W. Drummond, 1741.

______. *The Spiritual Maxims of Brother Lawrence, Together with The Character and Gathered Thoughts.* London: H. R. Allenson, (Heart and Life Booklets, No. 12), 1903(?).

Bruyère, Cécile J. *Spiritual Life and Prayer According to Holy Scripture and Monastic Tradition.* New York: Benziger Brothers, 1905.

Burke, Christy. *No Longer Slaves: The Mission of Francis Libermann (1802–1852).* Dublin: Columba Press, 2010.

Butler, Charles. *The Life of Fénelon, Archbishop of Cambray.* London: Longman, Hurst, Rees, and Orme, 1810.

_______. *The Life of Fénelon, To Which are Added the Lives of St Vincent of Paul and Henri-Marie de Boudon.* London: John Murray, 1819.

Camus, Jean Pierre. *The Beauties of St. Francis de Sales.* London: Longman, Rees, Orme, Brown, and Green, 1829.

_______. *A Draught of Eternitie. English Recusant Literature* 1558–1640, vol. 111. Menston: The Scolar Press, 1972.

_______. *The Spirit of St. Francis de Sales.* London: Burns Oates & Washbourne Ltd., 1925.

_______. *A Spirituall Combat,* 1632, in *English Recusant Literature* 1558—1640, vol. 189. London: The Scolar Press, 1974.

_______. *The Spiritual Director, Disinteressed. English Recusant Literature* 1558-1640, Vol. 181. London: The Scolar Press, 1974.

Canfield, Benedict. *A Bright Starre, Leading to, & Centering in, Christ our perfection. The third part of the Rule of Perfection.* London: Henry Overton, 1646.

_______. *The Holy Will of God: A Short Rule of Perfection.* London: Thomas Richardson and Sons, 1878.

_______. *The Rule of Perfection: Contayning a Breif* [sic] *and Perspicuous Abridgement of All the Whole Spiritual Life,* parts 1–2. Rouan, France: Cardin Hamilton, 1609.

Canisius, Peter. *The Devotion of Bondage & Introduction to the Catholic Faith. English Recusant Literature* 1558–1640, vol. 134. London: The Scolar Press, 1973.

Cepari, Virgilio. *The Life of St. Mary Magdalene of Pazzi*. London: Thomas Richardson and Son, 1849.

Challoner, Richard. *Considerations upon Christian Truths and Christian Duties Digested into Meditations for Every Day in the Year, For The First Six Months*, vol. 1. Philadelphia: Eugene Cummiskey, 1874.

_______. *Considerations upon Christian Truths and Christian Duties Digested into Meditations for Every Day in the Year, For The Last Six Months*, vol. 2. Philadelphia: Eugene Cummiskey, 1874.

_______. *The Garden of the Soul: A Manual of Spiritual Exercises, in Which are Included Many Devotions of Recent Practice, and Approved of by the Church*. London: R. Washbourne, 1872.

_______. *Think Well On't: Reflections on the Great Truths of the Christian Religion for Every Day in the Month*. Manchester: T. Haydock, 1801.

Chardon, Louis. *The Cross of Jesus*, vol. 1. St. Louis, MO: B. Herder Book Co., 1957.

_______. *The Cross of Jesus*, vol. 2. St. Louis, MO: B. Herder Book Co., 1959.

Chocarne, Bernard. *The Inner Life of the Very Reverend Pere Lacordaire*. London: R. Washbourne, 1878.

Cisneros, Gracia. *A Book of Spiritual Exercises and Directory for Canonical Hours*. London: Burns & Oates 1876.

Clerissac, Humbert. *The Mystery of the Church*. Cluny Media Edition, 2016.

Codrington, Thomas. *A Sermon Preached before their Majesties, in Saint James's, on Advent-Sunday*. London: Nathaniel Thompson, 1687.

Coleridge, Henry James. *The Baptism of the King: Considerations on the Sacred Passion*. London: Burns and Oates, 1884.

_______. *The Nine Months: The Life of Our Lord in the Womb*. London: Burns and Oates, 1885.

_______. *The Mother of the King: Mary During the Life of Our Lord*. London: Burns and Oates, 1886.

_______. *The Return of the King: Discourses on the Latter Days*. London: Burns and Oates, 1894.

Collins, Henry. *Heaven Opened; or, Our Home in Heaven, and the Way Thither*. London: Thomas Richardson and Son, 1880.

_______. *The Spirit and Mission of the Cistercian Order*. London: Simpkin Marhsall & Co., 1866.

_______. *Spiritual Conferences on the Mysteries of Faith and the Interior Life*. London: R. Washbourne, 1875.

Courbon, Abbe. *Familiar Instructions on Mental Prayer*, vols. 1 & 2. London: Joseph Masters, 1856.

_______. *Meditations on the Passion of our Lord Jesus Christ*. Dublin: Richard Grace and Son, 1833.

Crasset, John. *Christian Considerations; or, Devout Meditations for Every Day in the Year*. New York: P. O'Shea, 1864.

_______. *The Devotion of Calvary; or Meditations on the Passion of Our Lord and Saviour Jesus Christ*. Liverpool: Booker & Co., 1844.

_______. *Meditations for Every Day in the Year from the Christian Considerations of Father John Crasset, S.J.* London: R. Washbourne, 1888.

Croiset, John. *Devotion to the Sacred Heart of Jesus*. London: Burns & Lambert, 1863.

_______. *A Spiritual Retreat for One Day in Every Month*. London: Printed by Thomas Hales, 1704.

Cross, Nicholas. *The Cynosura, or a Saving Star That Leads to Eternity Discovered amidst the Celestial Orbs of David's Psalms, By Way of Paraphrase upon the Miserere*. London: I. Redmayne for Thomas Books, 1679.

_______. (Nicolas of the Holy Cross) *Pious Reflections, and Devout Prayers, on Several Points of Faith and Morality, from Man's Creation to His Consummation*. Doway: M. Mairesse, 1695.

Dalgairns, John Bernard. *The Devotion to the Heart of Jesus*. London: Thomas Richardson and Sons, 1853.

_______. *The Holy Communion, Its Philosophy, Theology, and Practice*. New York: The Catholic Publication House, 1868.

De Agreda, Mary. *The Mystical City of God: Complete Edition*. London: Catholic Way Publishing, 2013.

De Alacantra, Peter. *A Golden Treatise of Mental Prayer, With Divers Spiritual Rules and Directions*. Philadelphia: M. Fithian, 1844.

De Bausset, M.L.F. *The Life of Fénelon, Archbishop of Cambrai*, 2 vols. London: Sherwood, Neely, and Jones, 1810.

De Bergamo, Gaetano Maria. *The Humility of Heart*. Mandeville, LA: Founding Father Films Publishing, 2015.

_______. *Thoughts and Affections on the Passion of Jesus Christ For Every Day of the Year, Taken from Holy Scripture and the Writings of the Fathers of the Church*. New York: Benziger Brothers, 1905.

De Bernières-Louvigny, Jean. *The Interior Christian in Eight Books*. New York: The Catholic Publication Society, 1843.

De Bérulle, Pierre. *Discourses on the State and Grandeurs of Jesus: The Ineffable Union of the Deity with Humanity*. Washington, DC: Catholic University of America Press, 2023.

De Blois, Georges. *A Benedictine of the Sixteenth Century (Blosius)*. London: Burns and Oates, 1878.

De Bonilla, John. *Pax Animae: A Short Treatise.* (Attributed to Peter Alcantara). London: Burns & Oates, n.d.

De Bovilla, John. *The Quiet of the Soul.* London: Thomas Richardson and Sons, 1876.

De Castañiza, Juan. *The Spiritual Conflict and Conquest.* London: Burns and Oates, 1874.

_______. *The Spiritual Conflict and Conquest*, ed. Jerome Vaughan. London: Burns & Oates, Ltd., 1903.

De Caussade, Jean Pierre. *Abandonment to Divine Providence.* St. Louis: B. Herder Book Company, 1921.

_______. *On Prayer: Spiritual instructions on the Various States of Prayer According to the Doctrine of Bossuet, Bishop of Meaux.* New York: Benziger Brothers, 1931.

_______. *The Sacrament of the Present Moment.* San Francisco: HarperSanFrancisco Reissue edition, 2009.

De Chantal, Jane Frances Fremyot. *The Depositions of St. Jane Frances de Chantal in the Cause of the Canonisation of St. Francis de Sales* in *Library of St. Francis de Sales*, vol. 6. London: Burnes & Oates, Ltd., 1908.

_______. *Her Exhortations, Conferences and Instructions.* Westminster, MD: The Newman Bookshop, 1947.

_______. *Meditations for Retreats taken from Writings of St. Francis de Sales.* New York: Benziger Brothers, 1900.

_______. *Selected Letters of Saint Jane Frances de Chantal.* London: R. & T. Washbourne, Ltd., 1918.

De Chaugy, Françoise-Madeleine. *Life of Mother Marie Jacqueline Favre, to which is added Lives of other Mothers of the First Religious of the Visitation of Holy Mary.* London: R. Washbourne, 1876.

_______. *The Lives of S. Jane Frances de Chantal, St. Rose of Viterbo, and B. Mary of Oignies*, vol. II. London: Richardson and Son, 1852.

De Condren, Charles. *The Eternal Sacrifice.* London: Thomas Baker, 1906.

De Estella, *Meditations on the Love of God.* London: Burns & Oates, 1898.

_______. *Contempt for the World and the Vanities Thereof.* S. Omers: for John Heigham, 1622.

De Fonseca, Christopher. *Theion Enotikon: A Discourse of Holy Love, by which the Soul is United Unto God.* London: printed by J. Flesher, 1652.

De Granada, Luis. *Considerations on the Mysteries of the Faith.* London: Joseph Masters, 1862.

_______. *Counsels on Holiness of Life: Being the First Part of The Sinner's Guide.* London: Rivingtons, 1869.

_______. *The Conversion of a Sinner.* London: Printed by Thomas Creede, 1598.

_______. *An Excellent Treatise of Consideration and Prayer.* London: John Harison, 1601.

_______. *An Exhortation to Alms-Deeds.* London: J. P. Coghlan, 1775.

_______. *Fr. Granada's Meditations Containing Fourteen Devout Exercises for the Seven Days of the Week.* London: Joseph Browne, 1623.

_______. *Life of Dom Bartholomew of the Martyrs.* London: Thomas Baker, 1890.

_______. *A Memorial of a Christian Life.* New York: The Catholic Publication Society, 1870.

_______. *Meditations on the Lord's Prayer,* subjoined to the life of Nicolas Herman in *The Great Advantages that Arise to a Christian by Preserving in his Mind a constant Sense of the Divine Presence.* Edinburgh: Printed for Mr. W. Monro and W. Drummond, 1741.

_______. *Of Prayer and Meditation, Containing Fourteen Meditations for the Seven Days of the Week.* London: Printed by W.I. For Edward White, 1611.

_______. *The Sinner's Guide in Two Books.* Philadelphia: Henry McGrath, 1845.

_______. *Summa of the Christian Life,* vol. 1. St. Louis: TAN books, 1979.

_______. *Summa of the Christian Life,* vol. 2. St. Louis: TAN books, 1979.

_______. *Summa of the Christian Life,* vol. 3. St. Louis: TAN books, 1979.

De la Bedoyere, Michael. *The Archbishop and the Lady.* New York: Patheon, 1956.

De la Bouillerie, M. L'Abbe. *Hours Before the Altar; or, Meditations on the Holy Eucharist.* London: Richardson and Son, 1858.

_______. *The Eucharist and the Christian Life.* London: R. Washbourne 1875.

De la Colombière, Claude. *Faithful Servant: Spiritual Retreats and Letters of Blessed Claude La Colombière.* St. Louis, MO: B. Herder Book Co., 1960.

_______. *Sermons: vol. 1, Christian Conduct.* DeKalb, IL: NIU Press, 2014.

_______. *The Spiritual Direction of Saint Claude de la Colombière.* San Francisco: Ignatius Press, 1998.

De Laredo, Bernardino. *The Ascent of Mount Sion.* Ed. E. Allison Peers, New York: Harper & Brothers, 1950.

De Lehen, Edouard. *The Way of Interior Peace.* New York: Benziger Brothers, 1888.

De Liguori, Alphonsus. *Saint Alphonsus de Liguori Collection: 20 Books.* Aeterna Press, Kindle book, 2016.

_______. *Alphonsus de Liguori: Selected Writings.* New York: Paulist Press, 1999.

_______. *The Great Means of Salvation and of Perfection.* New York: Benziger Brothers, 1886.

_______. *The Glories of Mary.* New York: P. J. Kenedy & Sons, 1888.

_______. *The Holy Mass*, vol. 13 of *The Complete Works of Saint Alphonsus de Liguori, The Ascetical Works.* New York: Benziger Brothers, 1889.

_______. *The Holy Eucharist*, vol. 6 of *The Complete Works of Saint Alphonsus de Liguori, The Ascetical Works.* New York: Benziger Brothers, 1887.

_______. *The Passion and the Death of Jesus Christ.* New York: Benziger Brothers, 1887.

_______. *Preparation for Death.* Philadelphia: J. B. Lippincott & Co., 1869.

_______. *The True Spouse of Jesus Christ, or, The Nun Sanctified by the Virtues of Her State.* New York: Benziger Brothers, 1899.

_______. *Uniformity with God's Will.* Christian Classics Ethereal Library, https://www.ccel.org/ccel/alphonsus/uniformity.html

_______. *The Way of Salvation and Perfection*, vol. 2 of *The Complete Works of Saint Alphonsus de Liguori, The Ascetical Works.* New York: Benziger Brothers, 1886.

De Lombez, Ambrose. *A Treatise on Interior Peace.* New York: Alba House, 1996.

_______. *A Treatise on the Joy of the Christian Soul.* London: S. Anselm's Society, 1894.

De Losa, Francisco. *The Life of Gregory Lopez, a Hermit in America.* Boston: Henry V. Degan, 1856.

_______. *The Holy Life of Gregory Lopez, a Spanish Hermit in the West-Indies.* London, s.n., 1675.

De Montalembert, Charles. *Memoir of the Abbe Lacordaire.* London: Richard Bentley, 1863.

De Montfort, Louis. *God Alone: The Collected Writings of St. Louis Mary de Montfort.* Bay Shore, NY: Montfort Publications, 1988.

_______. *The Love of Eternal Wisdom.* Bay Shore, NY: Montfort Publications, 1960.

_______. *The Saint Louis de Montfort Collection.* London: Catholic Way Publishing, 2013.

_______. *The Secret of Sanctity Revealed to Mary.* Boston: Thomas B. Noonan & Co., 1887.

_______. *The Secret of the Rosary.* Bay Shore, NY: Montfort Publications, 2004.

_______. *True Devotion to Mary.* Bay Shore, NY: Montfort Publications, 1954.

De Osuna, Francisco. *The Third Spiritual Alphabet.* New York: Benziger Brothers, 1931.

De Paul, Vincent. *Some Counsels of S. Vincent de Paul, to which is appended The Thoughts of Mademoiselle le Gras.* London: Heath, Cranton & Ouseley, 1915.

_______. *Correspondence, Conferences, Documents*, vol. 9. New York: New City Press, 2005.

De Paz, Alvarez. *The Life of Our Lord Jesus Christ in Meditations.* London: B. Herder Book Co., 1933.

De Ponlevoy. *The Life of Father de Ravignan of the Society of Jesus.* Dublin: William Kelly, 1869.

De Ponte, Louis. *Meditations on the Mysteries of Our Holy Faith*, vol. 1. London: Richardson and Son, 1852.

_______. *Meditations on the Mysteries of Our Holy Faith*, vol. 2. London: Richardson and Son, 1852.

_______. *Meditations on the Mysteries of Our Holy Faith*, vol. 3. London: Richardson and Son, 1852.

_______. *Meditations on the Mysteries of Our Holy Faith*, vol. 4. London: Richardson and Son, 1853.

_______. *Meditations on the Mysteries of Our Holy Faith*, vol. 5. London: Richardson and Son, 1854.

_______. *Meditations on the Mysteries of Our Holy Faith*, vol. 6. London: Richardson and Son, 1854.

_______. *A Treatise on Mental Prayer.* London: Burns Oates & Washbourne Ltd., 1929.

De Ravignan, Gustave François Xavier. *Conferences on the Spiritual Life.* London: R. Washbourne, 1873.

_______. *On The Life and Institute of the Jesuits.* Philadelphia: W. J. Cunningham, 1845.

_______. *Ravignan's Last Retreat.* London: Burns and Oates, 1859.

De Rouville, Alexandre Joseph [Abbe d'Herouville]. *The Imitation of the Blessed Virgin.* London: Keating, Brown, & Keating, 1816.

De Sales, Francis. *Finding God's Will for You.* Manchester, NH: Sophia Institute Press, 1998.

_______. *Introduction to the Devout Life.* New York: Vintage Spiritual Classics, 2002.

_______. *Library of St. Francis de Sales*: vol. 1, *Letters to Persons in the World.* London: Burns & Oates, Ltd., 1894.

_______. *Library of St. Francis de Sales*: vol. 3, *The Catholic Controversy.* London: Burns & Oates, Ltd, 1909.

_______. *Library of St. Francis de Sales*: vol. 4, *Letters to Persons in Religion.* London: Burns & Oates, Ltd., 1909.

_______. *Library of St. Francis de Sales*: vol. 5, *The Spiritual Conferences.* London: Burns & Oates, Ltd., 1909.

_______. *Library of St. Francis de Sales*: vol. 6, I. *The Mystical Explanation of the Canticle of Canticles: By St. Francis de Sales; II. The Depositions of St. Jane Frances de Chantal in the Cause of the Canonisation of St. Francis de Sales.* London: Burns & Oates, Ltd., 1908.

_______. *Maxims and Counsels of St. Francis de Sales for Every Day of the Year.* Dublin: M. H. Gill & Son, 1884.

_______. *Mystical Exposition of the Canticle of Canticles.* DeSales University: Salesian Center for Faith & Culture, 2008.

_______. *The Mystical Flora: The Christian Life Under the Emblem of Plants.* Dublin: M.H. Gill & Son, 1877.

_______. *Practical Piety.* London: Burns and Lambert, 1851.

_______. *The Sermons of St. Francis de Sales*: vol. 4, *For Advent and Christmas.* Frederick, MD: Visitation Monastery, 1987.

_______. *The Sermons of St. Francis de Sales*: vol. 2, *On Our Lady.* Frederick, MD: Visitation Monastery, 1985.

_______. *The Spiritual Director of Devout and Religious Souls.* Dublin: printed by James Mehain, 1777.

_______. *St. Francis de Sales, Selected Letters*, ed. Elisabeth Stopp. New York: Harper & Brothers, 1960.

_______. *Sermons On Prayer.* https://www.theworkofgod.org/Library/Sermons/F_Sales.htm

_______. *Sermons on the Eucharist.* DeSales University, Salesian Center for Faith & Culture, 2005.

_______. *On the Preacher and Preaching.* Chicago: Regnery, 1964.

_______. *The Consoling Thoughts of St. Francis de Sales, Gathered From His Writings, and Arranged in Order by the Rev. Pere Huguet.* Dublin: M.H. Gill & Son, 1877.

_______. *Treatise on the Love of God.* Blacksburg, VA: Wilder Publications, 2011.

De Sales, Francis, and Jane de Chantal. *Letters of Spiritual Direction.* New York: Paulist Press, 1988.

De Sales, Francis, and Crasset, Jean. *The Secret of Sanctity According to St. Francis de Sales and Father Crasset, SJ.* New York: Benziger Brothers, 1892.

De Segur, Louis Gaston. *The Blind Friend of the Poor; Reminiscences of the Life and Works of Mgr. de Segur by One of His Spiritual Children.* New York: Benziger Brothers, 1883.

_______. *Confession: A Little book for the Reluctant.* New York: P. O'Shea, 1875.

_______. *Familiar Instructions and Evening Lectures on All the Truths of Religion*, vol. 1. London: Burns & Oates, 1878.

_______. *Familiar Instructions and Evening Lectures on All the Truths of Religion*, vol. 2. London: Burns & Oates, 1881.

_______. *On Holy Communion.* London: R. &T. Washbourne, Ltd., 1912.

_______. *Holy Communion.* New York: Paulist Press, 1915.

_______. *Plain Talk about the Protestantism of Today.* London: Thomas Richardson and Son, 1874.

_______. *Short and Familiar Answers to the Most Common Objections urged against Religion.* New York: P. O'Shea, 1880.

Doyle, Francis Cuthbert. *The Life of Gregory Lopez.* London: R. Washbourne, 1876.

_______. *Lectures for Boys*, vol. 1. *The Sundays of the Year, our Lady's Festivals; the Passion of our Lord; the Sacred Heart.* London: R. Washbourne, 1896.

_______. *Lectures for Boys,* vol. 2. London: R. &T. Washbourne, 1900.

_______. *Lectures for Boys,* vol. 3. London: R. &T. Washbourne, 1900.

_______. *Principles of Religious Life.* London: R. &T. Washbourne, Ltd, 1906.

Drane, Augusta Theodosia. *Life of Mother Margaret Mary Hallahan.* London: Longmans, Green, Reader, and Dyer, 1869.

_______. *The Life of St Dominic with Sketch of Dominican Order.* London: Burns Oates & Washbourne Ltd., 1857.

_______. *A Memoir of Mother Francis Raphael.* London: Longmans, Green and Co., 1904.

_______. *The Morality of Tractarianism.* London: William Pickering, 1850.

_______. *Songs in the Light and Other Poems.* London: Burns Oates & Washbourne, 1887.

_______. (Mother Frances Raphael) *The Spirit of the Dominican Order, Illustrated from the Lives of Its Saints.* London: R. &T. Washbourne, Ltd., 1910.

Duguet, Jacques Joseph. *The Characters and Properties of True Charity Displayed.* London: C. Davis, 1737.

_______. *The Principles of the Christian Faith*, vol. 1. Edinburgh: Printed

for G. Hamilton & J. Balfour, J. Traill, W. Miller, and J. Brown, 1755.
_______. *The Principles of the Christian Faith*, vol. 2. Edinburgh: Printed for G. Hamilton & J. Balfour, J. Traill, W. Miller, and J. Brown, 1755.

Elizabeth of the Trinity. *The Complete Works: Letters from Carmel*, vol. 2. Washington, DC: ICS Publications, 2014.

_______. *I Have Found God: Complete Works*, vol. 1. Washington, DC: ICS Publications, 2014.

_______. *The Praise of Glory: Reminiscences of Sr. Elizabeth of the Trinity.* London: R. & T. Washbourne Ltd., 1914.

_______. *Sister Elizabeth of the Trinity: Spiritual Writings. Letters, Retreats, and Unpublished Notes*, ed. M. M. Philipon. New York: P. J. Kenedy & Sons, 1962.

Eudes, John. *The Admirable Heart of Mary.* New York: P. J. Kenedy & Sons, 1948.

_______. *Letters and Shorter Works.* New York: P. J. Kenedy & Sons, 1948.

_______. *The Life and Kingdom of Jesus in Christian Souls.* New York: P. J. Kennedy & Sons, 1946.

_______. *Man's Contract with God in Baptism.* Philadelphia: Peter F. Cunningham, 1859.

_______. *Meditations on Various Subjects.* New York: P. J. Kenedy & Sons, 1947.

_______. *Sacred Heart of Jesus.* New York: P. J. Kenedy & Sons, 1946.

_______. *St. John Eudes: Selections from his Writings.* London: Burns Oates & Washbourne Ltd., 1925.

_______. *The Priest: His Dignity and Obligations.* New York: P. J. Kenedy & Sons, 1947.

Eymard, Peter. *The Divine Eucharist, First Series: The Real Presence.* New York: Fathers of the Blessed Sacrament, 1907.

_______. *The Divine Eucharist, Second Series: Holy Communion.* New York: The Sentinel Press, 1927.

_______. *The Divine Eucharist, Third Series: Retreats at the Feet of Jesus Eucharistic.* New York: Fathers of the Blessed Sacrament, 1909.

_______. *The Divine Eucharist, Extracts from the Writings and Sermons of Venerable Pierre-Julien Eymard, Fourth Series.* New York: Fathers of the Blessed Sacrament, 1912.

_______. *Eucharistic Handbook for Members of the People's Eucharistic League.* New York: The Sentinel Press, 1948.

_______. *How to Get More out of Communion.* Manchester, NH: Sophia Institute Press, 2000.

_______. *In the Light of the Monstrance.* New York: Blessed Sacrament Fathers, 1947.

_______. *Life and Letters of Saint Peter Julian Eymard*, vol. 1. Electronic version by Curia Generalizia, Congregation of the Blessed Sacrament, Rome, 2010.

_______. *Life and Letters of Saint Peter Julian Eymard*, vol. 2. Electronic version by Curia Generalizia, Congregation of the Blessed Sacrament, Rome, 2010.

_______. *Month of Saint Joseph*. New York: Sentinel Press, 1948.

_______. *Month of Our Lady of the Blessed Sacrament*. New York: Sentinel Press, 1903.

_______. *Rule of Life*. Congregation of the Blessed Sacrament, 1973.

Faber, Frederick. *All for Jesus: or, The Easy Ways of Divine Love*. Baltimore: John Murphy & Co., 1855.

_______. *Bethlehem*. London: Thomas Richardson and Son, 1860.

_______. *The Blessed Sacrament: or, The Works and Ways of God*. London: Burns Oates & Washbourne Ltd., 1861.

_______. *The Creator and the Creature, or, The Wonders of Divine Love*. London: Thomas Richardson and Son, 1857.

_______. *The Foot of the Cross: or, The Sorrows of Mary*. London: Thomas Richardson and Son, 1858.

_______. *Ethel's Book; or, Tales of the Angels*. London: Thomas Richardson and Son, 1858.

_______. *Growth in Holiness; or, The Progress of the Spiritual Life*. Baltimore: John Murphy & Co., 1855.

_______. *Notes on Doctrinal and Spiritual Subjects: Mysteries and Festivals*, vol. 1. London: Thomas Richardson and Son, 1872.

_______. *Notes on Doctrinal and Spiritual Subjects: The Faith and the Spiritual Life* vol. 2. London: Thomas Richardson and Son, 1866.

_______. *Spiritual Conferences*. New York: Benziger Brothers, 1800.

_______. *The Precious Blood; or, The Price of Our Salvation*. London: Burns & Oates, Ltd., 1860.

Falloux, Frederic Alfred Pierre, (Comte de). *Life and Letters of Madame Swetchine*. New York: The Catholic Publication House, 1869.

_______. *Tracts on the Church and Her Offices*. London: J. G. F. & J. Rivington, 1840.

Fathers of the Society of Jesus. *Sermons*, vol. 1. London: Burns and Oates, 1870.

_______. *Sermons*, vol. 2. London: Burns and Oates, 1872.

_______. *Sermons*, vol. 3. London: Burns and Oates, 1875.

Fénelon, François. *The Archbishop of Cambray's Pastoral Letter Concerning the Love of God*. London: Robert Nelson, 1715.

_______. *Christian Perfection.* New York: Harper & Brothers, 1947.
_______. *The Complete Fénelon.* Brewster, MA: Paraclete Press, 2008.
_______. *A Demonstration of the Existence of God.* London: John Murray, 1769.
_______. *An English Nun in Exile Translates the Spiritual Letters of Archbishop Fénelon to Madame Guyon.* http://www.umilta.net/cambray2.html
_______. *Dialogues of the Dead.* London: D. Browne, 1760.
_______. *Directions for a Holy Life, and the Attaining Christian Perfection.* London: Darton & Harvey, 1795.
_______. *Dissertation on Pure Love.* London: sold by G. Thomson, 1750.
_______. *Extracts from the Writings of Francis Fénelon, with some Memoirs of His Life,* ed. John Kendall. Philadelphia: Kimber, Conrad & Co., 1804.
_______. *Fénelon: Letters of Love and Counsel,* ed. John McEwen. New York: Harcourt, Brace & World, Inc., 1964.
_______. *Fénelon: Selected Writings.* New York: Paulist Press, 2006.
_______. *Letters and Reflections,* ed. Thomas Kepler. New York: The World Publishing Co., 1955.
_______. *Letters to the Duke of Burgundy.* Dublin: W. Watson, 1758.
_______. *Maxims of the Saints,* www.ccel.org/ccel/fenelon/maxims/maxims.htm.
_______. *On the Use of the Bible.* London: Booker, New Bond Street, 1837.
_______. *Pious Thoughts Concerning the Knowledge and Love of God.* London: W. and J. Innys, 1720.
_______. *Sixteen Short Sermons.* Boston: New-England Tract Society, 1815.
_______. *Spiritual Letters of Archbishop Fénelon. Letters to Men.* London: Rivingtons, 1877.
_______. *Spiritual Letters of Archbishop Fénelon. Letters to Women.* London: Longmans, Green, and Co., 1921.
_______. *Spiritual Letters of François de Salignac de La Mothe Fénelon* [to Countess Gramont]. Cornwall-on-Hudson, NY: Idlewild Press, 1945.
_______. *Spiritual Progress.* New York: M. W. Dodd, 1853.
_______. *The Seeking Heart.* Jacksonville, FL: SeedSowers Publishing, 1992.
_______. *Telemachus, son of Ulysses.* New York: Cambridge University Press, 1994.
_______. *Three Dialogues on Pulpit Eloquence.* Philadelphia: John McVey, 1897.

_______. *Thoughts on Spiritual Subjects.* Boston: Samuel G. Simpkins, 1843.

Foley, H. *The Life of Blessed Alphonsus Rodríguez.* London: Burns and Oates, 1873.

Froget, Barthelemy. *The Indwelling of the Holy Spirit in the Souls of the Just.* New York: Paulist Press, 1921.

Gabriel of Mary Magdalen. *Divine Intimacy: Meditations on the Interior Life for Every Day of the Liturgical Year.* Rockford, IL: TAN Books and Publishers, Inc., 1996.

Gallwey, Peter. *The Lady Chapel and Dr. Pusey's Peacemaker.* London: Burns, Lambert & Oates, 1865.

_______. *Salvage from the Wreck: A Few Memories of Friends Departed, Preserved in Funeral Discourses.* London: Burns & Oates, 1889.

_______. *The Watches of the Sacred Passion with Before and After*, vol. 1. London: Art and Book Company and Leamington, 1896.

_______. *The Watches of the Sacred Passion with Before and After*, vol. 2. London: Art and Book Company and Leamington, 1896.

_______. *Twelve Lectures on Ritualism*, vol. 1. London: Burns and. Oates, 1879.

_______. *Twelve Lectures on Ritualism*, vol. 2. London: Burns and. Oates, 1879.

Gavin, Martin. *Memoirs of Father P. Gallwey.* London: Burns & Oates, 1913.

Gay, Charles. *The Christian Life and Virtues Considered in the Religious State*, vol. 1. London: Burns & Oates, 1878.

_______. *The Christian Life and Virtues Considered in the Religious State*, vol. 2. London: Burns & Oates, 1878.

_______. *The Christian Life and Virtues Considered in the Religious State*, vol. 3. London: Burns & Oates, 1879.

_______. *The Religious Life and the Vows.* London: Burnes & Oates, 1989.

Gerbet, Olympe Philippe. *The Lily of Israel: The Life of the Blessed Virgin.* Dublin: M.H. Gill and Son, n.d.

_______. *Considerations on the Eucharist viewed as the Generative Dogma of Catholic Piety.* London: C. Dolman, 1840.

Gilbert, Alphonse. *A Gentle Way to God: The Spiritual Teaching of Francis Libermann CSSp.* London: Paraclete Press, 1990.

_______. *You Have Laid Your Hand on Me: a Message of Ven. Francis Libermann for Our Time.* Pittsburgh: Duquesne, University, 2021.

Gilli, Don Gaspar. *The Month of Mary According to the Spirit of St. Francis of Sales.* London: Robert Washbourne, 1890

Giraud, Sylvain-Marie. *Jesus Christ Priest and Victim*. London: R.&T. Washbourne, Ltd., 1914.

_______. *The Spirit of Sacrifice and the Life of Sacrifice in the Religious State*. New York: Benziger Brothers, 1905.

Goepfert, Prosper. *The Life of the Venerable Francis Mary Paul Libermann*. Dublin: M.H. Gill & Son, 1881.

Goldie, Francis. *The Life of St. Alonso Rodríguez*. London: Burns and Oates, 1889.

Gonnelieu, Jerome. *The Daily Exercises of a Christian Life*. London: Printed at S. Omer's, 1689.

Gorday, Peter J. *François Fénelon: A Biography—The Apostle of Pure Love*. Brewster, MA: Paraclete Press, 2012.

Grou, Jean Nicolas. *The Characteristics of True Devotion*. New York: Benziger Brothers, 1895.

_______. *The Christian Sanctified by the Lord's Prayer*. New York: Thomas Whitaker, 1885.

_______. *The Hidden Life of the Soul*, selections by Henrietta Lear. London: Rivingtons, 1871.

_______. *How to Pray*. London: Thomas Baker, 1901.

_______. *Manual for Interior Souls: A Collection of Unpublished Writings*. London: S. Anselm's Society, 1890.

_______. *The Interior of Jesus and Mary*, vol. 1. New York: Benziger Brothers, 1893.

_______. *The Interior of Jesus and Mary*, vol. 2. Dublin: James Duffy, 1847.

_______. *Meditations Upon the Love of God*. London: J.T. Hayes, 1905.

_______. *Morality, Extracted from the Confessions of Saint Austin*, vol. 1. London: J. P. Coghlan, 1791.

_______. *Morality, Extracted from the Confessions of Saint Austin*, vol. 2. London: J.P. Coghlan, 1791.

_______. *The Practical Science of the Cross in the Use of the Sacraments of Penance and the Eucharist*. London: Joseph Masters, 1871.

_______. *Self-Consecration, or the Gift of One's Self to God*. New York: E. & J.B. Young & Co., 1887.

_______. *The School of Jesus Christ*. London: Burns Oates & Washbourne Ltd., 1932.

_______. *The Spiritual Maxims of Père Grou*. London: J.T. Hayes, 1874.

Grunewald, Charles. *The Venerable Francis Mary Paul Libermann*. Detroit: Fathers of the Holy Ghost, 1902.

Guillore, François. *Self-Renunciation*. London: Rivingtons, 1871.

_______. *Spiritual Guidance*. London: Rivingtons, 1873.

Guyon, Jeanne. *A Short and Easy Method of Prayer*. https://www.ccel.org/ccel/g/guyon/prayer/cache/prayer.pdf.

_______. *Justifications*, 3 vols. Linden, MI: Peter-John Parisis, 2004.

_______. *On the Way to God: State of Union*. https://hendersonvilletinting.com/StudyingGodsWord/Guyon/JeanneGuyonOnTheWayToGod.pdf.

_______. *The Prison Narratives*. New York: Oxford University Press, 2012.

_______. *The Song of Songs of Solomon*. New York: A.W. Dennett, 1879.

_______. *The Unabridged Collected Works of Jeanne Guyon*. Kahley House Publishing, 2006.

Harpain, Marie Eustelle. *Angel of the Eucharist: The Writings of Marie-Eustelle Harpain*, translation and notes by J. Stephen Russell. Brooklyn, NY: Angelico Press, 2026.

Horstius, James Merlo. *The Paradise of the Christian Soul, Delightful for Its Choicest Pleasures of Piety of Every Kind*. London: Burns & Lambert, 1850.

Huby, Vincent. *The Spiritual Retreat of the Reverend Father Vincent Huby*. Philadelphia: Printed for Mathew Carey, 1795.

_______. *Spiritual Works of Pere Vincent Huby, S.J.* London: Burns Oates & Washbourne Ltd. 1930.

Ignatius of Loyola. *The Autobiography of St. Ignatius*. New York: Benziger Brothers, 1900.

_______ *Letters and Instructions of St. Ignatius Loyola*, vol. 1. St. Louis: B. Herder, 1914.

_______. *The Letters of St. Ignatius of Loyola*. Chicago: Loyola University Press, 1959.

_______. *The Spiritual Exercises of St. Ignatius*, transl. Louis Puhl. Westminster, MD: The Newman Press, 1951.

Janet, Paul. *Life and Works of Fénelon*. London: Sir Isaac Pitman & Sons, Ltd., 1914.

Jenks, Sylvester. *The Blind Obedience of an Humble Penitent: The Best Cure for Scruples*. London: Burns Oates and Washbourne, 1926.

_______. *A Contrite and Humble Heart*. Dublin: P. Wogan, 1799.

_______. *An Essay Upon the Art of Love Containing an Exact Anatomy of Love and all the Other Passions which Attend it*. London: s.n. 1702.

_______. *Practical Discourses Upon the Morality of the Gospel*, vol. 1. London: s.n., 1699.

_______. *Practical Discourses Upon the Morality of the Gospel*, vol. 2. London: s.n., 1700.

John Evangelist of Boisleduc (Balduke). *The Kingdom of God in the Soul*.

London: Sheed & Ward, 1930.

John of Ávila. *Audi, Filia—Listen, O Daughter.* New York: Paulist Press, 2006.

_______. *The Holy Ghost.* London: Scepter Limited, 1959.

_______. *Letters of Blessed John of Ávila.* London: Burns & Oates Ltd., 1904.

John of St. Samson. *Prayer, Aspiration and Contemplation.* New York: Alba House, 1975.

John of the Angels. *Conquest of the Kingdom of God.* St. Louis, MO: B. Herder Book Co., 1957.

_______. (Juan de Los Angeles) *The Loving Struggle between God and the Soul in which the triumphs and greatness of love are treated and by which is taught the most excellent way for the affections.* London: The Saint Austin Press, 2001.

John of the Cross. *The Complete Works of Saint John of the Cross,* vol. 1. London: Longman, Green, Longman, Roberts & Green, 1864.

_______. *The Complete Works of Saint John of the Cross,* vol. 2. London: Longman, Green, Longman, Roberts & Green, 1864.

Kelly, Bernard. *Life Began at Forty: The Second Conversion of Francis Libermann.* Dublin: Paraclete Press, 2005.

Koren, Henry J. *The Spiritans: A History of the Congregation of the Holy Ghost.* Spiritan Series 1. Pittsburgh: Duquesne University Press, 1958.

Lacordaire, Henri-Dominique. *Jesus Christ, God, God and Man. Conferences Delivered at Notre Dame in Paris.* London: Chapman and Hall, 1884.

_______. *Conferences of the Rev. Pere Lacordaire, Delivered in the Cathedral of Notre Dame, in Paris.* New York: P. O'Shea, 1870.

_______. *Letters to Young Men.* London: Art and Book Company, 1903.

_______. *Life: Conferences Delivered at Toulouse.* New York: P. O'Shea, 1875.

_______. *Life of Saint Dominic.* London: Burns and Oates, 1883.

_______. *Saint Mary Magdalene.* London: Thomas Richardson and Sons, 1860.

_______. *An Historical Sketch of the Order of St Dominic; or, a Memorial to the French People.* New York: P. O'Shea, 1869.

_______. *The Testament of Henri-Dominique Lacordaire.* Translated by the Brothers George and Richard Christian, 2010.

Lallemant, Louis. *The Spiritual Doctrine of Father Louis Lallemant,* ed. Frederick Faber. London: Burns & Lambert, 1855.

_______. *The Spiritual Doctrine of Louis Lallemant,* ed. Patricia Ranum. Boston: Boston College Institute of Jesuit Sources, 2016.

Lancicius, Nicholas (Mikolaj Lczycki). *Select Works vol. 1: The Yearly Eight Days' Retreat and How to Profit by It.* London: Burns & Oates, 1884.

_______. *Select Works vol. 2: On Rash Judgments, and On Aridity.* London: Burns & Oates, 1881.

Landriot, Jean-François. *The Valiant Woman: A Series of Discourses Intended for the use of Women living in the World.* London: Burns, Oates & Company, 1872.

_______. *Sins of the Tongue and Jealousy in Woman's Life; Followed by Discourses on Rash Judgments, Patience, and Grace.* London: Burns and Oates, 1873.

_______. *Conferences on the Holy Spirit.* Oxford: A.R. Mowbray & Co., 1899.

Languet de Gergy, Jean-Joseph. *Confidence in the Mercy of God.* London: R. Washbourne, 1876.

Lansperger, John. *An Epistle of Jesus Christ to the Faithful Soul.* London: John Philp, 1867.

Lawrence, Brother. See "Brother Lawrence."

Lear, Henrietta Louisa Sidney Farrer. *Bossuet and His Companions.* London: Rivingtons, 1874.

_______. *Fénelon, Archbishop of Cambrai: a Biographical Sketch.* London: Rivingtons, 1877.

_______. *St. Francis de Sales: Bishop and Prince of Geneva.* London: Rivingtons, 1876.

_______. *A Dominican Artist: A Sketch of the Life of the Rev. Pere Besson of the Order of St. Dominic.* London: Rivingtons, 1872.

_______. *Henry Dominique Lacordaire: A Biographical Sketch.* London: Rivingtons, 1887.

_______. *The Revival of Priestly Life in the Seventeenth Century in France.* London: Rivingtons, 1873.

_______. *A Selection from The Spiritual Letters of S. Francis de Sales*, ed. Lear. New York: E.P. Dutton and Company, 1876.

_______. *Weariness.* New York: James Pitt, 1884.

_______. *The Light of the Conscience.* London: Rivingtons, 1880.

Lebrun, Charles. *The Spiritual Teaching of St. John Eudes.* London: Sands & Co., 1934.

Lee, G. *The Life of Venerable Francis Libermann: Original Texts.* Fort Colins, CO: R.A. McCaffrey, 1999.

Leen, Edward. *Our Blessed Mother: Talks on Our Lady.* New York: P.J. Kenedy & Sons, 1946.

_______. *The Church Before Pilate.* Silver Spring, MD: The Preservation

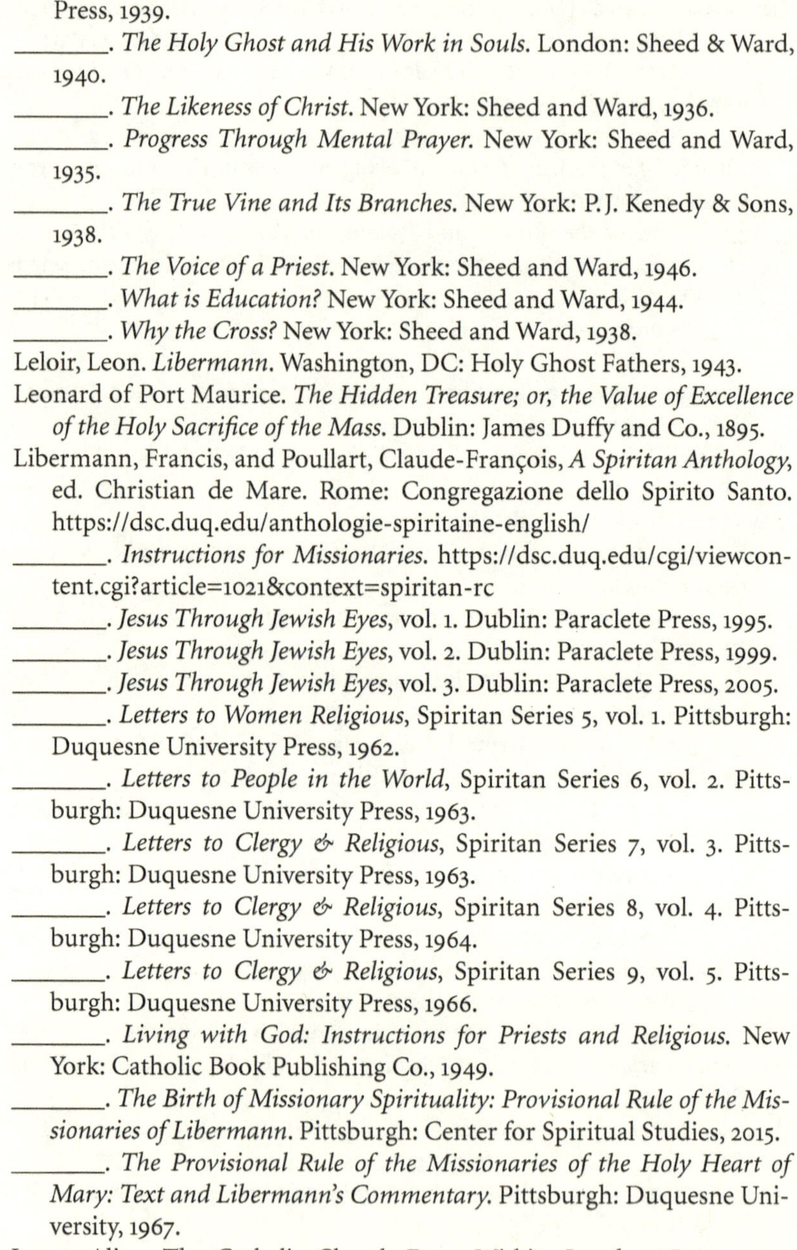

Press, 1939.

_______. *The Holy Ghost and His Work in Souls.* London: Sheed & Ward, 1940.

_______. *The Likeness of Christ.* New York: Sheed and Ward, 1936.

_______. *Progress Through Mental Prayer.* New York: Sheed and Ward, 1935.

_______. *The True Vine and Its Branches.* New York: P.J. Kenedy & Sons, 1938.

_______. *The Voice of a Priest.* New York: Sheed and Ward, 1946.

_______. *What is Education?* New York: Sheed and Ward, 1944.

_______. *Why the Cross?* New York: Sheed and Ward, 1938.

Leloir, Leon. *Libermann.* Washington, DC: Holy Ghost Fathers, 1943.

Leonard of Port Maurice. *The Hidden Treasure; or, the Value of Excellence of the Holy Sacrifice of the Mass.* Dublin: James Duffy and Co., 1895.

Libermann, Francis, and Poullart, Claude-François, *A Spiritan Anthology,* ed. Christian de Mare. Rome: Congregazione dello Spirito Santo. https://dsc.duq.edu/anthologie-spiritaine-english/

_______. *Instructions for Missionaries.* https://dsc.duq.edu/cgi/viewcontent.cgi?article=1021&context=spiritan-rc

_______. *Jesus Through Jewish Eyes,* vol. 1. Dublin: Paraclete Press, 1995.

_______. *Jesus Through Jewish Eyes,* vol. 2. Dublin: Paraclete Press, 1999.

_______. *Jesus Through Jewish Eyes,* vol. 3. Dublin: Paraclete Press, 2005.

_______. *Letters to Women Religious,* Spiritan Series 5, vol. 1. Pittsburgh: Duquesne University Press, 1962.

_______. *Letters to People in the World,* Spiritan Series 6, vol. 2. Pittsburgh: Duquesne University Press, 1963.

_______. *Letters to Clergy & Religious,* Spiritan Series 7, vol. 3. Pittsburgh: Duquesne University Press, 1963.

_______. *Letters to Clergy & Religious,* Spiritan Series 8, vol. 4. Pittsburgh: Duquesne University Press, 1964.

_______. *Letters to Clergy & Religious,* Spiritan Series 9, vol. 5. Pittsburgh: Duquesne University Press, 1966.

_______. *Living with God: Instructions for Priests and Religious.* New York: Catholic Book Publishing Co., 1949.

_______. *The Birth of Missionary Spirituality: Provisional Rule of the Missionaries of Libermann.* Pittsburgh: Center for Spiritual Studies, 2015.

_______. *The Provisional Rule of the Missionaries of the Holy Heart of Mary: Text and Libermann's Commentary.* Pittsburgh: Duquesne University, 1967.

Lovat, Alice. *The Catholic Church From Within.* London: Longmans,

Green & Co., 1901.
Mackey, H.B. *Four Essays on the Life and Writings of S. Francis de Sales, Doctor of the Church*. London: Burns and Oates, 1883.
Malaval, François. *A Simple Method of Raising the Soul to Contemplation: In the Form of a Dialogue*. London: J. M. Dent and Sons Ltd., 1931.
Malinkowski, F.X. "The Holy Spirit in Francis Libermann." *Spiritan Horizons Journal*, Issue 10, Fall 2015, 7–18.
_______. *Meeting the Holy Spirit in the Writings of Francis Libermann: Original Texts*. https://dsc.duq.edu/libermann-collection/58/.
Maria Magdalena de' Pazzi. *Selected Writings*. New York: Paulist Press, 2000.
Marie of the Incarnation. *The Autobiography of Venerable Marie of the Incarnation, O.S.U., Mystic and Missionary*. Chicago: Loyola University Press, 1964.
Mary of St. Peter. *The Golden Arrow: The Autobiography and Revelations of Sister Mary of St. Peter on Devotion to the Holy Face of Jesus*. Charlotte, NF: TAN Books, 2012.
Massillon, John-Baptist. *Sermons by John-Baptist Massillon*. London: Thomas Tegg, 1839.
Michel, Jacques. *A Treatise on Despondency in the Pursuit of Piety, Followed by One on Temptations*. Cincinnati: John P. Walsh, 1865.
Milner, *A Funeral Discourse on the Death of the Venerable and Right Reverend Richard Challoner*. London: J.P. Coghlan, 1781.
Monnin, Alfred. *Life of Saint John-Baptist Vianney, Curé d'Ars*. London: Burns Oates & Washbourne, 1862.
_______. *The Spirit of the Curé of Ars*. London: Burns, Lambert, and Oates, 1865,
More, Gertrude. *The Holy Practices of a Divine Lover, or The Saintly Ideot's [sic] Devotions*. London: Sands & Co., 1909.
_______. *The Writings of Gertrude More*. London: R.&T. Washbourne, Ltd., 1910.
Mudge, James. *Fénelon: The Mystic*. New York: Eaton and Mains, 1906.
Nepveu, François. *The Hidden Life*. London: J. Masters, 1871.
_______. *Meditations for Every Day in the Month*. New York: Benziger Brothers, 1911.
_______. *The Method of Mental Prayer, Rendered Practical and Easie for all sorts of Persons*. London: Thomas Hales, 1694.
_______. *Of the Love of our Lord Jesus Christ, and the Means of Acquiring It*. London: Burns, Oates, & Co., 1869.
_______. *The Spirit of Christianity, or the Conformity of the Christian*

with Christ. New York: Edward Dunigan & Brother, 1859.

Neumayr, Francis. *The Science of the Spiritual Life.* London: Burns and Oates, 1876.

Nieremberg, John Eusebius. *Of Adoration in Spirit and Truth.* London: Burns, Oates & Co., 1871.

_______. *The Difference Between Temporal and Eternal.* Dublin: James Duffy and Co., 1884.

_______. *The Marvels of Divine Grace: Meditations Based on the "Glories of Divine Grace" original treatise by Fr. Nieremberg,* ed. Alice Lady Lovat. London: R. & T. Washbourne, Ltd., 1917.

_______. *The Marvels of Divine Grace,* ed. Wm. J. Doheny, Notre Dame, IN: Ave Maria Press, 1977.

Nouet, Jacques. *The Octave of Corpus Christi; or, the Mystical Life of our Lord in the Blessed Sacrament.* London: Thomas Richardson and Son, 1847.

_______. *Meditations on the Life of our Lord.* Dublin: Browne & Nolan, Ltd., 1956.

_______. *The Life of Jesus Christ, in Glory: Daily Meditations.* London: J. H. Parker, 1847.

Oddi, Longaro Degli. *Life of the Blessed Master John of Ávila.* London: Burns and Oates, Ltd., 1898.

Olier, Jean-Jacques. *Catechism of an Interior Life.* Baltimore: Murphy & Co., 1852.

Partridge, F. J. M. A. *Gaston de Segur, A Biography, Condensed from the French Memoir by the Marquis de Segur.* London: Burns and Oates, 1884.

Paul of the Cross, *The Spiritual Diary of St. Paul of the Cross,* translated Silvan Rouse. https://passionist.org/wp-content/uploads/2025/09/Diary_Rouse_cp.pdf.

_______. *Flowers of the Passion.* New York: Benziger Brothers, 1893.

Peers, E. Allison *The Mystics of Spain.* London: George Allen & Unwin, Ltd., 1951.

_______. *Studies of the Spanish Mystics,* vol. 1. London: The Sheldon Press, 1927.

Philip, Sister Mary. *A Jesuit at the English Court: The Life of Venerable Claude de la Colombière.* London: Burns Oates & Washbourne Ltd., 1922.

Philipon, M. M. *The Sacraments in the Christian Life.* Westminster, MD: The Newman Press, 1954.

_______. *The Spiritual Doctrine of Sister Elizabeth of the Trinity.* Westminster, MD: The Newman Press, 1948.

Pollien, François, ed. Joseph Tissot. *The Interior Life Simplified and Reduced to Its Fundamental Principle*. London: Burns Oates & Washbourne Ltd., 1927.

Pond, Kathleen. *The Spirit of the Spanish Mystics: An Anthology of Spanish Religious Prose from the Fifteenth to the Seventeenth Century*. London: Burns & Oates, 1958.

Pourrat, Pierre. *Christian Spirituality*, vol. 3. *Later Developments, Part 1: From the Renaissance to Jansenism*. Westminster, MD: The Newman Press, 1953.

_______. *Christian Spirituality*, vol. 4. *Later Developments, Part 2: From Jansenism to Modern Times*. Westminster, MD: The Newman Press, 1955.

Premord, Charles Leonore. *The Rules of a Christian Life*. Taunton: J.W. Marriott, 1834.

_______. *Reflections on Communities of Women and Monastic Institutes*. Taunton: J. Poole, 1815.

Purcell, Mary. *The Quiet Companion: The Life of Peter Faber, SJ*. Chicago: Loyola Press, 1970.

Precious Pearl of Hope in the Mercy of God, The: Answers to Certain Difficulties Which are a Hindrance to Hope. London: Burns and Oates, 1878.

Quadrupani, R.P. [Carlo Giuseppe]. *Light and Peace: Instructions for Devout Souls to Dispel their Doubts and Allay Their Fears*. St. Louis, MO: B. Herder Book Co., 1918.

_______. *The Christian Instructed: Precepts for Living Christianly in the World*. London: James Burns, 1849.

Quarre, John. *A Spiritual Treasure: Containing our Obligations to God, and the Vertues Necessary to a Perfect Christian*. London: for Thomas Dring, 1664.

_______. *Devout Entertainments of a Christian Soule*. Paris, 1648.

Ramiere, Henri. *The Apostleship of Prayer, a Holy League of Christian Hearts United with the Heart of Jesus*. Baltimore: John Murphy & Co., 1866.

Ramsay, Andrew Michael. *The Life of François Fénelon, Archbishop and Duke of Cambray*. London: printed for Paul Vaillant, 1723.

Rigoleuc, Jean. *Walking with God: Or, Dwellers in the Recreation House of the Lord*. London: Thomas Richardson and Son, 1859.

Rodríguez, Alonso. *St. Alphonsus Rodríguez: Autobiography*. London: Geoffrey Chapman: London, 1964.

Rodríguez, Alphonsus. *The Practice of Christian and Religious Perfection*, vol. 1. London: James Duffy, 1861.

_______. *The Practice of Christian and Religious Perfection*, vol. 2. London: James Duffy, 1861.

_______. *The Practice of Christian and Religious Perfection*, vol. 3. London: James Duffy, 1861.

Rogacci, Benedict. *Holy Confidence; or, Simplicity with God*. London: Burns, Oates & Co., 1869.

_______. *The Christian Reformed in Mind and Manners*. London: Burns and Oates, 1877.

Saint-Jure, Jean Baptiste. *Christ our Teacher*. Baltimore: McCauley & Kilner, 1891.

_______. *The Holy Life of Monsieur de Renty, a Late Nobleman of France*. London: printed for Benj. Tooke, 1684.

_______. *The Religious: A Treatise on the Vows and Virtues of the Religious State*, vol. 1. New York: P. O'Shea, 1882.

_______. *The Religious: A Treatise on the Vows and Virtues of the Religious State*, vol. 2. New York: P. O'Shea, 1882.

_______. *The Spiritual Man; or, The Spiritual Life Reduced to its First Principles*. London: Burns and Oates, 1878.

_______. *A Treatise on the Knowledge and Love of Our Lord Jesus Christ*, vol. 1. New York: P. O'Shea, 1870.

_______. *A Treatise on the Knowledge and Love of Our Lord Jesus Christ*, vol. 2. New York: P. O'Shea, 1875.

_______. *A Treatise on the Knowledge and Love of Our Lord Jesus Christ*, vol. 3. New York: P. O'Shea, 1875.

_______. *Union with Our Lord Jesus Christ in His Principal Mysteries for All Seasons of the Year*. New York: D. & J. Sadlier & Co., 1876.

Saint-Jure, Jean Baptiste and Claude de la Colombière. *Trustful Surrender to Divine Providence*. Charlotte, NC: TAN Books and Publishers, 1983.

Sanders, E.K. *Fénelon: His Friends and His Enemies* 1651–1715. London: Longmans, Green, and Co., 1901.

Scaramelli, John Baptist. *Directorium Asceticum; or, Guide to the Spiritual Life*, vol. 1. New York: Benziger Bros, 1902.

_______. *Directorium Asceticum or, Guide to the Spiritual Life*, vol. 2. New York: Benziger Bros, 1902.

_______. *Directorium Asceticum or, Guide to the Spiritual Life*, vol. 3. New York: Benziger Bros, 1902.

_______. *Directorium Asceticum or, Guide to the Spiritual Life*, vol. 4. New York: Benziger Bros, 1902.

Scupoli, Lawrence. *The Spiritual Combat, with The Path of Paradise*. London: James Burns, 1845. Translator Pusey.

_______. *The Spiritual Combat of Dom Lorenzo Scupoli.* London: Methuen & Co., 1909. Translator Barns.

_______. *The Spiritual Combat and A Treatise on Peace of Soul.* Charlotte, NC: Tan Classics, 2010. Translators William Lester and Robert Mohan.

Segneri, Paul. *The Devout Client of Mary Instructed in the Motives and Means of Serving Her Well.* London: Burns & Lambert, 1857.

_______. *The Knowledge of Ourselves; With Practical Thoughts of Humility Divided into Meditations for Every Day in the Week.* York: C. Croshaw, 1834.

_______. *Lenten Sermons*, vol. 1. New York: Christian Publication House, 1872.

_______. *Lenten Sermons*, vol. 2. New York: Christian Press Association, 1874.

_______. *The Manna of the Soul: Meditations for Every Day of the Year*, vol. 1. New York: Benziger Brothers, 1892.

_______. *The Manna of the Soul: Meditations for Every Day of the Year*, vol. 2. New York: Benziger Brothers, 1892.

_______. *The Messenger of the Sacred Heart of Jesus, Organ of the Apostleship of Prayer*, vol. 2, July to December. Dublin: M.H. Gill and Son, 1884.

_______. *The Panegyrics of Father Segneri, of the Society of Jesus.* London: R. Washbourne, 1877.

_______. *The Quaresimale of P. Paolo Segneri*, London: Joseph Masters, 1869.

_______. *Sentimenti; or, Lights in Prayer.* London: Burns & Oates, 1876.

_______. *The Penitent Instructed.* London: 1703.

_______. *True Wisdom: Or Considerations for Every Day of the Week.* 1716.

Stopp, Elisabeth. *Madame de Chantal: Portrait of a Saint.* Westminster, MD: The Newman Press, 1963.

_______. *Hidden in God: Essays and Talks on St. Jane Frances de Chantal.* Philadelphia: St. Joseph's University Press, 1999.

Surin, John-Joseph. *The Foundations of The Spiritual Life: Drawn from the Book of the Imitation of Jesus Christ.* London: James Burns, 1844.

_______. *Into the Dark Night and Back: The Mystical Writings of Jean-Joseph Surin.* Leiden: Brill, 2019.

_______. *The Spiritual Letters of Father Surin.* London: Art & Book Co., 1892.

Swetchine, Madame. *The Writings of Madam Swetchine*, ed. de Falloux. Boston: Roberts Brothers, 1869.

Sylvain, Adrien. *Gold Dust: A Collection of Golden Counsels for the Sanctification of Daily Life.* New York: Fredrick A. Stokes Co., 1894.

_______. *Golden Sands: A Collection of Little Counsels for the Sanctification and Happiness of Daily Life.* New York: Benziger Brothers, 1882.

Teresa of Ávila. *The Interior Castle; or, the Mansions.* London: T. Jones, 1852.

_______. *Life of Saint Teresa Written by Herself.* New York: P. J. Kenedy & Sons, 1870.

_______. *Saint Teresa of Ávila Collected Works.* Washington, DC: ICS Publications, 1987.

_______. *The Way of Perfection.* New York: A Doubleday Image Book, 1964.

Teresa Gertrude of the Blessed Sacrament. *Jesus, the All-Beautiful.* London: Burns and Oates, 1910.

_______. *The Heart of Jesus of Nazareth: Meditations on the Hidden Life.* London: R. & T. Washbourne, 1906.

_______. *The Voice of the Sacred Heart: A collection of Devotional Exercises for Private Use, Specially adapted to the Requirements of the Sacred Heart, to Whom it is Affectionately Dedicated.* London: R. & T. Washbourne, 1911.

Tesniere, Albert. *Blessed Peter Julian Eymard: the Priest of the Eucharist.* New York: Fathers of the Blessed Sacrament, 1936.

Thérèse of Lisieux. *The Autobiography of Saint Thérèse of Lisieux: the Story of a Soul.* New York: Image Books, 1989.

_______. *Thoughts of the Servant of God: Thérèse of the Child Jesus.* New York: P. J. Kenedy & Sons, 1915.

Thompson, William M., ed. *Bérulle and the French School: Selected Writings.* New York: Paulist Press, 1989.

Thompson, Edward Healy. *The Life of Jean-Jacques Olier.* London: Burns and Oates, 1885.

_______. *The Life of St. Aloysius Gonzaga.* London: Burns & Oates, 1867.

_______. *The Life of the Baron de Renty; or, Perfection in the World Exemplified.* London: Burns & Oates, 1873.

_______. *The Life of Henri-Marie Boudon, Archdeacon of Evreux.* London: Burns and Oates, 1880.

_______. *The Life of Marie-Estelle Harpain, the Semptress of Saint-Pallais, called "The Angel of the Eucharist."* London: Burns, Oates & Co., 1868.

_______. *The Life and Glories of St. Joseph.* London: Burns & Oates, 1891.

Tissot, Joseph. *The Art of Profiting by our Faults.* New York: Benziger Brothers, 1889.

Trochu, Francis. *The Curé d'Ars: A Shorter Biography.* Westminster, MD: The Newman Press, 1955.

_______. *The Curé d'Ars: St. Jean-Marie-Baptiste Vianney According to the Acts of the Process of Canonization and Numerous Hitherto Unpublished Documents.* London: Burns, Oates & Washbourne Ltd., 1927.

Tronson, Louis. *Examination of Conscience Upon Special Subjects.* Oxford: Rivingtons, 1870.

Ullathorne, William. *The Autobiography of Archbishop Ullathorne, With Selections from His Letters.* London: Burns & Oates, 1892.

_______. *Christian Patience: The Strength and Discipline of the Soul.* London: Burns & Oates, 1886.

_______. *The Endowments of Man Considered in their Relations with His Final End.* London: Burns & Oates, 1880.

_______. *The Groundwork of the Christian Virtues.* London: Burns & Oates, 1890.

_______. *The Immaculate Conception of the Mother of God. An Exposition.* London: Richardson and Son, 1855.

Van Kaam, Adrian. *A Light to the Gentiles.* Eugene, OR: Wipf & Stock, 2009.

Van der Kley, Francesca. *Marian Mystic: A Short Life of St Mary Magdalen de' Pazzi.* Chicago, Carmelite Third Order Press, 1957.

Vaubert, T. F. (Luc). *The Holy Exercise of the Presence of God.* St. Louis: P. Fox, 1871.

Vercruysse, Bruno. *Practical Meditations for Every Day in the Year on the Life of Our Lord Jesus Christ: Composed Chiefly for the Use of Religious by a Father of the Society of Jesus*, vol. 1. London: Burns Oates & Washbourne, 1868.

_______. *Practical Meditations for Every Day in the Year on the Life of Our Lord Jesus Christ: Composed Chiefly for the Use of Religious by a Father of the Society of Jesus*, vol. 2. London: Burns Oates & Washbourne, 1868.

Vianney, John. *Sermons of the Curé of Ars.* Chicago: H. Regnery, 1960.

_______. *The Little Catechism of the Curé of Ars.* Rockford, IL: TAN books, 1951.

_______. *Thoughts of the Curé of Ars*, trans. Pauline Stump. Boston: Flynn & Mahony, 1896.

_______. *Thoughts of the Curé d'Ars*, compiled and arranged by W.M.B. Rockford, IL: TAN Books, 1967.

_______. *Sermons for the Sundays and Feasts of the Year.* Long Prairie, MN: The Neumann Press, 1995.

Visitation Sisters, *The Life of Jeanne Charlotte de Brechard.* New York: Longmans, Green and Co., 1924.

Von Cochem, Martin. *Cochem's Explanation of the Holy Sacrifice of the*

Mass. New York: Benziger Brothers, 1896.
_______. *The Four Last Things: Death. Judgment. Hell. Heaven.* New York: Benziger Brothers, 1899.
Walsh, Eugene. *The Priesthood in the Writings of the French School: Berulle, de Condren, Olier.* Washington DC: The Catholic University of America Press, 1949.
Watson, Thomas. *Sermons on the Sacraments.* London: Burns and Oates, 1876.

Index of Names

www.ingramcontent.com/pod-product-compliance
Lightning Source LLC
LaVergne TN
LVHW100525110826
845146LV00002B/783

* 9 7 9 8 8 9 2 8 0 1 8 9 8 *